A REVIEW GUIDE
FOR THE
FUNDAMENTALS OF
CRIMINAL INVESTIGATION

Sixth Edition

A REVIEW GUIDE
FOR THE
FUNDAMENTALS OF
CRIMINAL INVESTIGATION

Sixth Edition

By

Charles E. O'Hara & Gregory L. O'Hara

By

GREGORY L. O'HARA

CHARLES C THOMAS • PUBLISHER, LTD.
Springfield • Illinois • U.S.A.

Published and Distributed Throughout the World by

CHARLES C THOMAS · PUBLISHER, LTD.
2600 South First Street
Springfield, Illinois 62794-9265

© *1998 by* CHARLES C THOMAS · PUBLISHER, LTD.
ISBN 0-398-06880-1

Library of Congress Catalog Card Number: 98-17048

With THOMAS BOOKS *careful attention is given to all details of manufacturing
and design. It is the Publisher's desire to present books that are satisfactory as to their
physical qualities and artistic possibilities and appropriate for their particular use.*
THOMAS BOOKS *will be true to those laws of quality that assure a good name
and good will.*

*Printed in the United States of America
CR-R-3*

Library of Congress Cataloging in Publication Data

O'Hara, Gregory L.
    A review guide for the Fundamentals of criminal investigation.
sixth edition by Charles E. O'Hara & Gregory L. O'Hara / by
Gregory L. O'Hara.
        p.   cm.
    ISBN 0-398-06880-1 (pbk.)
    1. Criminal investigation--Problems, exercises, etc. I. O'Hara,
Charles E. Fundamentals of criminal investigation. II. Title.
HV8073.039 1994 Suppl.
363.25--dc21   98-17048
                                                                          CIP

PREFACE

This review book is designed to help the reader learn the *Fundamentals of Criminal Investigation*. Each question is constructed so that the correct answer when combined with it will form a statement that can be reread and learned. When you are finished testing yourself on the material and inserting the answers, you will have a collection of the important points of each chapter.

For the most part, there are three types of questions: (1) a fill-in-the-blank question; (2) a complete-the-sentence question; and (3) an "all of the following...except:" question. With the first two varieties, you can underline the correct answer and insert it into or at the end of the question to form a completed statement. With the third type, *cross out the word "except" and the correct answer* to form a collection of three significant sentences that can then be reviewed.

The letter representing the correct answer for each question appears at the end of each chapter along with the number of the textbook page from where the question originated. Also included are the number and letter of the general subdivisions of each chapter to help locate the references for those who are using other editions of this textbook.

Much of the wording of the questions are from the original editions of this textbook written by Charles E. O'Hara. If this review guide brings the reader to a greater knowledge and understanding of this complex subject, it will have served its purpose.

G.L.O.

CONTENTS

Page

A REVIEW GUIDE
FOR THE
FUNDAMENTALS OF
CRIMINAL INVESTIGATION

Sixth Edition

Chapter 1
METHODS OF INVESTIGATION

Questions:

1. A criminal investigator is a person who collects:

   a. facts.   c. theories.
   b. suspects.   d. ideas.

2. All of the following are aims of the criminal investigator except:

   a. identifying the guilty party.
   b. locating the guilty party.
   c. providing evidence of a suspect's guilt.
   d. prosecuting the guilty party.

3. Investigation is _____; hence, it must be discussed in terms of precepts and advice rather than laws and rigid theories.

   a. a science   c. a craft
   b. an art   d. an abstract discipline

4. By the application of the three "I's," the investigator gathers the facts which are necessary to establish the guilt or innocence of the accused in a criminal trial. The three "I's" include all of the following except:

   a. Information.   c. Identification.
   b. Interrogation.   d. Instrumentation.

5. An investigation may be considered a success if:

   a. the guilty party is identified and apprehended.
   b. the accused is proven guilty in court.
   c. the *corpus delicti* can be established.
   d. all of the available information relevant and material to the issues of the case are uncovered.

6. Many crimes are not able to be solved because:

   a. there are no eyewitnesses available.
   b. there is insufficient evidence available.
   c. there is no discernible motive.
   d. there are too many suspects.

7. The word _____ is used here to describe the knowledge which the investigator gathers from other persons.

    a. interview
    b. interrogation.

    c. information
    d. instrumentation

8. A crime involving greed, such as larceny or robbery, when perpetrated by a professional criminal is usually solved by:

    a. analyzing physical evidence.
    b. interrogating a suspect.

    c. discerning a motive.
    d. information.

9. _____ is the simple questioning of a person who has no personal reason to withhold information.

    a. An interview
    b. An interrogation

    c. A discussion
    d. A conversation

10. _____ is the questioning of a suspect or other person who may normally be expected to be reluctant to divulge information.

    a. An interview
    b. An interrogation

    c. An accusation
    d. A confrontation

11. In a homicide case where there are no eyewitnesses, a suspect will improve his chances for acquittal by:

    a. talking to the police but not about the crime.
    b. making up a simple but false account of his actions.
    c. blaming the crime on some other known criminal.
    d. refusing to make any statement at all.

12. Even after being given Miranda warnings, a suspect will frequently talk to police because the normal person:

    a. believes he is truly innocent.
    b. believes he can fool the police.
    c. is possessed by an irresistible desire to talk.
    d. enjoys the give and take of interrogation.

13. To become proficient in the art of interrogation requires:

    a. only a natural gift of insight into people.
    b. years of constant practice.
    c. periods of reflection and inactivity.
    d. just a little common sense.

14. Instrumentation includes the application of scientific instruments and methods as well as technical methods to the detection of crime. All of the following are examples of instrumentation except:

a. fingerprint systems.
b. criminalistics.
c. interrogation techniques.
d. surveillance equipment.

15. The application of scientific instruments and methods to crime detection is specifically called the study of:

a. criminalistics.
b. criminal investigation.
c. evidence collection.
d. police science.

16. Instrumentation is of considerable importance in:

a. cases where there is an abundance of physical evidence.
b. cases where there is no physical evidence.
c. typical larceny or robbery cases.
d. cases where there are a number of eyewitnesses.

17. It is important for the investigator:

a. to be an expert in criminalistics.
b. not to rely on technical methods.
c. to be an expert in many technical methods.
d. to know the technical aids that are available to him and to know their limitations.

18. _____ is an excellent means of identifying a criminal as well as a major objective of every investigation.

a. An eyewitness identification
b. Circumstantial evidence
c. Proof of a motive
d. An admission or confession

19. All of the following statements are true except:

a. A confession may be denied in court unless an affirmative show of voluntariness is present.
b. A confession can be used to establish the *corpus delicti* or the fact that a crime has been committed.
c. A confession must be supported by other corroborative evidence.
d. A confession can be used to identify the criminal.

20. The ideal eyewitness identification of a suspect is made by several persons who witness the commission of the crime and:

a. have seen the suspect once before.
b. are very familiar with the suspect.
c. have never seen the suspect before.
d. can't remember if they have seen the suspect.

21. An identification by circumstantial evidence involves:

    a. eyewitness testimony.
    b. an admission or confession.
    c. an inference from a proven fact.
    d. establishing the *corpus delicti.*

22. All of the following are common types of circumstantial evidence except:

    a. eyewitness testimony.
    b. proof of motive.
    c. proof of opportunity.
    d. physical evidence at the crime scene.

23. Establishing the fact that a crime has been committed is called proving the:

    a. elements of the offense.
    b. motive.
    c. circumstantial evidence.
    d. *corpus delicti.*

24. The term _____ refer(s) to the conditions which must be fulfilled by the evidence before it can be said that the guilt of the accused has been proven.

    a. elements of the offense
    b. motive
    c. circumstantial evidence
    d. *corpus delicti*

25. The _____ provide(s) a framework for the investigator in the development of a case.

    a. elements of the offense
    b. motive
    c. circumstantial evidence
    d. *corpus delicti*

26. In the first general element (that the accused did or omitted to do the acts as alleged), the identity of the accused must be established and his _____ the acts clearly shown.

    a. knowledge of
    b. consciousness of the unlawfulness of
    c. motive for
    d. causal connection with

27. _____ is that which induces the criminal to act, such as for revenge or personal gain.

    a. Intent
    b. Motive
    c. Malice
    d. Desire

28. The _____ of an action is the accomplishment of the act, the desire to achieve the consequences of an act.

    a. intent
    b. motive
    c. malice
    d. essence

29. _____ is a legal term meaning the intent to do injury to another.

    a. Motive
    b. Malice
    c. Assault
    d. Mayhem

30. The importance of the proof of motive depends upon the nature of the crime. Motive is often of little value in all of the following crimes except:

    a. robbery.   c. larceny.
    b. burglary.   d. murder.

31. _____ is forming a general theory from an examination of particular details.

    a. Inductive reasoning   c. Intuition
    b. Deductive reasoning   d. Inference

32. _____ is the application of a general theory to a particular instance to see if it explains that instance.

    a. Inductive reasoning   c. Intuition
    b. Deductive reasoning   d. Inference

33. In a criminal investigation, the best hypothesis is chosen on the basis of _____ and a high degree of probability.

    a. simplicity   c. consistency with the known facts
    b. complexity   d. creativity

34. _____ is a term used to refer to those clues encountered accidentally, which sometimes play an important part in the solution of a crime.

    a. Opportunity   c. Intuitional
    b. Chance   d. Accidental

35. _____ refers to the sudden and unexpected insight that clarifies a problem where reasoning has reached an impasse.

    a. Opportunity   c. Chance
    b. Inductive reasoning   d. Intuition

36. All of the following statements about criminal investigation are true except:

    a. The basic purpose of criminal investigation is the discovery of the truth concerning a criminal event.
    b. A prejudiced investigator is a contradiction in terms.
    c. An investigator collects only the evidence that would establish the guilt of a particular suspect.
    d. An investigator has an equal interest in facts that inculpate as well as exonerate a suspect.

Answers:

1. a	p. 5, 1.	13. b	p. 11, 3.	25. a	p. 18, 10.
2. d	p. 5, 1.	14. c	p. 11, 4.	26. d	p. 18, 10b.
3. b	p. 5, 1.	15. a	p. 11, 4.	27. b	p. 19, 10c.
4. c	p. 5, 1.	16. a	p. 12, 4.	28. a	p. 19, 10c.
5. d	p. 6, 1.	17. d	p. 12, 4.	29. b	p. 19, 10c.
6. b	p. 6, 1.	18. d	p. 13, 6a.	30. d	p. 19, 10c.

Chapter 2

THE INVESTIGATOR'S NOTEBOOK

Questions:

1. All of the following types of information would be appropriate for an investigator's notebook except:

    a. a description of the appearance and location of objects at the crime scene.
    b. the official report of the investigation.
    c. interviews with witnesses.
    d. a description of the odors and atmosphere of the crime scene.

2. An experienced investigator uses a notebook because:

    a. it is a legal requirement to do so.
    b. it is always necessary to use information from a notebook when writing the report.
    c. ordinarily, an investigator cannot remember all of the important data in a case.
    d. the sight of the investigator's notebook encourages candid interviews.

3. Much of the data collected in the notebook will not appear in the report of the investigation because:

    a. at the outset of an investigation, it is not easy to determine which data is significant.
    b. most of the data collected will turn out to be inaccurate.
    c. most of the data collected will be confidential.
    d. the notebook must first be examined for accuracy by a defense attorney in court.

4. The investigator's notebook may contain all of the following types of descriptive information about the crime scene except:

    a. the true location and condition of objects.
    b. the odor and general atmosphere of the area.
    c. the representational or the schematic image of the crime scene.
    d. the inventory of articles of value.

5. A defense counsel may examine the investigator's notebook if:

    a. he thinks it may contain evidence that will exonerate his client.
    b. the investigator uses it to refresh his memory while testifying in court.
    c. it is illegible and needs to be deciphered.
    d. the investigator is requested to relinquish it in a polite manner.

6. One of the conditions sometimes placed on the use of the investigator's notebook in court is that:

    a. it contains no cryptic or vague descriptions in it.
    b. all of the information in it is accurate.
    c. it contains original notes taken at the time of the investigation.
    d. all of the information in it is relevant.

7. Having a bound notebook written in ink suggests that:

    a. significant changes in the notebook were made at a later date.
    b. significant changes in the notebook were not made at a later date.
    c. some pages are probably missing.
    d. many erasures were made.

8. Having the notes of only one investigation in a notebook not only prevents confusion but also:

    a. keeps the investigator concentrating on only one case.
    b. keeps the investigator from writing unintelligible comments.
    c. prevents the unauthorized disclosure of information from a separate investigation.
    d. makes the loss of a notebook less of a problem.

9. Notes are gathered in:

    a. chronological order determined by the investigative steps or the receipt of information.
    b. a logical order that is apparent from the beginning of the case.
    c. a completely random order as long as all important notations are made.
    d. no apparent order to confuse an examining defense counsel.

10. Care and accuracy should be used when recording notes. One important reason for this is the possibility of a court examination of the notebook. Another important reason is:

    a. that another investigator might at some point have to assume responsibility for the investigation.
    b. that the supervisor might want to make changes in the investigator's note book.
    c. that the investigator knows exactly what he does everyday.
    d. that the investigator may be able to change the entries at a later date.

11. All of the following statements about notetaking of interviews are true except:

    a. The notes should include case identification, hour, date, place of interview, and identification of the person being interviewed.
    b. A summary of the interview should be included.
    c. Important statements should be recorded verbatim if possible.
    d. When dealing with a reluctant witness, a notebook should be drawn out immediately at the start of the interview.

12. In a major case, where a number of interviews must be conducted, having _____ would be the most helpful and practical solution to the problem of note-taking.

    a. extra investigators
    b. extra notebooks
    c. a portable tape recorder
    d. the interviewees speak slower

Answers:

1. b	p. 29, 1.	5. b	p. 30, 1d.	9. a	p. 31, 3.
2. c	p. 29, 1.	6. c	p. 30, 1d.	10. a	p. 31, 3.
3. a	p. 30, 1b.	7. b	p. 31, 2.	11. d	p. 31, 3.
4. c	p. 30, 1c.	8. c	p, 31, 2.	12. c	p. 32, 4.

Chapter 3

REPORT WRITING

Questions:

1. The report of investigation serves all of the following purposes except:

    a. as an official record of the investigation.
    b. as a source of leads for other investigators.
    c. as a repository for all of the details of an investigation.
    d. as a basis for prosecutive action by the district attorney.

2. The investigator's report should reflect the basic qualities of expository style which includes being all of the following except:

    a. clear and brief.
    b. imaginative and opinionated.
    c. objective and impartial.
    d. accurate and complete.

3. The report of investigation should include all of the following findings of the investigator except:

    a. information both favorable and unfavorable to the suspect.
    b. leads that produce positive as well as negative results.
    c. information that is both relevant and irrelevant to the case.
    d. statements and opinions of subjects and witnesses clearly presented as such.

4. In order to eliminate unwarranted and misleading suspicions, the report should include:

    a. neither positive nor negative findings.
    b. only positive findings.
    c. only negative findings.
    d. both positive and negative findings.

5. In major cases, status reports should be made:

    a. at regular intervals.
    b. only when new significant information has been uncovered.
    c. only after a suspect has been identified.
    d. when all leads have been developed.

6. After the subject has been identified by his full name in the report, it is customary to subsequently refer to him by:

    a. his full name in capital letters.
    b. his full name in lower-case letters.
    c. his last name in capital letters.
    d. his last name in lower-case letters.

7. The office in which the complaint was received or which has jurisdiction over the area where the offense took place is called the:

    a. auxiliary office.   c. headquarters.
    b. office of origin.   d. investigative agency.

8. When the status of a case is "pending," this means that:

    a. the investigation is continuing.
    b. the district attorney has presented the case to the court.
    c. the investigation depends upon the results of following a particular lead.
    d. the investigation is closed.

9. The synopsis on the cover sheet of the report is:

    a. a detailed narrative account of the investigation.
    b. the investigator's opinions, conclusions, and recommendations.
    c. a list of possible sources of information.
    d. a brief description of the offense and a summary of the major investigative steps taken.

10. The "Details" section of the report contains:

    a. a narrative account of the investigation.
    b. the conclusions and recommendations of the investigator.
    c. the undeveloped leads.
    d. the inclosures or exhibits.

11. In the part of the report containing the administrative data, all of the following information should be included except:

    a. the date, the file number, and the name of the subject.
    b. the nature of the case and the name of the complainant.
    c. the investigator's conclusions and recommendations.
    d. the name of the investigator and the office of origin.

12. An "uncontacted" possible source of information is called:

    a. a confidential informant.   c. a subject.
    b. a material witness.   d. an undeveloped lead.

13. The inclosure or exhibit section of the report may contain all of the following except:

    a. photographs and sketches of the crime scene.
    b. a list of undeveloped leads.
    c. identification photographs.
    d. photocopies of checks.

14. In his report the investigator:

    a. may refer to himself in the third person.
    b. may not refer to himself in the third person.
    c. must refer to himself only in the first person.
    d. must refer to himself only in the third person.

15. A closing report may be filed in all of the following circumstances except:

    a. on the successful conclusion of the case.
    b. when all leads are exhausted.
    c. when the investigator is assigned a more important case.
    d. on orders from a higher authority.

16. In the investigator's report, the identity of a confidential informant:

    a. should be disclosed.
    b. should never be disclosed.
    c. should be disclosed if he is the only witness to a major crime.
    d. should be disclosed at the discretion of the investigator.

17. If practical, the statement of a subject should be set forth verbatim which means:

    a. the substance of his remarks should be recorded.
    b. a summary of his statements should be written.
    c. what the subject intends to say should be written.
    d. the subject's exact words should be transcribed.

18. All of the following are advantages of this system of filing reports except:

    a. It provides reviewing authorities the means of checking on the work of the investigator.
    b. It provides order, method, and routine to investigative activity.
    c. It provides a method of collecting and recording irrelevant and immaterial information.
    d. It gives supervisors the assurance there are no obvious omissions in the investigation.

Answers:

1. c	p. 34, 2.	7. b	p. 37, 6a.	13. b	p. 39, 6f.
2. b	p. 34, 4.	8. a	p. 37, 6a.	14. a	p. 40, 6g.
3. c	p. 35, 4.	9. d	p. 38, 6b.	15. c	p. 41, 9.
4. d	p. 35, 5.	10. a	p. 38, 6c.	16. b	p. 41, 10a.
5. a	p. 36, 5.	11. c	p. 39, 6d.	17. d	p. 42, 10c.
6. c	p. 36, 6a.	12. d	p. 39, 6e.	18. c	p. 43, 11.

Chapter 4

CRIME SCENE SEARCH

Questions:

1. The search of the crime scene is often the most important part of the investigation of crimes that involve:

    a. little physical activity.   c. much physical activity.
    b. much mental activity.   d. a quick getaway.

2. Traces are left at the scene, when the criminal comes in contact with the crime scene in a forceful manner. This frequently occurs in all of the following crimes except:

    a. burglary.   c. homicide.
    b. forgery.   d. assault.

3. The investigator must be concerned with the transfer of evidence not only from the criminal to the crime scene but also from the crime scene to the:

a. investigator.
b. victim.
c. witness.
d. criminal.

4. Samples of characteristic dust, seeds, and soil from the crime scene area are collected in anticipation of finding traces:

a. on the victim.
b. on the investigator.
c. at other crime scenes.
d. on a suspect.

5. On first arriving at the crime scene, the investigator should do all of the following except:

a. Identify the person who first notified the police.
b. Determine the perpetrator by direct inquiry.
c. Collect all available evidence.
d. Safeguard the area.

6. All of the following personnel would be helpful for the crime scene search except:

a. an officer in charge and an assistant.
b. a report writer and an interrogator.
c. a sketcher and a photographer.
d. an evidence collector and a measurer.

7. When first arriving at the scene of the crime, it is important for the investigator to:

a. stand aside and make an estimate of the situation.
b. telephone his supervisor for advice.
c. begin the crime scene search.
d. begin collecting evidence.

8. In the initial steps of the crime scene search, it is important for the investigator to be careful not to _____ articles of evidence.

a. evaluate
b. handle
c. discuss
d. photograph

9. The basic search of the crime scene should be guided primarily by:

a. method.
b. intuition.
c. analysis.
d. imagination.

10. Once a plan of search has been decided upon, it should be followed:

a. loosely.
b. determinedly.
c. until a better plan is developed.
d. indifferently.

11. When collecting evidence, the investigator should be guided in his selection by:

    a. the principle that anything may be evidence.
    b. the purpose that the evidence may serve.
    c. the principle that every piece of evidence should be collected.
    d. the principle that less is more.

12. As a basic guide for its collection, evidence may be looked upon as establishing all of the following except:

    a. the *corpus delicti* or the fact that the crime was committed.
    b. the *modus operandi* or the method of operation of the perpetrator.
    c. the thoroughness of the investigation.
    d. the identity of the guilty person.

13. If the crime scene is indoors, the search plan will:

    a. follow a predetermined indoor crime scene plan.
    b. follow the intuition of the investigator.
    c. be either the strip or zone method.
    d. be determined by the size of the room and its contents.

14. In the _____ method, the area to be searched is blocked out in the form of a rectangle and the searchers proceed along paths parallel to the base of the rectangle.

    a. zone   c. double strip
    b. grid   d. strip

15. The double strip or _____ method is a modification of the strip method where the rectangle is traversed parallel to the base and then parallel to the side.

    a. grid   c. wheel
    b. zone   d. spiral

16. In the _____ method, the searchers follow a circular pattern beginning on the outside and circling in toward the center.

    a. wheel   c. spiral
    b. zone   d. grid

17. In the _____ method, each searcher is assigned a subdivision of a quadrant to search.

    a. strip   c. grid
    b. double strip   d. zone

18. In the _____ method, the searchers begin at the center and proceed outward along radii.

   a. wheel   c. zone
   b. spiral   d. strip

19. The process of picturing the circumstances of a crime is called _____ the crime.

   a. evaluating   c. imagining
   b. reconstructing   d. analyzing

20. Reproducing the positions of articles and the actions of the persons during the occurrence is called:

   a. physical reproduction.   c. physical reconstruction.
   b. mental reproduction.   d. mental reconstruction.

21. In the mental reconstruction of the crime, the investigator should test his theory for:

   a. believability.   c. consistency.
   b. imagination.   d. redundancy.

22. The mental reconstruction of a crime should be conducted from the point of view of:

   a. the investigator.   c. the victim.
   b. a witness.   d. the criminal.

23. A theory concerning the actions of the criminal must be consistent with:

   a. the evidence.
   b. the conclusions of other investigators.
   c. what the investigator would do in a similar situation.
   d. intelligent guesswork.

24. The purpose of developing a theory for the crime is to:

   a. plan a course of investigative action.
   b. complete the crime scene search.
   c. supplement the physical reconstruction of the crime.
   d. complete the investigative report.

Answers:

   1. c   p. 47, 1.   9. a   p. 50, 5.   17. d   p. 52, 6c.
   2. b   p. 47, 1.   10. b   p. 50, 5.   18. a   p. 52, 6d.

3. d	p. 47, 1.	11. b	p. 50, 5.	19. b	p. 56, 9.
4. d	p. 47, 1.	12. c	p. 50, 5.	20. c	p. 56, 9a.
5. c	p. 48, 2.	13. d	p. 50, 6.	21. c	p. 56, 9b.
6. b	p. 49, 3.	14. d	p. 51, 6a.	22. d	p. 56, 9b.
7. a	p. 49, 4.	15. a	p. 51, 6a.	23. a	p. 56, 9b.
8. b	p. 49, 4.	16. c	p. 52, 6b.	24. a	p. 56, 9b.

Chapter 5

PHOTOGRAPHING THE CRIME SCENE

Questions:

1. The purpose of the crime scene photographs is to convey as fully as possible an understanding of what happened at the crime scene from _____ point of view.

    a. the investigator's
    b. the victim's
    c. the suspect's
    d. an objective

2. The number and kind of photographs needed depend a great deal on all of the following except:

    a. the type of crime and its seriousness.
    b. the complexity of the crime scene and the size of the premises.
    c. knowing the identity of the suspect and whether he has confessed.
    d. the amount and importance of the physical evidence present at the crime scene.

3. Ordinarily, it will be unproductive to extensively photograph _____ crime scene because so few traces of the event will be left behind.

    a. a burglary
    b. an armed robbery
    c. a murder
    d. an arson

4. As a general rule, it is better to take too many photographs at the crime scene than too few because:

    a. an apparently insignificant object may later turn out to be an important piece of evidence.
    b. the laboratory often loses or improperly develops the film.
    c. the investigator will frequently take pictures with the camera out of focus.
    d. objects are often substituted after the investigator has left.

5. All of the following are important uses of crime scene photographs except:

   a. to provide a permanent record that will be kept on file.
   b. to help investigators and prosecutors to know and understand the details of the case.
   c. to allow newspaper reporters to provide their readers with informative pictures.
   d. to convey in court to the judge and jury an objective representation of the scene.

6. Among the investigative purposes that crime scene photographs may serve include all of the following except:

   a. to establish the *corpus delicti* or the fact that the crime has been committed.
   b. to suggest to a witness how he should prepare or change his testimony.
   c. to refresh the investigator's memory so that he can mentally reconstruct the crime.
   d. to avoid excessive handling of the physical evidence.

7. All of the following are evidence rules governing the admissibility of photographs except:

   a. the object which is represented should be material and relevant.
   b. the photograph should not unduly incite prejudice or sympathy.
   c. the photograph should not portray evidence that will incriminate a suspect.
   d. the photograph should be free from distortion.

8. When evidence is said to be material and relevant, this means:

   a. it is physical evidence and related to an issue.
   b. it is physical and significant evidence.
   c. it is tangible and related to an issue.
   d. it is significant and related to an issue.

9. Distortion that misrepresents the crime scene may be caused by all of the following except:

   a. pointing the camera so as to obscure certain objects.
   b. tilting the camera upward or downward.
   c. exposing or developing film in a way that misrepresents the tones.
   d. holding the camera close to an object to create a larger image.

10. Proper perspective may be maintained by keeping the camera at eye level with the lens pointed so that it is at a _____ -degree angle with an opposing wall.

   a. 30   c. 60
   b. 45   d. 90

11. _____are the representation of colors in black-and-white photography.

    a. Pigments   c. Perspectives
    b. Tones   d. Focal lengths

12. The two most widely used cameras for crime scene photography are the 4 x 5 press and the:

    a. 35mm.   c. videotape camera.
    b. polaroid.   d. fingerprint camera.

13. Color film is especially suited for photographing:

    a. tool marks.   c. bruises.
    b. furniture.   d. weapons.

14. Ideally, when photographing the crime scene, the investigator should be prepared to use:

    a. black-and-white film only.
    b. color film only.
    c. both black-and-white and color film.
    d. neither black-and-white nor color film.

15. At a homicide crime scene, _____ general view photograph(s) should be taken.

    a. only one   c. no
    b. two   d. at least four

16. The investigator photographs the body of the deceased in relationship to the furniture in the room because the arrangement may suggest:

    a. the economic or social status of the victim.
    b. how orderly and tidy the victim was.
    c. the actions of the victim immediately preceding death.
    d. the possibility of recovering physical evidence there.

17. Two photographs are needed for a significant object less than 6 inches in length. The first should be at close range to show a larger image. The second should be at approximately _____ feet to bring the background in view.

    a. 6 ft.   c. 20 ft.
    b. 12 ft.   d. 30 ft.

18. A _____ is the general name for a device placed in the field of view which aids in the interpretation of a photograph.

    a. locator   c. sign
    b. ruler   d. marker

19. If markers are to be used in the crime scene photographs, it will be necessary to first take another set of pictures of the scene in its original state in order to:

    a. keep the markers from concealing part of the evidence.
    b. avoid distracting the jurors when they view the picture.
    c. avoid the charge of tampering with evidence.
    d. show the jurors that you do not need visual aids to establish your points.

20. There are three types of markers that are generally used: (1) rulers; (2) location markers; and (3) small signs with:

    a. numbers.   c. arrows.
    b. measurements.   d. identifying data.

21. In order to show the size of an object in a crime scene photograph, a _____ is placed in the field of view.

    a. location marker   c. ruler
    b. numbered sign   d. arrow

22. Arrows and numbered signs are kinds of markers used to convey _____.

    a. size   c. identifying data
    b. location   d. date and time

23. When photographing a tool mark, _____ should be used.

    a. a wide-angle lens   c. a fingerprint camera
    b. a normal lens   d. photomacrography

24. In a homicide case, all of the following should be considered part of the crime scene except:

    a. the approach to the crime scene.
    b. the suspect's hideout.
    c. the exit from the crime scene.
    d. an adjoining area where a struggle took place.

25. A complete record of identifying and technical data for each photograph should be kept in a notebook or:

    a. in a "photo log."
    b. in the report of investigation.
    c. on the identifying marker.
    d. in the crime scene sketch.

26. All of the following are true statements about videotaping the crime scene except:

 a. When the crime scene is extensive, a videotape can show the relationship of seemingly unrelated photographs.
 b. A videotape can serve as a substitute for the usual crime scene photographers.
 c. A videotape can capture the general atmosphere of the crime scene.
 d. A videotape can be used to record the spectators at the crime scene in order to discover a witness or a suspect.

27. A videotape is an ideal form of evidence commonly used for all of the following crimes except:

 a. embezzlement cases.
 b. insurance frauds.
 c. "buy and bust" narcotics cases.
 d. drunken driving cases.

28. A "posed photograph" is sometimes used:

 a. in a photo-lineup.
 b. to illustrate the testimony of witnesses.
 c. as a substitute for the crime scene photograph.
 d. to induce a suspect to confess.

Answers:

1. d	p. 59, 1.	11. b	p. 62, 2c.	21. c	p. 64, 3d.
2. c	p. 59, 1.	12. a	p. 63, 3.	22. b	p. 64, 3d.
3. b	p. 59, 1.	13. c	p. 63, 3.	23. d	p. 65, 3e.
4. a	p. 59, 1.	14. c	p. 63, 3.	24. b	p. 65, 3f.
5. c	p. 60, 1.	15. d	p. 64, 3a.	25. a	p. 66, 3h.
6. b	p. 60, 1c.	16. c	p. 64, 3b.	26. b	p. 68, 5.
7. c	p. 62, 2.	17. a	p. 64, 3c.	27. a	p. 69, 5.
8. d	p. 62, 2a.	18. d	p. 64, 3d.	28. b	p. 70, 6.
9. d	p. 62, 2c.	19. c	p. 64, 3d.		
10. d	p. 62, 2c.	20. d	p. 64, 3d.		

Chapter 6

CRIME SCENE SKETCH

Questions:

1. The crime scene sketch serves all of the following purposes except:

 a. presents the visual appearance of the crime scene.
 b. presents the actual measurements of the distances between objects.
 c. locates and identifies certain objects that are hidden in photographs.
 d. identifies certain objects that are not clearly visible in photographs.

2. The drawing made by the investigator at the crime scene is called:

    a. the projection sketch.   c. the rough sketch.
    b. the template.   d. the finished drawing.

3. All of the following statements concerning the rough sketch are true except:

    a. The scale of the drawing may be approximate.
    b. Measurements may be approximate.
    c. It may be used as the basis for the finished drawing.
    d. No changes should be made to the original after leaving the crime scene.

4. The crime scene sketch made primarily for courtroom presentation is called:

    a. the projection sketch.   c. the rough sketch.
    b. the courtroom drawing.   d. the finished drawing.

5. All of the following statements about the finished drawing are true except:

    a. It is based on the rough sketch.
    b. The measurements are exact.
    c. It need not be drawn to scale.
    d. A person skilled in drawing should make the sketch.

6. All of the following equipment would be useful to the investigator in making the rough sketch at the crime scene except:

    a. a soft pencil and a clipboard.
    b. a drawing set, a drafting board, and India ink.
    c. a compass to indicate direction.
    d. a steel tape for accurate measurement.

7. Measurements establishing the location of a movable object must be:

    a. based on an immovable object.
    b. based on another movable object.
    c. based solely on compass direction.
    d. accomplished with a template.

8. The direction of the sketch is determined by:

    a. a measuring tape.   c. a template.
    b. the scale of the drawing.   d. a compass.

9. The crime scene sketch should include:

    a. all objects that may have a bearing on the investigation.
    b. all immovable objects, such as walls, windows, and plumbing fixtures.
    c. all of the furniture in the room.
    d. all movable and immovable objects.

10. A _____ is a pattern used in drawing furniture, plumbing fixtures, dead bodies, and other crime scene objects.

    a. compass   c. polar coordinate
    b. projection sketch   d. template

11. The _____ is an explanation of the symbols used to identify objects in a sketch.

    a. scale   c. title
    b. legend   d. compass

12. A crime scene sketch of a room which shows all four walls and which looks like a cardboard box that has been flattened is called:

    a. a rough sketch.   c. a projection sketch.
    b. a finished drawing.   d. a computer sketch.

13. The simplest way to locate an object in the crime scene sketch of a room is:

    a. to measure the distances from two mutually perpendicular walls to the object.
    b. to measure the distance between the object and another movable object.
    c. by giving the polar coordinates of the object.
    d. to measure the distance from the object to two parallel walls.

14. All of the following statements accurately describe the advantages of a computer generated crime scene sketch except:

    a. All of the lines of the sketch will be straight and without erasures.
    b. Multiple copies can be printed readily.
    c. Rescaling the drawing can be accomplished easily.
    d. A computerized system requires the operator to have artistic ability.

Answers:

1. a	p. 72, 1.	6. b	p. 73, 1c.	11. b	p. 74, 2e.
2. c	p. 72, 1a.	7. a	p. 73, 2a.	12. c	p. 75, 3.
3. b	p. 72, 1a.	8. d	p. 73, 2b.	13. a	p. 75, 4a.
4. d	p. 72, 1b.	9. a	p. 73, 2c.	14. d	p. 77, 5.
5. c	p. 72, 1b.	10. d	p. 74, 2c.		

Chapter 7

CARE OF EVIDENCE

Questions:

1. _____ may be defined generally as the articles and materials which are found in connection with an investigation that assists in the discovery of the facts.

    a. Evidence
    b. Associative evidence

    c. Circumstantial evidence
    d. Physical evidence

2. Investigators may find it helpful when looking for evidence at the crime scene to classify it according to:

    a. the investigative purpose it may serve.
    b. the rules of evidence.
    c. the laboratory techniques to be used.
    d. the chronological order of discovery.

3. When classifying physical evidence found at the crime scene, an investigator will find that an article of evidence will most commonly belong to:

    a. only one category.
    b. several categories.

    c. all of the categories.
    d. none of the categories.

4. _____ are objects or substances that tend to establish that a crime has been committed.

    a. Associative evidence
    b. *Corpus delicti* evidence

    c. Identifying evidence
    d. Tracing evidence

5. _____ are objects and substances that link the suspect to the crime scene or the offense.

    a. Associative evidence
    b. *Corpus delicti* evidence

    c. Identifying evidence
    d. Tracing evidence

6. _____ are objects and substances that tend to directly establish who the perpetrator is.

    a. Associative evidence
    b. *Corpus delicti* evidence

    c. Identifying evidence
    d. Tracing evidence

7. _____ are articles that assist the investigator in locating the suspect.

    a. Associative evidence
    b. *Corpus delicti* evidence

    c. Identifying evidence
    d. Tracing evidence

8. All of the following are forms of information or skills which will assist the investigator in recognizing valuable physical evidence except:

   a. a knowledge of the law of evidence.
   b. the ability to recreate imaginatively the commission of the crime.
   c. the ability to photograph and sketch crime scenes.
   d. a knowledge of scientific laboratory techniques and the conclusions which may be derived from their use.

9. In order to introduce physical evidence in a trial, all of the following conditions must be fulfilled except:

   a. The article must be properly identified.
   b. The chain of custody must be proved.
   c. The evidence must be shown to be competent, that is, material and relevant.
   d. The evidence must be examined by a laboratory expert.

10. The proof of identity implies that the investigator who first found the object can testify that the exhibit offered in evidence is _____ the object he discovered at the crime scene.

   a. similar to
   b. the same as
   c. almost the same as
   d. not dissimilar to

11. Protecting evidence by accounting for each change of possession is called maintaining the chain of:

   a. custody.
   b. command.
   c. collection.
   d. protection.

12. Each transfer of evidence must not only be recorded but also be:

   a. observed.
   b. witnessed.
   c. photographed.
   d. receipted.

13. The protection of physical evidence serves two major purposes. First, physical evidence is often _____ in nature and carelessness in handling may result in a loss of its value as a clue.

   a. volatile
   b. durable
   c. fragile
   d. complex

14. Second, physical evidence must be presented in court in:

   a. a condition exactly the same as it was at the time of the offense.
   b. a condition similar to the way it was at the time of the offense.
   c. any condition as long as it is recognizable as evidence from the offense.
   d. any condition as long as it is identifiable as evidence from the offense.

15. Alterations in physical evidence are commonly caused by all of the following except:

    a. natural causes, such as exposure to the elements.
    b. negligence and accident, such as careless handling or packing.
    c. intentional changes or loss by investigators.
    d. intentional damage or theft by unauthorized personnel.

16. All unauthorized personnel should be excluded from the crime scene because of the possibility of unintentional damage to the physical evidence by inadvertently being stepped on or handled. This is most likely to occur:

    a. prior to the discovery of its significance.
    b. after it has been photographed.
    c. while it is being collected.
    d. while it is being transported.

17. Often the investigator will receive an article of evidence when he is not at the crime scene and he does not have his evidence collecting equipment. He should:

    a. leave the evidence there and return later with the proper equipment.
    b. telephone another investigator and ask him to bring an evidence kit.
    c. improvise a method of collecting the evidence.
    d. always carry an evidence kit when on an investigation.

18. Known specimens which are used when examining questioned evidence for similarities and differences are called:

    a. associative evidence.   c. representative samples.
    b. evidence samples.   d. standards of comparison.

19. The choice of evidence container will depend on all of the following except:

    a. the size of the specimen.
    b. the investigative purpose the evidence will serve.
    c. the fragility of the evidence.
    d. the physical state, whether liquid or solid, of the evidence.

20. Evidence should be stored in:

    a. an evidence room maintained by the investigative agency.
    b. a locked file cabinet in the investigator's office.
    c. a locked crime-scene unit vehicle.
    d. a scientific laboratory where it can be examined.

21. Each deposit or removal of evidence from storage should be recorded by:

    a. the investigator.
    b. the investigator's supervisor.
    c. the person depositing or receiving the evidence.
    d. the officer in charge of the evidence room.

22. When collecting evidence in the form of organic matter, such as food, blood, or tissue, special consideration should be given to:

    a. its size and shape.
    b. its physical state, whether liquid or solid.
    c. the factors of time and temperature.
    d. its color and hardness.

23. All of the following statements are true except:

    a. Blood will deteriorate when exposed to high temperatures.
    b. For long-term storage, blood should be permitted to freeze solidly.
    c. Ideally, liquid blood and other perishable specimens should be placed in refrigeration as soon as possible after collection.
    d. Organic matter naturally decomposes unless preventive measures are taken.

24. As a general rule, when dealing with perishable evidence, preservative should be added:

    a. routinely.
    b. at the first sign of decomposition.
    c. after determining what the evidence will be used for.
    d. after consulting with a laboratory expert.

25. Most of the errors committed in connection with evidence take place in the _____ of samples.

    a. collection   c. preservation
    b. protection   d. identification

26. All of the following are common errors involving the collection of evidence except:

    a. collecting an insufficient sample.
    b. collecting too large a sample.
    c. failure to supply standards of comparison and control samples.
    d. contaminating evidence by placing one sample in contact with another.

27. In a homicide investigation, a potentially significant stain found on a wood or linoleum floor should be collected by:

    a. scraping the stain off the floor.
    b. scraping the stain off the floor and cutting off part of the unstained floor.
    c. cutting off part of the stained floor.
    d. cutting off part of the stained and part of the unstained floor.

28. The removal of fixed evidence may depend upon all of the following except:

    a. the size and weight of the evidence.
    b. the color and texture of the evidence.
    c. the importance of the evidence to the case.
    d. the seriousness of the case.

29. In a homicide case, a potentially significant tool impression found on a bedroom door should be collected by:

    a. removing the door.
    b. photographing the tool impression.
    c. casting (using clay or silicone rubber to replicate it) the tool impression.
    d. both photographing and casting the tool impression.

30. The most common forms of physical evidence found at the crime scene are:

    a. bloodstains.
    b. hairs and fibers.
    c. articles bearing fingerprints.
    d. dirt, soil, and other particles.

31. Papers which may have fingerprints on them should be handled with _____ and placed in a cellophane envelope.

    a. latex gloves
    b. tongs or forceps
    c. two fingers at the edge
    d. a spatula

32. All of the following types of evidence are *usually* placed in filter paper before being put in a pillbox or other suitable containers except:

    a. hairs and fibers.
    b. soil and dirt particles.
    c. dried blood and semen scrapings.
    d. bullets and buckshot pellets.

33. In a "druggist fold," filter paper is folded into _____ in both directions forming a square interior compartment.

    a. eighths
    b. quarters
    c. thirds
    d. halves

34. Wet clothing should be air-dried before being packed into:

    a. a paper bag for each article of clothing.
    b. a paper bag for each person's clothes.
    c. a plastic evidence bag for each article of clothing.
    d. a plastic evidence bag for each person's clothes.

35. When handling blood or other biological evidence, the investigator should wear latex gloves *primarily*:

    a. to make sure test tubes do not slip from his hand.
    b. to protect against contamination of the evidence from perspiration and other biological residue on the hands.
    c. to protect against infection by the hepatitis and the aids virus.
    d. for convenience in cleaning up after completing the evidence collection.

36. When there is a large pool of blood present at the crime scene, the investigator should use an eye dropper or syringe and collect approximately _____ of blood in a test tube and a second sample of equal amount if DNA analysis may be performed.

a. 2cc
b. 5cc

c. 20cc
d. 50cc

37. If DNA analysis is to be performed, liquid blood should be preserved:

a. with sodium fluoride.
b. with EDTA.

c. by air-drying.
d. by refrigeration only.

38. Dried blood or semen stains on porous material that can neither be moved or scraped may be collected with:

a. a moist swab.
b. a scalpel or razor.

c. a tweezers.
d. a syringe.

39. When using an eyedropper, scalpel, or swab to collect bloodstains, each instrument should be:

a. used only once.
b. changed after collecting several stains.
c. used on only the stains from one person.
d. used on all of the stains.

40. All semen and saliva evidence should be _____ before being packaged and sent to the laboratory.

a. refrigerated
b. preserved

c. air-dried
d. moistened

41. _____ is extremely difficult to see once it is dried.

a. Blood
b. Semen

c. Saliva
d. Paint

42. When a paint smear adheres to the surface of a vehicle, it is necessary to use a metal scalpel to cut off a paint chip, about 1/2 inch square, which would include:

a. only the smear.
b. the smear and the top layer of paint.
c. the smear and all the layers of paint except the undercoat.
d. the smear, all the layers of paint, and the undercoat, until bear metal is reached.

43. Evidence should be properly marked or labeled for identification as it is being:

    a. discovered.
    b. photographed.
    c. collected.
    d. examined in the laboratory.

44. Placing the initials of the investigator on an article of evidence that is found or received at the crime scene is called:

    a. marking.
    b. initialing.
    c. identifying.
    d. labeling.

45. A mark of identification should be placed on:

    a. solid objects.
    b. solid objects having a volume of approximately 1 cubic inch or greater.
    c. solid objects having a volume less than approximately 1 cubic inch.
    d. none of the solid objects.

46. After the articles of evidence have been placed in separate containers, these containers should then be:

    a. marked.
    b. initialed.
    c. sealed.
    d. labeled.

47. After sealing the container, the investigator's initials and the date should be placed:

    a. on the seal.
    b. on the container only.
    c. to extend from the seal to the container.
    d. on a separate label.

48. After the evidence container has been sealed, a label should be attached to the container bearing:

    a. the owner of the articles name and address.
    b. the identifying case information.
    c. the initials of the investigator and the date.
    d. the address where the evidence will be sent.

49. When a bullet is collected as evidence, the steps taken by the investigator would occur in the following order:

    a. marking, placing in a pillbox, sealing, and then labeling.
    b. placing in a pillbox, marking, sealing, and then labeling.
    c. marking, placing in a pillbox, labeling, and then sealing.
    d. placing in a pillbox, marking, labeling, and then sealing.

50. When marking a document, the investigator's initials and the date should be inscribed with a fine-pointed pen:

    a. on the front upper-right hand corner only.
    b. anywhere on the back.
    c. only on the gummed label that will be attached to the cellophane envelope in which the document will be placed.
    d. where the marking will not affect the examination.

51. In order to avoid unnecessarily defacing a firearm, it is best to mark it on an inconspicuous area of the frame such as:

    a. on the bottom under the trigger guard.
    b. on the top above the cylinder.
    c. on the side below the cylinder.
    d. on the side behind the cylinder.

52. A firearm should be marked on the frame and on any part that may leave an imprint on the bullet or cartridge case and is:

    a. removable with tools.   c. not removable.
    b. removable without tools.   d. unusual.

53. If the evidence weapon is a revolver containing loaded cartridges and fired cases, the investigator should do all of the following except:

    a. Diagram the rear face of the cylinder to show the position of each cartridge.
    b. Number the cartridges to correspond to the numbering of the chambers on the diagram.
    c. Mark the rear face of the cylinder on both sides of the chamber which lay under the firing pin.
    d. Send the loaded weapon to the laboratory.

54. A bullet should be marked:

    a. on its base.   c. on its nose.
    b. on its side.   d. only if it is deformed.

55. A fired cartridge case should:

    a. be marked on its base.
    b. be marked on its outer surface near the base.
    c. be marked inside the mouth.
    d. not be marked at all.

56. In submitting a firearm for examination, the investigator should try to supply approximately ten cartridges of ammunition of the same type used in the weapon to serve as:

    a. additional evidence.   c. physical evidence.
    b. associative evidence.   d. standards of comparison.

57. Articles of clothing are best marked by an inked inscription on the _____ of the garment.

a. label
b. collar
c. cuff
d. lining

58. A plaster cast should be marked on:

a. the front while the plaster is wet.
b. the back while the plaster is wet.
c. the front after the plaster has dried.
d. the back after the plaster has dried.

59. For the identification of a crime scene photograph, the print may be marked on _____ and the date and the place of the photograph.

a. the front with the investigator's name
b. the reverse with the investigator's name
c. the front with the photographer's name
d. the reverse with the photographer's name

60. When requesting the FBI to examine evidence, a letter of transmittal should indicate the essential facts of the case and must state that the evidence _____ examined by an expert other than the one at the FBI Laboratory.

a. will be
b. may be
c. has been
d. has not and will not be

Answers:

1. d	p. 79, 1.	21. d	p. 85, 5h.	41. c	p. 91, 8d.
2. a	p. 79, 1.	22. c	p. 85, 6.	42. d	p. 91, 8d.
3. b	p. 79, 1.	23. b	p. 86, 6b.	43. c	p. 91, 9.
4. b	p. 80, 1a.	24. d	p. 86, 7.	44. a	p. 93, 9a.
5. a	p. 80, 1b.	25. a	p. 86, 8.	45. b	p. 93, 9a.
6. c	p. 80, 1c.	26. b	p. 86, 8.	46. c	p. 93, 9b.
7. d	p. 80, 1d.	27. d	p. 87, 8b.	47. c	p. 93, 9b.
8. c	p. 80, 2.	28. b	p. 88, 8d.	48. b	p. 94, 9c.
9. d	p. 81, 3.	29. a	p. 88, 8d.	49. a	p. 94, 9c.
10. b	p. 81, 3.	30. c	p. 89, 8d.	50. d	p. 95, 9d.
11. a	p. 81, 4.	31. b	p. 89, 8d.	51. a	p. 96, 9d.
12. d	p. 81, 4.	32. d	p. 89, 8d.	52. b	p. 96, 9d.
13. c	p. 82, 5.	33. c	p. 89, 8d.	53. d	p. 96, 9d.
14. b	p. 82, 5.	34. a	p. 89, 8d.	54. a	p. 96, 9d.
15. c	p. 82, 5a.	35. c	p. 89, 8d.	55. c	p. 96, 9d.
16. a	p. 83, 5b.	36. b	p. 90, 8d.	56. d	p. 97, 9d.
17. c	p. 84, 5e.	37. b	p. 90, 8d.	57. d	p. 97, 9d.
18. d	p. 84, 5f.	38. a	p. 90, 8d.	58. b	p. 97, 9d.
19. b	p. 84, 5g.	39. a	p. 90, 8d.	59. d	p. 97, 9d.
20. a	p. 85, 5h.	40. c	p. 91, 8d.	60. d	p. 99, 10.

Chapter 8
INTERVIEWS

Questions:

1. The effectiveness of an investigator is largely dependent upon his ability to:

    a. identify suspects.
    b. obtain information.
    c. collect evidence.
    d. trace fugitives.

2. When building a case, the investigator must be able to develop in people who are usually _____ a willingness to give information, to testify, and to make formal written statements.

    a. friends
    b. associates
    c. acquaintances
    d. strangers

3. The technique of systematically questioning the people living near or frequenting the crime scene in order to locate someone who can provide information about the crime is called:

    a. building the case.
    b. tracing the fugitive.
    c. canvassing the neighborhood.
    d. interviewing the witnesses.

4. The primary purpose of conducting the systematic interviews of the people in a neighborhood is to find a _____ or someone who can provide facts about the crime.

    a. suspect
    b. witness
    c. victim
    d. complainant

5. Ideally, the canvass should take place:

    a. at the same time of day as when the crime occurred.
    b. in the evening or on the weekend when people are available to answer questions.
    c. at different times of day in order to talk to as many people as possible.
    d. in the morning when people are more alert and eager to answer questions.

6. The neighborhood canvass is usually carried out by:

    a. one investigator.
    b. a pair of investigators.
    c. either one or two investigators.
    d. a team of investigators.

7. _____ is the questioning of a person who is believed to possess knowledge that is of official interest to the investigator.

    a. A canvass
    b. An investigation
    c. An interview
    d. An interrogation

8. After each interview, the novice investigator should subject his performance to a critical review by checking the quantity and quality of the information obtained and the extent to which he _____ the subject.

a. earned the respect of
b. allayed the fears of
c. established rapport with
d. controlled the interview with

9. The investigator as an interviewer should have the qualities of all of the following except:

a. a salesman.
b. a debater.
c. an actor.
d. a psychologist.

10. Because a completely voluntary offer of information is the ideal result of an interview, the investigator must endeavor:

a. to persuade the subject of the benefits of talking to him.
b. to lead the subject to reveal more than he had intended.
c. to overwhelm the subject with the importance of the case.
d. to win the confidence of the subject.

11. The primary trait which the interviewer should possess is the forcefulness of personality which induces the subject to _____ the interviewer:

a. be careful what he says to
b. be ashamed not to talk to
c. trust and confide in
d. avoid arguing with

12. In order to establish rapport with a subject, it is necessary to share common interests. For this reason, the investigator should have:

a. an extensive higher education as well as practical knowledge.
b. close friends from every walk of life with whom he can discuss his experiences.
c. membership in a number of community organizations.
d. a wide range of practical knowledge as well as an acquaintance with the habits and temperament of people from all walks of life.

13. A background interview of a businessman or a representative of a large company would usually take place:

a. in the subject's office during office hours.
b. in the subject's office after office hours.
c. in the investigator's office during office hours.
d. in the investigator's office after office hours.

14. In order to obtain the maximum amount of information in a routine criminal case, the investigator should schedule the interview:

   a. whenever the subject decides he would like it.
   b. during office hours when the subject can fit it into his schedule.
   c. whenever the investigator has the time and inclination to go into the matter in detail.
   d. whenever the subject has the leisure to devote his full attention to the matter.

15. In important criminal cases, the investigator should arrange to interview the witnesses in places other than their homes or offices:

   a. so that they are not embarrassed in front of their family and colleagues.
   b. so that they cannot secretly record the interview.
   c. to protect the investigator from hostile friends and relatives.
   d. to keep the witness from feeling confident and thus controlling the kind and amount of information given.

16. As a general principle, an interview should take place as soon as possible after the event while the information is fresh in the mind of the witness and he has had little time to think about:

   a. any unpleasant consequences of giving the information.
   b. the investigator's motive in asking for information.
   c. requesting monetary compensation for his help in the case.
   d. why the event happened.

17. On first meeting the subject of an interview, the investigator, in order to avoid any misunderstanding, should begin by:

   a. showing his credentials and informing the subject of his identity.
   b. explaining the nature of the crime he is investigating and informing the subject of the type of information he is looking for.
   c. asking the subject for identification so that the investigator can be certain of the identity of the person he is talking to.
   d. informing the subject of his rights and that he has no obligation to speak to an investigator.

18. When conducting an interview, the investigator should do all of the following except:

   a. Before interviewing a witness, mentally review the case and consider what information the witness can contribute.
   b. Give the witness every opportunity to give a complete account without interruptions.
   c. Insist on "yes" and "no" answers to important questions as a preparation for testimony in court.
   d. After the witness has told his story, review it with him and request him to amplify certain points.

19. When questioning a witness about his story, the investigator should do all of the following except:

   a. Control the interview so that complete and accurate information that is responsive to the questions is obtained.
   b. Correlate information obtained from one witness with that obtained from others so that important facts are corroborated.
   c. Point out all discrepancies, falsehoods, and inaccuracies as they become apparent and request an immediate and complete explanation.
   d. Treat questionable points by rewording queries and asking additional questions.

20. When questioning a witness all of the following rules should be followed except:

   a. Ask only one question at a time to avoid confusing the witness.
   b. The answer to a question should be suggested in the question so that the investigator can obtain the type of information that he is looking for.
   c. Questions should be simple because long, complicated questions serve only to confuse and irritate.
   d. Never insist on "yes" and "no" answers because it is unfair to the witness and results in inaccurate information.

21. "Would you care to sign this statement?" is a poorly formulated question because:

   a. it suggests that a negative reply would be acceptable.
   b. it suggests that a positive reply would be acceptable.
   c. it is not expressed politely.
   d. it is too ambiguous.

22. "Could I possibly interview you at ten o'clock tomorrow morning?" should be rephrased by saying:

   a. "Would you like to be interviewed tomorrow morning at ten o'clock?"
   b. "Please may I interview you tomorrow morning at ten o'clock?"
   c. "Wouldn't it be enjoyable to meet tomorrow morning at ten o'clock for an interview?"
   d. "I have the interview set for ten o'clock tomorrow morning?"

23. The investigator must display confidence and authority when interviewing a witness because:

   a. a witness will only cooperate if he is intimidated.
   b. any wavering on the investigator's part will encourage evasion and a resistance to tell the whole story.
   c. a display of sympathy and understanding by the investigator will never elicit the truth from a reluctant witness.
   d. the average witness secretly enjoys controlling the interview and manipulating the investigator.

24. Two principles should guide the investigator in maintaining control of digression: (1) The subject must be kept on the point being discussed and (2) The subject must be prevented from:

    a. answering the questions too succinctly.
    b. progressing through the narrative too quickly.
    c. going into detail about essential matters.
    d. going into detail about nonessential matters.

25. All of the following are techniques the investigator should use to control digression except:

    a. precise questioning.   c. skipping by guessing.
    b. shunting.   d. suggesting the answer in the question.

26. _____, which means constructing the question carefully in order to restrict the range of information which the subject can give in answer, is the investigator's most effective device in controlling digression.

    a. Precise questioning.   c. Skipping by guessing
    b. Shunting   d. Suggesting the answer in the question

27. _____ consists in asking a question which relates the digression to the original line of questioning.

    a. Precise questioning   c. Skipping by guessing
    b. Shunting   d. Suggesting the answer in the question

28. _____ consists of passing over intermediate details of a long narrative by speculating as to the probable outcome of the various stages of the subject's recital.

    a. Precise questioning   c. Skipping by guessing
    b. Shunting   d. Suggesting the answer in the question

29. Young children ordinarily do not make good witnesses because of their tendency to:

    a. intentionally deceive.   c. be motivated by jealousy and dislikes.
    b. be imaginative and inventive.   d. be vindictive.

30. The intense preoccupation of _____ with themselves prevents them from being ideal witnesses.

    a. children   c. young persons
    b. boys and girls   d. middle-aged persons

31. _____ are often ideal witnesses because they are aware of their fellow beings at other age levels and their faculties and judgement are usually unimpaired.

    a. Boys and girls   c. Middle-aged persons
    b. Young persons   d. Older persons

32. The investigator should endeavor to classify the subject as soon as possible after beginning the interview in order to:

    a. establish control of the interview.
    b. determine whether the subject is telling the truth.
    c. organize and hence simplify the myriad details of the case.
    d. adjust his method of interviewing to the personality and attitude he is encountering.

33. The technique of asking a great many questions that the subject cannot deny knowing the answers to and then shifting to relevant questions is effective for dealing with the _____ type.

    a. know-nothing   c. inebriated
    b. disinterested   d. suspicious

34. Flattery is an effective technique when interviewing the _____ types.

    a. know-nothing and suspicious   c. talkative and honest
    b. disinterested and inebriated   d. deceitful and timid

35. Creating the impression that the investigator knows a good deal about the case and that this knowledge may be used against the subject if he does not cooperate is an effective technique for dealing with the _____ type.

    a. know-nothing   c. suspicious
    b. disinterested   d. timid

36. Threatening to redirect the investigation against the subject on a charge of obstruction of justice is a technique to be used against the _____ witness.

    a. talkative   c. deceitful
    b. honest   d. timid

37. The most difficult kind of interview is with the type of subject that:

    a. is deceitful   c. is boastful and egotistical.
    b. is timid.   d. refuses to talk.

38. In the interview with the _____, the investigator should convince him of his interest and complete cooperation in the case while privately forming an opinion of his reliability.

    a. victim   c. complainant
    b. informant   d. person complained of

39. Before the interview with the _____, the investigator should review the elements of the offense and this person's record and reputation. Questioning should be impartial and probing.

    a. victim   c. complainant
    b. informant   d. person "complained of"

40. The _____ should be flattered. He should be permitted to talk freely and then questioned for details.

    a. victim
    b. informant

    c. complainant
    d. person "complained of"

41. In the interview with the _____, the investigator should be sympathetic and listen to the complete story. He should not offer any opinion and just devote himself to gathering the facts.

    a. victim
    b. informant

    c. complainant
    d. person "complained of"

42. During the interview, the investigator will be forming a judgement on the credibility of the witness based on all of the following except:

    a. physical mannerisms.
    b. style of dress.

    c. emotional state.
    d. frankness and content of statements.

43. Because the appearance of a notebook may instill excessive caution in the subject, the investigator must make a judgement as to when it should be used depending on the _____ of the matter being discussed.

    a. importance
    b. significance

    c. criminality
    d. sensitivity

44. After the investigator puts the pertinent information in writing, he should ask the subject to:

    a. draw conclusions.
    b. list other possible sources.
    c. sign the statement.
    d. make his recommendation on what direction the investigation should proceed.

45. _____ may be defined as a sleep-like state of heightened awareness and concentration. In this state, the subject becomes aware of those experiences, stored in his subconscious memory, that were repressed, forgotten, or that he was not fully conscious of at the time of their occurrence.

    a. Concentration
    b. Meditation

    c. A cognitive interview
    d. Hypnosis

46. The "television technique," in which the subject while under hypnosis is told to imagine he is watching a videotape of the crime, is advantageous for all of the following reasons except:

   a. Watching the crime on television is less frightening than reliving the actual crime.
   b. Replaying the event as an imaginary videotape allows the subject to pause on important images.
   c. The subject becomes very receptive to the suggestions of the hypnotist.
   d. The subject can provide a more complete account of the crime because the hypnotist can take as long as he needs to run through the videotape.

47. Courts severely restrict the use of testimony from a witness who has been hypnotized because:

   a. the witness may acquire misleading or false information by being overly receptive to the hypnotist.
   b. a witness will recall so many inconsequential and irrelevant details that it will confuse the jury.
   c. a mind that has been hypnotized can no longer be counted on to function normally since it has been under the control of a hypnotist.
   d. they believe that hypnosis has no scientific basis and should be rejected as superstition.

48. The cognitive interview is a series of techniques designed to help the witness:

   a. understand the nature of the crime he has just witnessed.
   b. relate to the problems of the suspect and victim of the crime.
   c. understand what it means to be a witness and his role in the investigative process.
   d. enhance memory recall in order to recollect the details of a crime.

49. All of the following techniques are used in the cognitive interview except:

   a. trying to picture all of the possible ways a crime like the one under consideration can be committed.
   b. speaking freely about the crime without hurry or interruption.
   c. mentally recreating the period before, during, and after the crime.
   d. recalling every detail of the crime, no matter how insignificant.

50. All of the following techniques are used in the cognitive interview except:

   a. considering the events of the crime in a different sequence such as reverse order.
   b. considering the events from another point of view such as the victim's or the suspect's.
   c. associating the sense perceptions of the events to people, places, and things that are familiar to him.
   d. mentally selecting a possible suspect and imagining that he is committing the crime.

Answers:

1. b	p. 103, 1.	18. c	p. 110, 8.	35. c	p. 116, 11d.
2. d	p. 104, 1b.	19. c	p. 111, 8c.	36. c	p. 117, 11g.
3. c	p. 104, 1c.	20. b	p. 111, 8c.	37. d	p. 118, 11j.
4. b	p. 104, 1c.	21. a	p. 112, 8c.	38. c	p. 118, 12a.
5. a	p. 104, 1c.	22. d	p. 112, 8c.	39. d	p. 118, 12b.
6. d	p. 105, 1c.	23. b	p. 112, 8c.	40. b	p. 119, 12c.
7. c	p. 105, 2.	24. d	p. 113, 9.	41. a	p. 119, 12d.
8. c	p. 105, 3.	25. d	p. 113, 9.	42. b	p. 119, 13.
9. b	p. 106, 4.	26. a	p. 113, 9a.	43. d	p. 120, 14.
10. d	p. 106, 4a.	27. b	p. 113, 9b.	44. c	p. 120, 14.
11. c	p. 106, 4b.	28. c	p. 114, 9c.	45. d	p. 120, 15.
12. d	p. 107, 4c.	29. b	p. 114, 10a.	46. c	p. 121, 15.
13. a	p. 107, 5a.	30. c	p. 115, 10b.	47. a	p. 121, 15.
14. d	p. 107, 5b.	31. c	p. 115, 10c.	48. d	p. 122, 16.
15. d	p. 108, 5c.	32. d	p. 116, 11.	49. a	p. 122, 16a.
16. a	p. 108, 5d.	33. a	p. 116, 11a.	50. d	p. 122, 16d.
17. a	p. 108, 6.	34. b	p. 116, 11b.		

Chapter 9

INTERROGATIONS

Questions:

1. Before interrogating a suspect in custody, the interrogator should do all of the following except:

    a. Identify himself as a law enforcement officer.
    b. Explain the nature of the offense and the wish to question him about it.
    c. Explain to him the sentencing for an outright acknowledgement of guilt.
    d. Advise the suspect of his *Miranda* rights.

2. All of the following are part of the *Miranda* warnings except:

    a. You have the right to remain silent.
    b. Anything you say can be used against you in court.
    c. You have the right to legal counsel.
    d. If you cannot afford a lawyer, the state will appoint one for you and send you a bill for his services.

3. In his response to the *Miranda* warnings, the suspect may choose to remain silent, may request counsel, or may _____ his rights.

    a. assert   c. affirm
    b. waive   d. deny

4. Proof of a waiver of rights by the accused may only take the form of:

   a. an express statement.   c. answering a question.
   b. silence.   d. a lengthy denial of guilt.

5. The *Miranda* decision restricts the use of information gathered by the police from a suspect in custody by means of:

   a. a volunteered statement.   c. a confession freely made.
   b. any statement.   d. interrogation.

6. An individual enters a police station and states that he wishes to confess a crime. The police officer should:

   a. read the person his *Miranda* rights.
   b. call for a court appointed lawyer.
   c. write down his statement.
   d. ask the individual if he really wants to make a statement.

7. General questioning, without *Miranda* warnings, of people at the scene of the crime who are not under restraint is:

   a. prohibited.   c. poor police practice.
   b. permitted.   d. only sometimes permitted.

8. When there is an immediate threat to public safety such a the presence of a loaded weapon or a bomb, an arresting officer may question a suspect in custody without first giving *Miranda* warnings. This public safety exception to the *Miranda* rule was created by the Supreme Court in 1984 in:

   a. *New York v. Quarles.*   c. *Gideon v. Wainwright.*
   b. *Powell v. Alabama.*   d. *Argesinger v. Hamlin.*

9. The existence of a threat to the public safety is determined by an objective standard, namely, whether:

   a. a threat actually exists.
   b. it is highly probable that a threat actually exists.
   c. a reasonable police officer in this situation would conclude that a threat exists.
   d. the answers given by the suspect are suspicious.

10. In 1932, in _____, also called the "Scottsboro Boys" rape case, the Supreme Court declared that the Constitution guarantees the right to counsel in state court trials whenever the defendant's life is at stake.

   a. *New York v. Quarles*   c. *Gideon v. Wainwright*
   b. *Powell v. Alabama*   d. *Argesinger v. Hamlin*

11. _____ required the state to furnish free legal counsel to poor defendants in all felony cases.

    a. *Miranda v. Arizona*   c. *Argesinger v. Hamlin*
    b. *Powell v. Alabama*   d. *Gideon v. Wainwright*

12. In _____, the Supreme Court ruled that a person in police custody had a right to legal counsel during interrogation.

    a. *Miranda v. Arizona*   c. *Argesinger v. Hamlin*
    b. *Powell v. Alabama*   d. *Gideon v. Wainwright*

13. _____ required the state to furnish free legal counsel to poor defendants whenever imprisonment is to be considered as punishment.

    a. *Miranda v. Arizona*   c. *Argesinger v. Hamlin*
    b. *New York v. Quarles*   d. *Gideon v. Wainwright*

14. A _____ is an offense ordinarily punishable by a sentence of less than a year or a fine.

    a. felony   c. violation
    b. misdemeanor   d. summons

15. In many jurisdictions, it is perceived that a defendant who insists on his right to counsel in misdemeanor cases are treated _____ other defendants.

    a. more fairly than   c. more harshly than
    b. more leniently than   d. the same as

16. In major cities that are swamped with drug offenders, legal representation can best be described as:

    a. excellent.   c. minimal.
    b. good.   d. nonexistent.

17. A questioning of a person suspected of having committed an offense or of a person who is reluctant to divulge information is called:

    a. information gathering.   c. an interrogation.
    b. an interview.   d. an inquiry.

18. A(n) _____ is a person, other than a suspect, who is requested to give information concerning an incident or a person.

    a. witness   c. complainant
    b. informant   d. source

19. A(n) _____ is a person whose guilt is considered on reasonable grounds to be a possibility.

    a. subject
    b. suspect
    c. perpetrator
    d. offender

20. The term _____ is used to represent the person who is being interviewed or interrogated.

    a. subject
    b. suspect
    c. witness
    d. interviewee

21. The primary purpose of interrogation is to obtain:

    a. a confession from the guilty party.
    b. an admission from which guilt can be inferred.
    c. information that will further the investigation.
    d. the identities of all persons involved in a crime.

22. All of the following may be purposes of interrogation except:

    a. to develop additional leads.
    b. to learn the identity of accomplices.
    c. to learn of the existence and the location of physical evidence.
    d. to force the subject to make an admission or confession.

23. The interrogator must be able to impress his subject and inspire confidence:

    a. through the use of formal authority.
    b. because his personality commands respect.
    c. because he is completely in sympathy with the subject.
    d. by detailing the consequences of noncooperation.

24. The most important acquired characteristic of an interrogator is his:

    a. self-control.
    b. acting ability.
    c. general knowledge.
    d. ability to observe and interpret.

25. All of the following are adjectives that describe the personality characteristics of the ideal investigator except:

    a. alert.
    b. emotional.
    c. persevering.
    d. logical.

26. As a man of integrity, the interrogator should:

    a. never make promises at all.
    b. make promises only when necessary to obtain confessions in major cases.
    c. only make promises he can keep.
    d. feel obligated to fulfill only those promises that have been recorded in the interrogation log.

27. All of the following are abilities that are helpful in interrogating a suspect except:

a. to antagonize or intimidate. c. to observe and interpret.
b. to maintain self-control. d. to feign anger or sympathy.

28. It is of great importance for the investigator to develop an effective personality that will induce in the subject:

a. a desire to appease. c. fear of giving the wrong answer.
b. a desire to respond. d. the need to be evasive.

29. All of the following recommendations would be helpful to the interrogator except:

a. The interrogator must control any physical mannerism that may distract or antagonize the subject.
b. The interrogator must always be in command of the situation.
c. The speech of the interrogator should be adapted to the subject's cultural level.
d. Euphemisms to describe the suspect's conduct should never be used.

30. All of the following statements about interrogation are true except:

a. Civilian dress is more likely to inspire confidence and friendship in a criminal than a uniform.
b. The interrogator should maintain the attitude that he is seeking the truth rather than seeking to convict or punish.
c. The interrogator should identify himself at the outset of the interrogation and show his credentials.
d. The investigator should try never to be left alone with the subject during the interrogation.

31. All of the following statements about the design and use of the interrogation room are true except:

a. A room with a single door and no windows is preferred to avoid interruptions and distractions.
b. The subject and the investigator should be seated with no large furniture between them.
c. An object or picture should be placed prominently in the room so that both investigator and subject can focus on it to relax and relieve tension.
d. The subject should be seated with his back to the door to deprive him of the hope of interruptions or distractions.

32. An interrogation room should be equipped with all of the following technical aids except:

a. a tape or video recorder. c. a polygraph.
b. a hidden microphone. d. a two-way mirror.

33. An interrogation _____ is essentially a form on which the investigator maintains in chronological order a record of the time periods of interrogation together with a time record of necessities and privileges requested by and granted to the subject.

   a. log
   b. record

   c. report
   d. summary

34. To pursue a logical line of questioning, the interrogator should possess all of the following except:

   a. a thorough knowledge of the particular case under investigation.
   b. a firm belief in the guilt of the subject.
   c. a mental outline of the elements of the offense.
   d. a mental outline of the mode of proof required to substantiate each element.

35. In the work of interrogation, the following principle should guide the investigator:

   a. The simplest approach is the best if it achieves the desired result.
   b. A complex crime always requires a complex solution.
   c. The investigator must always give the appearance of knowing more than the subject does.
   d. The more you confuse the subject, the more likely he will make a mistake.

36. To be admissible in court, a confession must be _____ and trustworthy and it must have been obtained by civilized police practices.

   a. intelligent
   b. thorough

   c. voluntary
   d. clear

37. In determining whether undue pressure has been exerted on the subject, the courts make use of what is called the _____ test.

   a. interrogation technique
   b. totality of circumstances

   c. interrogation log
   d. police civilized practices

38. All of the following statements concerning the use of trickery and deception as interrogation techniques are true except:

   a. Trickery and deception should be avoided in those cases where a straight forward approach can achieve the same results.
   b. Trickery or deception will not by itself invalidate a confession.
   c. Trickery and deception may be used even if it is likely to lead the subject into a false confession.
   d. The use of trickery and deception is one of the factors considered in the totality of circumstances test for voluntariness.

39. The choice of interrogation technique should depend on all of the following except:

   a. the nature of the crime under investigation.
   b. the character of the subject.
   c. the investigator's like or dislike of the subject.
   d. the investigator's personality and limitations.

40. All of the following are interrogation techniques practiced by experienced investigator's except:

   a. promising a shorter sentence if the subject confesses.
   b. befriending the subject and helping him to make things right.
   c. pretending to know every detail of the crime under investigation.
   d. informing the subject falsely that his accomplice has implicated him.

41. Most of the interrogation techniques described in this text involve the investigator pretending to have more _____ than he actually has.

   a. authority   c. concern
   b. intelligence   d. evidence

42. One of the first lessons to be learned by the inexperienced investigator is the unfortunate ease with which he can:

   a. be deceived by the subject.   c. lose control of the interrogation.
   b. be controlled by the subject.   d. get sidetracked by digression.

43. When the interrogator senses that his tactics are not getting him anywhere, he should:

   a. end the interrogation as soon as possible.
   b. take a break and come back after additional planning.
   c. call in another interrogator to help.
   d. become angry with the subject and demand answers.

44. In detecting deception, the interrogator draws his conclusions not only from the inconsistencies and improbabilities in the subject's statement but also from the _____ of the subject discernible in his features and mannerisms or in his unconscious behavior.

   a. emotional reaction   c. subconscious state
   b. physical state   d. understanding

45. Observed physiological changes in the subject, such as a quickened heartbeat, a change in breathing, blushing, perspiring, and dryness of mouth, are usually consistent with a state of:

   a. guilt only.   c. both nervousness and guilt.
   b. nervousness only.   d. neither nervousness nor guilt.

46. The _____ measures and records changes in blood pressure, pulse rate, breathing, and the resistance of the skin to a small electrical current.

    a. polygraph
    b. lie detection test
    c. psychological stress evaluator
    d. general acceptance test

47. The most important element in the process of detecting deception is:

    a. the quality and accuracy of the test machine.
    b. the qualified examiner.
    c. the treatment of the subject before, during, and after the test.
    d. the construction and order of the questions.

48. _____ questions enable the examiner to establish a norm for the subject's reactions to questions free of emotional content.

    a. Relevant
    b. Provocative
    c. Neutral or irrelevant
    d. Subtle

49. The guilty person's fears usually tend to increase during the test. The nervousness of the innocent person tends to _____ during the test.

    a. decrease
    b. also increase
    c. remain the same
    d. disappear

50. *Frye v. United States* set forth criteria for the judicial acceptance of a scientific advancement. To be admissible, a principle or procedure must have already received _____ from the scientists in the particular field to which it belongs.

    a. universal acceptance
    b. general notice
    c. no criticism
    d. general acceptance

51. Information obtained by means of the polygraph is _____ accepted as direct evidence in a court of law.

    a. generally
    b. often
    c. not generally
    d. in important cases

52. All of the following are probably not fit subjects for a polygraph test except the person who:

    a. has a heart condition or a respiratory disorder.
    b. is insane or mentally ill.
    c. is a hardened criminal.
    d. is under the influence of alcohol or a sedative.

53. The questions to be used in a lie detector test should be constructed by the examiner to be all of the following except:

    a. short and simple.
    b. open to interpretation.
    c. easily understood.
    d. requiring only a "yes" or "no" answer.

54. The polygraph examiner is interested in the subject's reaction to the _____ of the question.

    a. immediate sense   c. hidden meaning
    b. complexity   d. puzzling nature

55. A questioning technique used by polygraph experts that involves a series of relevant (concerning the offense) and irrelevant (not concerning the offense) questions mixed together in a planned order is called the _____ test.

    a. general acceptance   c. peak of tension
    b. general question   d. *Frye*

56. A questioning technique used by polygraph experts that involves a series of questions leading up to one that involves a specific detail of the offense is called the _____ test.

    a. general acceptance   c. peak of tension
    b. general question   d. *Frye*

57. Most unsatisfactory lie detector examinations are attributable to two main factors: (1) unsuitable subjects; and (2) _____ .

    a. unprepared examiners   c. too complicated questions
    b. unreliable machines   d. unexpected interruptions

58. In order to insure the success of a polygraph examination, the investigator should follow all of the following rules except:

    a. Do not wait until the last minute to ask a person to take the test.
    b. Use it to screen a large number of possible suspects to identify the guilty party.
    c. Do not tell a suspect everything you know about the offense.
    d. Be sure to investigate the case before you ask a person to take the test.

59. The Psychological Stress Evaluator (PSE) is a form of a lie detector that is based on the principle that internal stress is reflected in the:

    a. pulse rate.   c. audible variations of the voice.
    b. breathing rate.   d. inaudible variations of the voice.

Answers:

1. c	p. 126, 1.	21. c	p. 134, 6.	41. d	p. 144, 12d.		
2. d	p. 126, 1d.	22. d	p. 135, 6.	42. c	p. 146, 13.		
3. b	p. 128, 2c.	23. b	p. 135, 7.	43. b	p. 147, 13d.		
4. a	p. 128, 2c.	24. c	p. 136, 7a.	44. a	p. 147, 14.		
5. d	p. 130, 3a.	25. b	p. 136, 7b.	45. c	p. 148, 14a.		

6. c	p. 130, 3a.	26. c	p. 137, 7d.	46. a	p. 149, 14b.
7. b	p. 130, 3b.	27. a	p. 137, 7f.	47. b	p. 149, 14b.
8. a	p. 130, 3c.	28. b	p. 137, 8.	48. c	p. 149, 14b.
9. c	p. 130, 3c.	29. d	p. 138, 8c.	49. a	p. 149, 14b.
10. b	p. 131, 4a.	30. d	p. 139, 8g.	50. d	p. 149, 14b.
11. d	p. 131, 4b.	31. c	p. 139, 9b.	51. c	p. 150, 14b.
12. a	p. 131, 4c.	32. c	p. 140, 9d.	52. c	p. 150, 14c.
13. c	p. 131, 4d.	33. a	p. 140, 9e.	53. b	p. 151, 14e.
14. b	p. 132, 4e.	34. b	p. 141, 10.	54. a	p. 152, 14e.
15. c	p. 132, 4e.	35. a	p. 141, 11.	55. b	p. 152, 14f.
16. c	p. 133, 4f.	36. c	p. 142, 11a.	56. c	p. 152, 14f.
17. c	p. 134, 5a.	37. b	p. 142, 11b.	57. a	p. 153, 14h.
18. a	p. 134, 5b.	38. c	p. 142, 11f.	58. b	p. 154, 14h.
19. b	p. 134, 5c.	39. c	p. 143, 12.	59. d	p. 155, 15.
20. a	p. 134, 5d.	40. a	p. 143, 12.		

Chapter 10

ADMISSIONS, CONFESSIONS, AND WRITTEN STATEMENTS

Questions:

1. Ideally, a confession should be taken:

   a. in an oral form only.
   b. in a written statement only.
   c. in both an oral and a written form, with the oral statement preferred.
   d. in both an oral and a written form, with the written statement preferred.

2. All of the following statements about confessions are true except:

   a. Almost half of all felony defendants make a confession.
   b. The written confession is legal proof that the suspect committed the crime.
   c. Often the written confession is not considered admissible in court.
   d. The investigator should develop the proof of the elements of the offense independently of the written confession.

3. Confessions have been called "the prime source of other evidence" because:

   a. it is easier to discuss the crime with the suspect than with the victim.
   b. it is always difficult to obtain information from witnesses.
   c. the suspect has more information about the details of the crime than anyone else.
   d. because the introduction of all other evidence depends upon the admissibility of the confession.

4. _____ is a self-incriminatory statement by the subject falling short of an acknowledgment of guilt. It is an acknowledgment of a fact or circumstance from which guilt may be inferred.

a. An admission
b. A confession

c. A deposition
d. An affirmation

5. According to the *Miranda* decision, before an individual in custody makes any incriminating statement he:

a. must always be given *Miranda* warnings.
b. must be given *Miranda* warnings only if his statement acknowledges guilt.
c. need not be given *Miranda* warnings.
d. need not be given *Miranda* warnings only if the statement denies guilt.

6. _____ is a direct acknowledgement of the truth of the guilty fact as charged or of some essential part of the commission of the criminal act itself.

a. An admission
b. A confession

c. A deposition
d. An affirmation

7. Before the prosecution may use any statement arising from custodial interrogation, the investigator must first demonstrate through his own testimony and that of witnesses that the statement is:

a. truthful.
b. voluntary.

c. inculpatory (incriminating).
d. exculpatory (exonerating).

8. _____ is the testimony of a witness reduced to writing under oath, before a person empowered to administer oaths.

a. An admission
b. A confession

c. A deposition
d. An affirmation

9. Written statements should be taken especially from all of the following except:

a. a reluctant witness.
b. an eager witness.
c. a witness who changes his mind often.
d. a witness who will be unable to attend the trial.

10. The most desirable form of written confession is one in which:

a. the subject writes his own comprehensive statement without guidance.
b. the investigator gives the subject a list of the essential points to be covered in the subject's written statement.
c. the subject delivers his statement orally to the investigator who writes the statement.
d. the investigator prepares the statement by writing his version of the information given by the subject.

11. It is of great importance, particularly in a confession, that the written statement:

  a. include all of the information that the subject has related about the crime.
  b. include all the elements of the crime and the facts associating the suspect to these elements.
  c. be composed entirely by the subject to insure that it is authentic and voluntary.
  d. be composed for the most part by the investigator to make sure that the elements of the crime are included.

12. After the written confession has been prepared for signature, witnesses will be introduced and the subject and the witnesses will sign the document. This is done so that the witnesses will be able to later testify to all of the following except:

  a. that the subject read and revised the entire document.
  b. that the subject understood the contents of the confession.
  c. that the subject knew what he was doing and acted voluntarily.
  d. that the subject's statement is true and correct.

13. If the subject is to be sworn to the written confession, _____ will administer the oath.

  a. the subject   c. an attorney
  b. a witness   d. the investigator

14. After obtaining a written confession, the investigator should review the confession in relation to the charge. All of the following points should be considered except:

  a. Have the elements of proof been established?
  b. What substantiating evidence is needed to support the facts contained in the confession.
  c. What additional confessions can be obtained to corroborate the information found in this confession.
  d. Is there sufficient evidence independent of the confession to show that the offense has been committed by someone.

15. *A confession must be voluntary and trustworthy, and it must have been obtained by civilized police practices.* This is the test employed by state and federal courts for the _____ of a confession.

  a. admissibility   c. truthfulness
  b. reliability   d. voluntariness

16. A summary of the procedural safeguards for meeting the test of admissibility will include all of the following except:

   a. the fourfold warning and proof of waiver.
   b. the investigator's and witness's testimony to the voluntariness of the confession.
   c. the subject having to sign his statement.
   d. the record of the interrogation, including the interrogator's notes and the interrogation log.

17. _____ is the direct application of illegal physical methods such as beatings.

   a. Duress
   b. Torture
   c. Coercion
   d. Psychological constraint

18. _____ is the imposition of restrictions on physical behavior such as prolonged detention in a dark cell.

   a. Duress
   b. Torture
   c. Coercion
   d. Psychological constraint

19. _____ is the unlawful restraining of the free action of the will by threats or other methods of instilling fear. For example, suggesting that harm may come to the suspect, his relatives, or his property.

   a. Duress
   b. Torture
   c. Coercion
   d. Psychological constraint

20. When obtaining from the suspect a waiver of his rights, deception and trickery may:

   a. be used if it is not of such a nature as to make an innocent man confess.
   b. be used if the suspect is later given an explanation.
   c. sometimes be used if the acts are not inherently coercive.
   d. never be used.

21. All of the following deceptions may be used in obtaining a confession except:

   a. Informing the suspect that his accomplice just confessed.
   b. Informing the suspect that he has failed a polygraph test.
   c. Promising the suspect that he will be released from custody.
   d. Pretending that his fingerprint has been found on a weapon.

22. All of the following are promises that may render a confession inadmissible except:

   a. a promise that the suspect will receive a pardon.
   b. a promise that the investigator will explain the crime to the suspect's wife.
   c. a promise that the suspect will receive a lighter sentence.
   d. a promise that the suspect will be prosecuted for only one of several crimes.

23. During the course of the interrogation, if the suspect confesses to two different crimes the investigator should draw up:

    a. two separate confessions, one for each crime.
    b. only one confession for the crime presently under consideration.
    c. only one confession listing both crimes.
    d. two identical confessions listing both crimes on each.

24. In order for the confession of a suspect not to be used against his accomplice in court, the accomplice, when first learning of the confession, must:

    a. remain silent.   c. deny it
    b. agree with it.   d. ignore it

25. When a defendant testifies in court in his own defense, a confession obtained in violation of the *Miranda* rules may:

    a. be introduced as substantive evidence against the defendant.
    b. be used to challenge his testimony.
    c. be accepted as an admissible confession.
    d. never be used.

26. If wrong police methods have been used, it is possible to later obtain a valid confession by:

    a. showing that the threats or other abusive influences have been removed.
    b. having a different investigator assigned to interrogate the subject.
    c. having the investigator formally admit his mistakes in a sworn statement.
    d. forcing the subject to submit to another properly run interrogation.

Answers:

1. d	p. 158, 1.	10. a	p. 165, 11.	19. d	p. 171, 17c.		
2. b	p. 159, 2.	11. b	p. 165, 12.	20. d	p. 171, 18.		
3. c	p. 159, 2.	12. d	p. 166, 13.	21. c	p. 172, 18b.		
4. a	p. 160, 4.	13. d	p. 168, 14.	22. b	p. 172, 18b.		
5. a	p. 161, 4.	14. c	p. 169, 15c.	23. a	p. 172, 19a.		
6. b	p. 161, 5.	15. a	p. 169, 16a.	24. c	p. 173, 19b.		
7. b	p. 161, 6.	16. c	p. 169, 16b.	25. b	p. 173, 19c.		
8. c	p. 163, 8.	17. c	p. 170, 17a.	26. a	p. 173, 20.		
9. b	p. 163, 9.	18. a	p. 170, 17b.				

Chapter 11

RECORDING INTERVIEWS AND INTERROGATIONS

Questions:

1. Relying on simple memory to record interviews rather than written notes may sometimes be preferable because:

    a. the appearance of paper and pencil may cause the subject to be more cautious in his responses.
    b. written notes tend to include too much detailed information.
    c. mental notes may be more accurate.
    d. it gives the investigator the appearance of great mental ability, thus helping him control the interview.

2. In recording interviews and interrogations in important criminal cases:

    a. a stenographer should always be present.
    b. written notes will be sufficient in all cases.
    c. tape recording or videotaping are preferable to written notes.
    d. written notes supplemented with mental notes will be sufficient in all cases.

3. Overt recordings are made:

    a. without the subject's knowledge.
    b. when the subject is "friendly to the prosecution."
    c. when the subject is "unfriendly to the prosecution."
    d. when the subject is reluctant to divulge information.

4. Surreptitious recordings are:

    a. rarely used in criminal investigation.
    b. used with willing witnesses anxious to go on record.
    c. made without the knowledge of the subject.
    d. made with the permission of the subject.

5. Ideally an interrogation should take place in:

    a. the investigator's office using a portable recording device.
    b. a mutual agreeable meeting place with the investigator "wired" with a microphone and a small recorder.
    c. the subject's home or office with a listening device surreptitiously installed.
    d. an interrogation room with a permanent recording installation.

6. A recording of an interrogation are used for all of the following purposes except:

   a. as evidence in court.
   b. to confront the subject with inconsistencies in his story.
   c. to confront associates with information given by the subject to induce a confession.
   d. to confront the investigator with inconsistencies in the investigation.

7. An investigator may interrupt an interrogation after the first recital of the story in order to:

   a. review the recording for inconsistencies and then plan the strategy for the next interrogation.
   b. give the subject more time to think about his story and remove any inconsistencies.
   c. give the subject more time to consult his lawyer about his story.
   d. test the recording equipment to see if it is working properly.

8. When tape recording an interview, it is important for the investigator to do all of the following except:

   a. When there are several interviewees, refer to each by name as often as possible.
   b. Describe and identify all objects referred to in the recording.
   c. Identify all of the laws that were broken or referred to in the recording.
   d. Completely describe all of the physical actions referred to in the recording.

9. All of the following are advantages of videotaping a confession except:

   a. It provides the strongest possible evidence that a confession was voluntary.
   b. It eliminates the need for a trained technician.
   c. It protects the police from false allegations of coercion.
   d. It increases guilty pleas, saving court costs.

10. All of the following are true statements except:

   a. A written confession should be obtained before the videotaping begins.
   b. Normally, permission is requested from the subject to videotape an interrogation.
   c. The suspect is requested to waive his rights on videotape.
   d. A clock should not be continuously in view during videotaping.

Answers:

1. a	p. 175, 1a.	5. d	p. 177, 3b.	9. a	p. 181, 6.
2. c	p. 176, 2.	6. d	p. 178, 4b.	10. d	p. 181, 6b.
3. b	p. 176, 3a.	7. a	p. 178, 4b.		
4. c	p. 177, 3b.	8. c	p. 179, 5.		

Chapter 12
INFORMANTS

Questions:

1. It is necessary for the investigator to cultivate informants because:

    a. an investigator should know who lives in his area.
    b. it is important to keep the general population under surveillance.
    c. the informant may commit a crime.
    d. many important cases are solved with the help of informants.

2. An informer may have a variety of motives for providing information. The investigator should:

    a. deal only with individuals with understandable motives.
    b. deal only with honest informers.
    c. evaluate all information in light of the informer's motive.
    d. accept all information uncritically, no matter what the motive.

3. Vanity, civic-mindedness, fear, repentance, revenge, jealously, and remuneration are among the many motives that lead an informer to reveal information. One may infer from this that:

    a. emotional motives lead to more reliable information than economic motives.
    b. economic motives lead to more reliable information than emotional motives.
    c. motives for informing are as varied and complex as the human character.
    d. neither emotional or economic motives lead to reliable information.

4. Besides direct payment for information there are other economic motives for the informer such as:

    a. to insure police protection for his own illegal pursuits.
    b. to eliminate the competition by informing on them.
    c. to avoid taxes by working for law enforcement.
    d. to have the investigator steer customers to his own illegal activities.

5. An investigator should safeguard the identity of an informant, first, as a matter of ethical practice and, second, because failure to do so would mean that:

    a. the investigator might lose a valuable source of information.
    b. the investigator's superior might lose confidence in him.
    c. the investigator might lose the respect of the community.
    d. the informer might charge more for future help.

6. In general a confidential informant will not be called to testify in court and a confidential communication from an informant cannot be disclosed in court. An exception will be made when the confidential informant is:

   a. requested to testify by the investigator.
   b. the sole source of essential evidence in a case.
   c. one of the people who can verify the testimony of the accused.
   d. no longer useful as a source of information.

7. All of the following statements are true except:

   a. The informant should be treated considerately.
   b. The investigator should fulfill all ethical promises made to the informant.
   c. The investigator should let the informant control his area of the investigation.
   d. The proper name of the informant should not be used on the telephone.

8. In communicating with an informant the investigator should:

   a. meet secretly in the investigator's office.
   b. have the informant telephone at odd hours using his real name as identification.
   c. vary the circumstances of the meetings so that a recognizable pattern is avoided.
   d. never meet with an informant.

9. When dismissing an informant:

   a. a record should be kept of the reason for the dismissal.
   b. all records of the informant should be destroyed to preserve his confidentiality.
   c. he should not be given a reason for his dismissal.
   d. the investigator should henceforth disavow any knowledge of his existence.

10. The investigator may form an estimate of the reliability of an informant by:

   a. checking for consistency with information obtained from other sources.
   b. testing his honesty by the use of trick questions.
   c. evaluating his criminal record.
   d. questioning his friends about his reliability.

11. When dealing with anonymous persons who voluntarily offer information by telephone, the investigator should draw out all of the relevant information before the call ends. The primary reason for this is that:

   a. the caller may change his story in a subsequent call.
   b. the caller will be difficult to identify without this information.
   c. ordinarily, an anonymous caller will not call back.
   d. the investigator should not spend his time waiting for telephone calls.

12. Information concerning the identity of the informant should be maintained in a central file because:

a. it is more convenient this way.
b. this arrangement is more confidential than the investigator's notebook.
c. the informant may not trust the investigator.
d. the informant belongs to the organization not to the investigator.

13. Information concerning the identity of the informant should be kept in a central file. All of the following statements are true except:

a. The file should be maintained by the supervisor.
b. The informants real name should appear in all reports.
c. The file should be classified confidential.
d. The informant should be assigned a code designation.

14. It may be said that private investigative work requires two major talents: the ability to conduct surveillances and:

a. the ability to collect physical evidence.
b. the ability to interrogate hardened criminals.
c. knowledge of how to circumvent standard law enforcement regulations.
d. ingenuity in developing information.

Answers:

1. d	p. 183, 1.	6. b	p. 186, 4.	11. c	p. 187, 8.
2. c	p. 184, 2.	7. c	p. 186, 5b.	12. d	p. 188, 10.
3. c	p. 184, 2.	8. c	p. 187, 6b.	13. b	p. 189, 10d.
4. b	p. 184, 2g.	9. a	p. 187, 7.	14. d	p. 189, 11.
5. a	p. 185, 4.	10. a	p. 187, 8.		

Chapter 13

TRACING AND SOURCES OF INFORMATION

Questions:

1. The term _____ is used to describe all of the procedures used in consulting the various sources of information in the search for persons.

a. intelligence
b. tracing

c. interrogation
d. surveillance

2. Because detectives have a ready access to personal interviews, they often have a tendency to rely on them exclusively and neglect to:

    a. telephone or visit the home.
    b. contact their confidential informants.
    c. conduct a research type of investigation.
    d. canvass the neighborhood.

3. An important preliminary step in searching for a person is to obtain the information necessary to:

    a. interrogate him successfully.   c. locate his associates.
    b. establish a mail cover.   d. identify him beyond question.

4. The first action the investigator should take in locating a missing or wanted person is to:

    a. telephone his home.   c. setup a mail cover.
    b. visit his home.   d. contact his relatives.

5. When inquiring about a missing or wanted person at his home, it is particularly important to obtain information concerning:

    a. his health.   c. his habits.
    b. his state of mind.   d. his occupation.

6. By requesting the post office to maintain a mail cover, the investigator will be able to keep track of the subject's:

    a. incoming mail.   c. incoming and outgoing mail.
    b. outgoing mail.   d. package deliveries.

7. With a mail cover in place, the post office will:

    a. open the subject's mail if it looks suspicious.
    b. open the subject's mail if it is requested by the investigator.
    c. not open the subject's mail, but will record the return address and post marks.
    d. forward the subject's mail to the investigator.

8. The purpose of sending a registered letter bearing a fugitives's name to the address of a relative is to induce the relative into:

    a. signing for the letter.   c. contacting the fugitive.
    b. destroying the letter.   d. contacting the post office.

9. In a criss-cross or reverse directory, telephone subscribers are listed according to their:

    a. first name.   c. business address.
    b. last name.   d. street address.

10. By looking up the address of the missing person in a criss-cross directory, the investigator can quickly compile a list of the names, addresses, and telephone numbers of all of his:

    a. relatives.   c. friends.
    b. neighbors.   d. family.

11. A pen register is a device that is attached to the telephone line which records:

    a. the phone numbers dialed.
    b. the phone numbers of the calls received.
    c. both the phone numbers dialed and those of the calls received.
    d. the phone numbers of long distance calls received.

12. The Federal Bureau of Investigation maintains all of the following sources of information except the:

    a. National Crime Information Center.
    b. National Firearms Tracing Center.
    c. Fingerprint and Criminal Identification Files.
    d. Known Professional Check Passers File.

13. The NCIC's _____ contains information and descriptive data on those persons for whom warrants have been issued.

    a. PROCHEK   c. Computerized Criminal History File
    b. Unidentified Person's File   d. Wanted Persons File

14. The National Crime Information Center exchanges information with _____ law enforcement agencies.

    a. only federal   c. only state
    b. federal and state   d. federal, state, and local

15. A _____ is the name given to a computerized file of instantly available information which can be rapidly transmitted.

    a. computer memory   c. storage and retrieval system
    b. data bank   d. personnel record

16. High-speed data retrieval systems are seen as a threat to an individual's right to:

    a. security.   c. prosperity.
    b. privacy.   d. an education.

17. All of the following proposals can help provide safeguards for the privacy of the individual except:

    a. Each person should be given access to his personal file to check for accuracy.
    b. Notice should be given to an individual for any request for personal information from his file.
    c. Personal data systems whose very existence is secret should be maintained.
    d. Data collected for one purpose should not be made available for other purposes.

18. Computer technology can facilitate on-the-street investigation by quickly delivering information so that the investigator has:

    a. personal information about a suspect.
    b. an understanding of a suspect's motivation.
    c. a legal basis for the apprehension of a suspect.
    d. a list of possible criminal activities of a suspect.

Answers:

1. b	p. 192, 1.	7. c	p. 194, 2d.	13. d	p. 202, 5a.
2. c	p. 192, 1.	8. c	p. 195, 2e.	14. d	p. 202, 5a.
3. d	p. 193, 2.	9. d	p. 195, 2f.	15. b	p. 205, 7a.
4. a	p. 193, 2a.	10. b	p. 195, 2f.	16. b	p. 205, 7c.
5. b	p. 194, 2b.	11. a	p. 196, 2g.	17. c	p. 206, 7c.
6. a	p. 194, 2d.	12. b	p. 202, 5.	18. c	p. 206, 8.

Chapter 14

MISSING PERSONS

Questions:

1. The Missing Persons Unit is concerned with all of the following classes of persons except:

    a. missing persons eighteen years of age or under.
    b. missing persons over eighteen years of age in full possession of their faculties.
    c. unidentified persons.
    d. unidentified dead.

2. A person who is sought by the police in connection with a crime is :

    a. a convict.   c. a wanted person.
    b. a missing person.   d. an unidentified person.

3. A Missing Persons Unit will be involved in cases where an individual over eighteen years old has disappeared and:

    a. has a tendency to commit crimes.
    b. has no close relatives.
    c. is affected by a serious mental or physical condition.
    d. travels across the country.

4. A Missing Persons Unit will be involved in cases where the circumstances of an adult's absence indicates:

    a. that he committed a crime.
    b. that he involuntarily disappeared.
    c. that he voluntarily disappeared.
    d. that he unexpectedly changed jobs.

5. Dead persons whose true identities are unknown and whose friends and relatives cannot be located are called:

    a. unidentified dead.
    b. unknown dead.
    c. unidentified persons.
    d. missing persons.

6. A patient suffering from Alzheimer's disease who requires police attention, does not know who he is or where he lives, and has not been reported missing may be classified as:

    a. a missing person.
    b. an unknown person.
    c. an unidentified person.
    d. an amnesiac.

7. Suicides are ordinarily motivated by:

    a. financial difficulties.
    b. boredom.
    c. the desire for change.
    d. a disappointment in love.

8. In solving disappearance cases, the investigator should primarily be concerned with:

    a. discovering possible motives.
    b. checking out alibis.
    c. establishing a corpus delicti.
    d. collecting physical evidence.

9. A common motive for simulating suicide is:

    a. to evoke sympathy.
    b. to evade apprehension.
    c. to inflict psychological revenge.
    d. to defraud insurance companies.

10. In simulated suicide cases, it is necessary for the perpetrator to leave clothes for identification in a situation where the absence of a body is plausible. The preferred method involves:

    a. swimming in the ocean.
    b. an accidental explosion.
    c. arson.
    d. hiring a hit man.

11. _____ account for a large percentage of disappearances.

    a. Homicides
    b. Suicides
    c. Unhappy marriages
    d. Simulated suicides

12. The voluntary disappearance of a married adult is ordinarily not in itself a crime. It can become so if it involves:

    a. abandoning one's property.
    b. not notifying the Motor Vehicle Bureau.
    c. abandoning a pregnant wife in destitute circumstances.
    d. lying to one's spouse.

13. When a dead body is recovered, the primary focus of police attention is on:

    a. interrogating the one who found the body.
    b. identifying the body.
    c. preserving the body.
    d. determining the exact time of death.

14. The following are true statements concerning missing persons except:

    a. There are no reliable statistics on missing persons.
    b. There are no official sources of information about missing persons who have changed their name.
    c. The FBI does not conduct searches for missing persons.
    d. It is practically impossible to disappear in today's society.

Answers:

1. b	p. 209, 1.	6. c	p. 210, 2c.	11. c	p. 213, 3g.
2. c	p. 209, 2a.	7. a	p. 211, 3b.	12. c	p. 213, 3g.
3. c	p. 209, 2a.	8. a	p. 211, 3b.	13. b	p. 213, 4a.
4. b	p. 209, 2a.	9. d	p. 211, 3c.	14. d	p. 216, 6c.
5. a	p. 209, 2b.	10. a	p. 211, 3c.		

Chapter 15
SURVEILLANCE

Questions:

1. Because surveillance involves systematic procedures and precautions, it can best be described as a _____ of observation.

    a. theory
    b. habit

    c. technique
    d. type

2. A failed surveillance in which the investigator is discovered will not only waste time but will also lead the suspect to:

    a. continue his criminal activities.
    b. take greater precautions.
    c. turn himself into the police before enough evidence can be obtained.
    d. turn away from his criminal activities.

3. Surveillance is the _____ observation of places, persons, and vehicles for the purpose of obtaining information concerning the identities or activities of subjects.

    a. overt
    b. remote

    c. conspicuous
    d. covert

4. The _____ is the person who maintains the surveillance or performs the observation.

    a. subject
    b. surveillant

    c. suspect
    d. observer

5. The _____ is the person or place being watched.

    a. subject
    b. object

    c. surveillant
    d. shadow

6. All of the following are kinds of surveillance except:

    a. surveillance of place.
    b. shadowing or tailing.

    c. tracing a fugitive.
    d. undercover investigation.

7. Surveillance of place would be helpful in all of the following crimes except:

    a. gambling.
    b. acting as a fence.

    c. illegal drug sales.
    d. assault and battery.

8. All of the following are typical objectives of place surveillance except:

   a. detecting criminal activities.
   b. discovering the identity of people frequenting an establishment.
   c. interviewing persons who frequent an establishment.
   d. providing a basis for obtaining a search warrant.

9. All of the following equipment may be important for maintaining a surveillance of a place except:

   a. a 35mm camera, a videotape camera, and telephoto lenses.
   b. a small telescope, binoculars, and a night-viewer.
   c. wiretap and recording apparatus.
   d. a battery-operated transmitter or "beeper."

10. A complete description of all the activities observed at the establishment under surveillance will be kept in the:

   a. investigator's notebook.   c. surveillance log.
   b. report of investigation.   d. photo log.

11. An investigator selected to shadow should possess all of the following characteristics except:

   a. a conspicuous appearance.
   b. qualities of perseverance and patience.
   c. the appearance of minding his own business.
   d. being resourceful, quick witted, and a fluent speaker.

12. Shadowing or tailing is simply the act of _____ a person.

   a. locating   c. observing
   b. following   d. investigating

13. All of the following are typical objectives of shadowing except:

   a. to detect evidence of criminal activity.
   b. to collect physical evidence.
   c. to establish the associations of a suspect.
   d. to find a wanted person.

14. Where only a general impression of a subject's habits and associates is necessary, _____ may be used.

   a. a close tail   c. a loose tail
   b. rough shadowing   d. undercover work

15. Where the subject must be shadowed and he is aware of this fact, _____ may be used.

   a. a loose tail   c. a close tail
   b. rough shadowing   d. undercover work

16. Where constant surveillance is necessary and extreme precautions must be taken against losing the subject, _____ should be used.

    a. rough shadowing   c. a close tail
    b. a loose tail   d. undercover work

17. Before undertaking a surveillance mission, the surveillant must have a complete description of the subject, especially how he appears from:

    a. the front.   c. the left side.
    b. the right side.   d. behind.

18. In preparing for a surveillance assignment, the investigator should do all of the following except:

    a. learn as much as possible about the subject.
    b. ask the subject's neighbors and friends about his habits, haunts, and social life.
    c. prepare a plausible "story," in case he is confronted by the subject.
    d. study the neighborhood, especially transportation lines and pedestrian routes.

19. The advantages of the ABC method of shadowing include all of the following except:

    a. One of the surveillants will be able to walk right alongside the subject without being noticed.
    b. An individual operative will be able to drop out of the tail, if the subject becomes suspicious of him.
    c. One of the surveillants will be able to view the subject from the other side of the street when he turns a corner or when he enters a building.
    d. The positions of the surveillants can be switched to prevent the subject from becoming to familiar with any one of them.

20. All of the following tactics are useful on a surveillance except:

    a. never hurrying to the corner to keep up with the subject.
    b. remaining as inconspicuous as possible.
    c. looking directly at the subject periodically.
    d. never walking directly behind the subject for too long.

21. The shadower runs the risk of being "made" which means he is:

    a. followed by the subject.
    b. recognized as a shadow by the subject.
    c. eluded by the subject.
    d. attracting the attention of the subject.

22. The shadower must avoid being "lost," which means:

    a. eluded by the subject.
    b. led around in circles, so that he does not know his location.
    c. recognized as a shadow by the subject.
    d. followed by the subject.

23. There is a tendency for an inexperienced surveillant to:

    a. "lose" the subject.
    b. to believe incorrectly that he has "lost" the subject.
    c. be "made" by the subject.
    d. to believe incorrectly that he has been "made" by the subject.

24. When the subject is convinced that he is being tailed, the surveillant must be very careful to avoid being _____ by the subject.

    a. "lost"   c. followed
    b. "made"   d. confused

25. When a subject boards a bus or train, and then jumps off the vehicle just before the doors closes while checking to see if any other person has jumped off, he is:

    a. eluding the surveillant.   c. confusing the surveillant.
    b. testing for a tail.   d. confronting the surveillant.

26. A person who follows the subject to make sure he is not being followed is called a:

    a. surveillant.   c. convoy.
    b. follower.   d. tail.

27. If the subject does have a convoy, the shadower must:

    a. continue to follow the subject.
    b. follow the convoy instead of the subject.
    c. confront the convoy.
    d. test for a tail.

28. The best solution to the problem of what vehicle the investigator should use on surveillance would be:

    a. to use the investigator's own car.
    b. to buy one car especially for this purpose.
    c to use the organization's own car.
    d. to use a rental car.

29. When parking near the subject's home or business establishment and waiting for the subject to emerge, the surveillant should choose a spot:

  a. on the next block.
  b. on the same block.
  c. at the nearest bus stop or fire hydrant.
  d. at the nearest legal parking place.

30. A surveillance log, which is a record of the day's observations, can and should be used for all of the following purposes except:

  a. as evidence in a criminal trial.
  b. as a tool for interrogation so that the investigator can pretend to have intimate knowledge of a suspect's activities.
  c. to monitor the alertness and the attitude of each surveillant.
  d. to evaluate the effectiveness of each surveillance operation.

31. For automobile surveillance, a miniature _____ can be attached to the understructure of the vehicle.

  a. receiver   c. bug
  b. recorder   d. transmitter or "beeper"

32. A _____ is an electronic device that is attached to a telephone wire which allows the investigator to hear both ends of a conversation.

  a. bug   c. recorder
  b. wiretap   d. pen register

33. A _____ is a miniature electronic device concealed in a room that receives and transmits the sound of voices.

  a. bug   c. recorder
  b. wiretap   d. pen register

34. All of the following are conditions under which a federal law enforcement officer may intercept a telephone conversation except:

  a. where one party consents.
  b. where the owner of the telephone consents.
  c. where there is a court order authorizing it.
  d. where an officer determines that an emergency situation involving national security or organized crime exists and later obtains judicial authorization.

35. Surveillance may be divided into three broad categories. _____ surveillance is concerned with what a person is doing or saying and consists of activities such as shadowing, wiretapping, hidden videotaping, and spying.

  a. Physical   c. Data
  b. Psychological   d. Technical

36. _____ surveillance is concerned with what a person is thinking and feeling and involves equipment such as lie detectors, employment forms, and personality tests.

a. Physical
b. Psychological

c. Data
d. Technical

37. _____ surveillance is concerned with what a person has done or has thought and consists of all of the official records as well as personal information collected in government and corporate computers.

a. Physical
b. Psychological

c. Data
d. Technical

38. The ultimate determinant in preserving the privacy of the individual must be:

a. the Supreme Court's protective rulings.
b. the ethical judgment of the individual investigator.
c. the federal laws controlling surveillance.
d. the policy of the local law enforcement agencies in enforcing the proper conduct of surveillance.

Answers:

1. c p. 220, 1.	14. c p. 223, 5.	27. b p. 230, 11.	
2. b p. 220, 1.	15. b p. 223, 5.	28. d p. 230, 13.	
3. d p. 220, 2.	16. c p. 223, 5.	29. a p. 232, 14.	
4. b. p. 221, 2.	17. d p. 224, 6.	30. c p. 232, 16.	
5. a p. 221, 2.	18. b p. 224, 6.	31. d p. 234, 18a.	
6. c p. 221, 2.	19. a p. 225, 7.	32. b p. 234, 18b.	
7. d p. 221, 2.	20. c p. 225, 8.	33. a p. 234, 18b.	
8. c p. 221, 3.	21. b p. 228, 9.	34. b p. 236, 19.	
9. d p. 222, 3b.	22. a p. 228, 9.	35. a p. 237, 20a.	
10. c p. 222, 3c.	23. d p. 229, 9.	36. b p. 237, 20a.	
11. a p. 222, 4.	24. c p. 229, 9.	37. c p. 237, 20a.	
12. b p. 223, 5.	25. b p. 229, 10.	38. b p. 239, 20c.	
13. b p. 223, 5.	26. c p. 230, 11.		

Chapter 16

UNDERCOVER ASSIGNMENTS

Questions:

1. Undercover work may be classified as a method of:

   a. surveillance.
   b. tracing.
   c. interrogation.
   d. identification.

2. In undercover work, the investigator assumes a different and unofficial identity in order to:

   a. identify a criminal.
   b. locate a criminal.
   c. obtain information about a criminal activity.
   d. sabotage a criminal activity.

3. Undercover work is a useful technique in crimes that involve:

   a. an individual.
   b. an unusual *modus operandi.*
   c. violence.
   d. an organization.

4. In all of the following crimes, undercover work would ordinarily be helpful except for:

   a. selling drugs.
   b. stalking.
   c. subversive activities.
   d. systematic theft.

5. Undercover work may be used to accomplish all of the following objectives except:

   a. obtaining evidence.
   b. checking the reliability of informants.
   c. establishing a fixed surveillance.
   d. interrogating suspects.

6. In addition to intelligence, the most important characteristics of the ideal undercover operative would include:

   a. patience and cheerfulness.
   b. obedience and humility.
   c. self-confidence and resourcefulness.
   d. pride and assertiveness.

7. As a general rule, the more complex the undercover assignment, the more attention the undercover agent must pay to:

   a. safety concerns.
   b. the suspect's rights.
   c. the details of his cover story.
   d. the admonitions of his supervisor.

8. The role of the employee is one of the simplest of undercover roles because it is not necessary:

    a. to know how to do the job.
    b. to explain one's presence at the job.
    c. to work extra hours.
    d. to talk with suspects.

9. The investigator's background story should :

    a. be completely true.   c. have some true elements.
    b. be completely false.   d. be highly imaginative.

10. All of the following statements concerning the undercover operative are true except:

    a. He must not possess any article which suggests his true identity.
    b. A firearm may be carried when it is compatible with his background story.
    c. Personal possessions should be obtained that are appropriate to the character assumed.
    d. A badge or other credential reflecting his true identity should be hidden on his person.

11. When making contact with the subject, ideally the undercover investigator:

    a. should control the meeting by introducing himself to the subject.
    b. should plan a crime and invite the subject to be an accomplice.
    c. create a situation where the subject becomes interested in and approaches him.
    d. prevail upon the subject's associates to arrange a meeting.

12. All of the following preparations for undercover work are recommended except:

    a. detailed plans for future crimes that would interest the subject of the investigation.
    b. a detailed checklist of the subject's character, habits, and history.
    c. knowledge of the geography of the area and characteristics of the inhabitants.
    d. a fictitious background and history for the new character of the investigator.

13. To avoid a charge of entrapment, the undercover investigator should:

    a. pretend to be a part of the criminal activity but not make any suggestions or render any real assistance.
    b. induce the subject to commit a crime and then not take part.
    c. provide suggestions for new areas of criminal activity that the subject might be interested in.
    d. only provide the means (money, getaway car, weapons) and never actually participate in the crime.

14. When on assignment, the undercover agent may do all of the following except:

    a. establish a regular pattern of meetings with his supervisor.
    b. use a pay phone to communicate with headquarters.
    c. take notes when necessary in a form that is only intelligible to the agent.
    d. occasionally send letters to headquarters, omitting the return address.

15. When an undercover assignment is completed, the investigator should:

    a. vanish without giving an explanation.
    b. identify himself as an agent in order to stop any further criminal activity.
    c. arrest the subject if enough evidence has been collected.
    d. give a plausible reason for his departure so that he can return if necessary at a later date.

16. Maintaining a large-scale undercover operation with a rented warehouse and several undercover operatives, is usually a technique for investigating:

    a. narcotic sales.   c. arson rings.
    b. burglary and "fencing."   d. bank robberies.

Answers:

1. a	p. 242, 1.	7. c	p. 245, 4.	13. a	p. 249, 6c.
2. c	p. 242, 1.	8. b	p. 245, 4c.	14. a	p. 250, 8.
3. d	p. 242, 1.	9. c	p. 247, 5c.	15. d	p. 251, 10.
4. b	p. 242, 1.	10. d	p. 248, 5d.	16. b	p. 251, 11.
5. d	p. 243, 2.	11. c	p. 248, 6b.		
6. c	p. 244, 3b.	12. a	p. 249, 6c.		

Chapter 17

ARSON

Questions:

1. There is difficulty in determining the number of arson fires each year for all of the following reasons except:

    a. the lack of fire marshalls to investigate suspicious fires.
    b. the lack of interest shown by fire departments in arson cases.
    c. the lack of witnesses because arson is a crime of stealth.
    d. the lack of physical evidence because it is often consumed in the fire.

2. Arson is a crime committed primarily by:

    a. young men.
    b. middle-aged businessmen.
    c. young men and women.
    d. older males.

3. Sometimes federal prosecutors will charge an arson suspect with mail fraud (involving false insurance claims) because:

    a. mail fraud is often a more serious offense.
    b. there are more postal inspectors than fire marshalls.
    c. arson is a much more difficult offense to prove.
    d. arson often involves a conspiracy.

4. Arson, or the malicious burning of another's house, is considered in common law to be a crime against:

    a. property.
    b. the security of a dwelling.
    c. the privacy of a dwelling.
    d. insurance companies.

5. To achieve the element of burning required for an arson offense, part of the structure must:

    a. be burned to the ground.
    b. show visible flames.
    c. be at least slightly damaged.
    d. be heated to the point of ignition.

6. To satisfy the requirement of being an "inhabited dwelling" for an aggravated arson charge, the building in question:

    a. must have people present in it.
    b. must in part be used as a dwelling.
    c. can be a barn or storage facility.
    d. could be used for a dwelling.

7. The legal term for the intent to do injury to another is called:

    a. revenge.
    b. malice.
    c. hatred.
    d. criminal design.

8. In an arson case, the prosecution must show that a burning was accomplished by:

    a. criminal design.
    b. malice.
    c. negligence.
    d. any of the above.

9. An attempted arson charge would be more appropriate than no charge or an arson charge in the following instance:

    a. The suspect gathered together incendiary materials.
    b. The suspect lit a match and the match went out.
    c. The suspect lit a match that burned a part of a building before going out.
    d. The suspect ignited a fire in a building which was extinguished immediately by the fire department.

10. For a charge of attempted arson, there must be at least _____ to carry out the intent.

    a. a criminal design   c. an overt act designed
    b. a criminal motive   d. the combustible materials

11. The *corpus delicti* of the offense is established by showing that: (1) there was a burning; and (2) the fire was willfully set (criminal design). All of the following may be offered as proof of the *corpus delicti* except:

    a. the discovery of an incendiary device or plant.
    b. elimination of all accidental and natural causes.
    c. an unsupported confession of the accused.
    d. the testimony of arson experts.

12. After establishing the *corpus delicti*, it is necessary to show that the accused committed the act with criminal intent. All of the following can be used as evidence except:

    a. articles associating the suspect with the scene such as tools or clothing.
    b. actions of the suspect demonstrating unfriendly relations with the owner of the building.
    c. suspicion by the owner that the suspect committed the crime.
    d. absence of any effort by the suspect to extinguish the fire.

13. In arson cases where there is a great dependence on circumstantial evidence, it is _____ to prove a motive.

    a. absolutely necessary   c. of little importance
    b. especially important   d. not necessary

14. Experience has shown that five motives predominate in arson cases: (1) economic gain; (2) concealment of a crime; and all of the following except:

    a. revenge, for reasons of jealousy and hatred;
    b. intimidation, such as gang members do to shop owners;
    c. pyromania, the uncontrollable urge to set fires;
    d. demonstration or display of fire-making ability;

15. All of the following are interests who may benefit economically from a fire except:

    a. the government, from insurance on its property.
    b. businesses wishing to eliminate competitors.
    c. contractors wishing to increase business.
    d. salvagers or "strippers" stealing copper pipes.

16. All of the following are types of pyromaniacs except:

   a. mentally deficient youths who enjoy watching fires.
   b. youths who pull fire alarms in order to see fire engines.
   c. the "hero type" who wishes to be a fireman.
   d. the sexual deviate who derives stimulation from setting fires.

17. All of the following are factors that determine the rate and extent of the spread of fire in a building except the:

   a. weather conditions.
   b. plumbing system.
   c. the building's construction materials.
   d. vegetation surrounding the building.

18. All of the following are accidental electrical causes of fire except:

   a. spontaneous combustion.
   b. arcing.
   c. sparking.
   d. overheating.

19. Combustible material may be solid, liquid, or gas, but strictly speaking only _____ burn.

   a. solids
   b. liquids
   c. gases
   d. powders

20. In order to have ignition, there must be: (1) a combustible material; (2) a source of heat to raise the temperature of the fuel to the kindling point; and (3) a supply of:

   a. oxygen.
   b. hydrogen.
   c. nitrogen.
   d. gasoline.

21. Liquids such as gasoline or ether with low flash points require at least a _____ for ignition.

   a. heating
   b. spark
   c. an open flame
   d. an oxidating agent

22. All of the following are liquids possessing excellent incendiary properties and are often used by arsonists as accelerants except:

   a. acetylene.
   b. alcohol.
   c. kerosene.
   d. turpentine.

23. All of the following are common gases that can cause fires by explosion when present in an enclosed area except:

   a. butane.
   b. carbon dioxide.
   c. natural gas.
   d. propane.

24. Some substances such as sodium, potassium, and calcium chloride generate intense heat on contact with:

    a. air.   c. water.
    b. oxygen.   d. fire.

25. Certain solids, called _____ , give off oxygen on decomposition thus aiding combustion.

    a. combustibles   c. incendiary agents
    b. inflammables   d. oxidizing agents

26. A _____ is a general term given to any device that is designed to ignite combustible material sometime after the initiating action.

    a. heater   c. streamer
    b. sparker   d. plant

27. Electrical switches, door bells, and short circuits in the presence of a gas or volatile fluid may be used as:

    a. heaters.   c. trailers.
    b. sparkers.   d. streamers.

28. A(n) _____ may be made out of candlewick, rope, or cloth saturated with an inflammable liquid. They are strung from room to room to provide a path for the fire.

    a. accelerant   c. sparker
    b. heater   d. streamer

29. The Molotov cocktail in the crude form of a soda bottle filled with _____ and a streamer of cloth or paper is the favorite incendiary device of rioters.

    a. natural gas   c. alcohol
    b. nitroglycerine   d. gasoline

30. The presence of _____ indicates that humid substances have come in contact with the hot combustible substances.

    a. steam   c. grey smoke
    b. white smoke   d. black smoke

31. _____ is produced by either incomplete combustion or by burning a petroleum based product such as rubber, tar, coal, or turpentine.

    a. steam   c. grey smoke
    b. white smoke   d. black smoke

32. Burning alcohol is characterized by a _____ flame; _____ flames may indicate the presence of a petroleum product.

    a. red ... blue   c. green ... red
    b. blue ... red   d. red ... green

33. All of the following are indications of arson except:

    a. a fire that burns exceptionally fast.
    b. a fire that spreads in an unusual direction.
    c. a fire that rises vertically until it reaches an obstacle and then travels horizontally.
    d. a fire that has more than one origin.

34. Turpentine, alcohol, kerosene, and gasoline are among the accelerants that have a characteristic:

    a. appearance.   c. feel.
    b. color.   d. odor.

35. A camcorder is especially useful at the scene of a suspected arson in progress not only for documenting the development of the fire but also for recording:

    a. the suspected origin of the fire.
    b. the entrance ways and exits of the building.
    c. the face of the arsonist who may be in a crowd of observers.
    d. the extent of the damage from the fire.

36. The difficulties that may be encountered in the search of an arson scene depend primarily on:

    a. the extent of the investigator's knowledge and experience.
    b. the extent to which the building has been consumed by the fire.
    c. the number of investigators assigned to the case.
    d. the degree of assistance given by the fire department.

37. When the investigator arrives at the scene of a suspected arson, he should do all of the following except:

    a. prevent unnecessary disturbance of the debris by restricting unauthorized personnel.
    b. halt the extinguishing of the fire, to protect the physical evidence from further damage.
    c. check the doors and windows of the building for evidence of a break.
    d. search for the location of the point of origin.

38. As the investigator draws closer to the point of origin, he will find the charring becoming:

a. more widespread.　　　　c. deeper.
b. more noticeable.　　　　d. more elongated.

39. Fire characteristicly burns upward and outward in a _____ -shaped pattern from the point of origin.

a. "A"　　　　c. "U"
b. "L"　　　　d. "V"

40. _____ is the pattern of thin irregular lines found in glass that has been exposed to high temperatures.

a. Alligatoring　　　　c. Searing
b. Crazing　　　　d. Spalling

41. _____ is the chipping, flaking, and discoloration of concrete or brick due to intense heat.

a. Alligatoring　　　　c. Searing
b. Crazing　　　　d. Spalling

42. _____ is the pattern of crevices on the surface of charred wood.

a. Alligatoring　　　　c. Searing
b. Crazing　　　　d. Spalling

43. The debris at the point of origin should be studied carefully for the primary purpose of determining:

a. the cause of the fire.　　　　c. the identity of the firesetter.
b. the extent of the damage.　　　　d. the distance the fire travelled.

44. With the use of a liquid accelerant, there is often a certain amount of spillage. The investigator should search for the traces of unburned accelerant, especially on the floor in the area _____ the point of origin.

a. above　　　　c. at the same level as
b. below　　　　d. at the exact location of

45. All of the following are especially useful methods of detecting the traces of accelerant in a burned building except:

a. looking for spillage or evidence of deep charring.
b. using a hydrocarbon vapor detector or "sniffer."
c. screening unburnt accelerant by attempting to light it.
d. using a dog trained to identify accelerants.

46. In examining the arson crime scene, the investigator should pay special attention to the sprinkler system and the alarm devices because they:

    a. usually don't work.
    b. are usually not turned on.
    c. may have been tampered with.
    d. may have been recently repaired.

47. The task of collecting physical evidence in an arson case is complicated by the _____ of the materials.

    a. filthy condition
    b. delicate condition
    c. dangerous nature
    d. large amount

48. Because residual accelerant may be the most important physical evidence, it must be protected especially from:

    a. contamination.
    b. leakage.
    c. evaporation.
    d. ignition.

49. Where straw or a like substance has been used in a "plant" the ashes will retain its characteristic:

    a. texture.
    b. shape.
    c. color.
    d. odor.

50. A search for fingerprints should be made, giving special attention to:

    a. door jambs.
    b. fire alarm boxes.
    c. window sills.
    d. containers for accelerants.

51. A careful study should be made of all _____ in the building because they are sometimes brought there by the arsonist and abandoned, thus providing a tracing clue.

    a. tools
    b. financial records
    c. heating appliances
    d. electrical appliances

52. In an arson fire designed to destroy financial records in order to conceal evidence of embezzlement or other regularities, a common mistake the novice arsonist makes is that:

    a. he leaves his fingerprints on papers at the scene.
    b. he fails to remove insurance policies from the office.
    c. he fails to realize that masses of papers are usually not completely destroyed by fire.
    d. he fails to call the fire department in a timely fashion.

53. All of the following are indications from the contents of a building that a fire in that building had been planned except:

    a. the removal of articles of value or of sentimental significance.
    b. the removal of insurance policies.
    c. account books arranged in a tented fashion on the desk.
    d. the loss of the lives of people trapped in the building.

54. When investigating a suspected arson in a commercial building, all of the following people should be interviewed extensively on their observations, whereabouts, and suspicions except:

    a. the security personnel and the firemen extinguishing the blaze.
    b. the employees and other occupants of the building.
    c. the customers doing business with the company.
    d. the owner of the company.

55. When investigating a suspected arson of a commercial building, the most important person to ask the security personnel to identify would be:

    a. the person who discovered the fire.
    b. the person who turned in the alarm.
    c. the first fireman to enter the building to put out the fire.
    d. the last person to leave the building before the fire.

56. Photographing the crime scene should proceed:

    a. according to the order of the search.
    b. according to the order of importance of the evidence.
    c. outwardly from the point of origin of the fire.
    d. according to the path taken by the firemen in extinguishing the blaze.

57. The investigator should provide the laboratory expert, examining the physical evidence in an arson case, all of the following pieces of information except:

    a. the type and construction of the burned building.
    b. a list of chemical agents used in extinguishing the fire.
    c. the cleaning and maintenance schedule of the building.
    d. the photographs and sketches indicating the points at which the evidence was collected.

58. The Property Insurance Loss Reporting System is a computerized record of all fire losses designed to:

    a. detect patterns of arson.
    b. identify potentially vulnerable buildings.
    c. be a reference collection of incendiary materials.
    d. spot a potential arsonist before he commits his first arson.

59. All of the following are common motives for deliberately burning an automobile except:

    a. to conceal evidence of a crime.
    b. to divert police attention from a crime happening in another location.
    c. to defraud an insurance company.
    d. as an act of vandalism.

60. It is _____ to accomplish the total loss of a vehicle from an automobile fire that was not set deliberately with an accelerant.

    a. easy
    b. extremely easy
    c. difficult
    d. extremely difficult

61. The possible points of origin of an automobile fire under the hood would include all of the following except the:

    a. fuel pump.
    b. transmission.
    c. carburetor.
    d. wiring.

62. All of the following are indications that a car was burnt deliberately with the use of incendiary substances except:

    a. the presence of burned spots on the paint.
    b. soot deposits on the underside of the frame.
    c. melted wiring.
    d. burned fan belt.

63. An examination of the car's accessories, such as a radio or tape deck, may indicate whether an automobile fire was deliberately set. The investigator should check to see if the radio _____ at the time of the fire.

    a. was removed
    b. was recently repaired
    c. was turned on
    d. was turned off

64. The owner's description of his automobile fire may be important to the investigator because he may unwittingly reveal:

    a. details of an accidental fire.
    b. details of a fire contrived with an inflammable material.
    c. inconsistencies in his description.
    d. a lack of understanding of automobile fires.

65. In some jurisdictions, the term _____ is used to describe the criminal burning of property other than a dwelling.

    a. simple arson
    b. aggravated arson
    c. automobile arson
    d. incendiary fire

Answers:

1. b	p. 255.	23. b	p. 267, 7a.	45. c	p. 275, 9e.
2. a	p. 255.	24. c	p. 267, 7a.	46. c	p. 276, 9h.
3. c	p. 257.	25. d	p. 267, 7a.	47. b	p. 276, 10.
4. b	p. 257, 1.	26. d	p. 267, 7b.	48. c	p. 277, 10a.
5. d	p. 257, 1a.	27. b	p. 268, 7b.	49. b	p. 277, 10b.
6. b	p. 257, 1b.	28. d	p. 268, 7b.	50. d	p. 277, 10c.
7. b	p. 258, 1c.	29. d	p. 269, 7b.	51. a	p. 278, 10f.
8. a	p. 258, 1c.	30. a	p. 270, 8a.	52. c	p. 278, 10g.
9. b	p. 258, 2.	31. d	p. 270, 8a.	53. d	p. 278, 11.
10. c	p. 258, 2.	32. b	p. 270, 8a.	54. c	p. 279, 12.
11. c	p. 259, 3a.	33. c	p. 270, 8a.	55. d	p. 280, 12c.
12. c	p. 260, 3b.	34. d	p. 271, 8a.	56. a	p. 280, 13.
13. b	p. 260, 4.	35. c	p. 272, 8b.	57. c	p. 281, 14.
14. d	p. 260, 4.	36. b	p. 272, 9.	58. a	p. 282, 15b.
15. a	p. 260, 4.	37. b	p. 273, 9a.	59. b	p. 287, 17.
16. b	p. 262, 4e.	38. c	p. 274, 9c.	60. d	p. 288, 18.
17. b	p. 263, 5.	39. d	p. 274, 9c.	61. b	p. 289, 19c.
18. a	p. 264, 6h.	40. b	p. 274, 9c.	62. c	p. 289, 19c.
19. c	p. 266, 7a.	41. d	p. 274, 9c.	63. a	p. 289, 19e.
20. a	p. 266, 7a.	42. a	p. 274, 9c.	64. b	p. 290, 20e.
21. b	p. 266, 7a.	43. a	p. 274, 9d.	65. a	p. 290, 21.
22. a	p. 266, 7a.	44. b	p. 275, 9e.		

Chapter 18

NARCOTICS VIOLATIONS

Questions:

1. Drug addiction is attributable to the availability of an addicting drug coupled with:

    a. enthusiastic peers.
    b. a desire for experimentation.
    c. a personality disorder.
    d. an underprivledged life.

2. _____ is the condition of habitually using a narcotic drug and having lost the power of self-control with respect to it.

    a. Addiction
    b. Physical dependence
    c. Psychological dependence
    d. Tolerance

3. _____ is a state in which a drug is necessary to maintain well-being due to physiological changes brought about by using the drug.

    a. Addiction
    b. Physical dependence
    c. Psychological dependence
    d. Tolerance

4. _____ is the adaptation of the body to the use of a drug making it necessary to increase the dosage to achieve the same results.

    a. Addiction   c. Psychological dependence
    b. Physical dependence   d. Tolerance

5. _____ is the association of a sense of satisfaction and mental well-being with the periodic administration of a drug leading a person to want to take that drug again and again because it feels good.

    a. Addiction   c. Psychological dependence
    b. Physical dependence   d. Tolerance

6. In the Controlled Substances Act, the term "opiate" includes not only opium derivatives but also:

    a. cocaine derivatives.   c. sedatives and tranquilizers.
    b. hallucinogens.   d. synthetic drugs similar in effect.

7. The _____ for the first time placed amphetamines, barbiturates, and hallucinogens under repressive controls.

    a. Drug Abuse Control Amendments (1965)
    b. Controlled Substances Act (1970)
    c. Narcotic Drug Import and Export Act (1922)
    d. Harrison Act (1914)

8. The _____ prohibited the importation and manufacture of heroin as well as the smoking of opium.

    a. Drug Abuse Control Amendments (1965)
    b. Controlled Substances Act (1970)
    c. Narcotic Drug Import and Export Act (1922)
    d. Harrison Act (1914)

9. The _____ taxed the importation, manufacture, distribution, and sale of narcotics.

    a. Drug Abuse Control Amendments (1965)
    b. Controlled Substances Act (1970)
    c. Narcotic Drug Import and Export Act (1922)
    d. Harrison Act (1914)

10. The _____ is the controlling federal statute for narcotics, superseding all other federal laws.

    a. Drug Abuse Control Amendments (1965)
    b. Controlled Substances Act (1970)
    c. Narcotic Drug Import and Export Act (1922)
    d. Harrison Act (1914)

11. The Uniform Controlled Substance Act was developed to encourage _____ to adopt similar drug laws not only to facilitate enforcement but also to benefit manufacturers, pharmacists, doctors, and their patients.

a. cities
b. states

c. the federal government
d. other countries

12. Opium is derived from the:

a. poppy plant.
b. coca shrub.

c. hemp plant.
d. peyote cactus.

13. Although opium may also be chewed or eaten, a distinguishing characteristic of opium ingestion is the use of the:

a. bent spoon.
b. medicine dropper.

c. hypodermic needle.
d. pipe.

14. The opium derivatives most commonly used illegally include all of the following except:

a. morphine.
b. heroin.

c. methadone.
d. codeine.

15. Morphine is usually sold as a white powder, a small quantity of which is wrapped in a glassine paper. In this form, it is called a:

a. deck.
b. cut.

c. mainline.
d. kit.

16. To achieve a more rapid and stimulating effect, the morphine user injects it directly in the blood stream. Someone using this method is called a(n):

a. addict.
b. junkie.

c. mainliner.
d. pusher.

17. All of the following are characteristics of the morphine user except:

a. withdrawal symptoms such as nausea and stomach pains.
b. contracted pupils that do not react normally to light.
c. exceptionally irrational behavior.
d. needle marks and dark blue scar tissue on the veins.

18. _____ is manufactured legally in the form of white tablets and is used as a sedative and an analgesic by the medical profession.

a. Morphine
b. Methadone

c. Heroin
d. Codeine

19. _____ is a weak natural alkaloid of opium which is used medically as a sedative in cough mixtures and as an analgesic in tablet form.

a. Morphine
b. Methadone

c. Heroin
d. Codeine

20. _____ is the most common drug in cases of narcotics addiction. It cannot be manufactured legally or used medically in the United States.

a. Morphine
b. Methadone

c. Heroin
d. Codeine

21. Aside from law enforcement officers acting in the performance of duty, the mere possession of _____ is ordinarily considered illegal.

a. morphine
b. methadone

c. heroin
d. codeine

22. The attraction of heroin for the drug dealer is its characteristic of being:

a. highly pleasurable.
b. highly addictive.

c. rare and expensive.
d. difficult to obtain.

23. The person most responsible for spreading drug addiction to the young is:

a. the pusher.
b. the parent or uncle.

c. the youthful enthusiastic user.
d. the older experienced addict.

24. Meperidine, methadone, Dilaudid, and Percodan are chemically synthesized drugs designed to be used as substitutes for the opium derivatives. These are called:

a. barbiturates.
b. amphetamines.

c. synthetic analgesics.
d. minor tranquilizers.

25. Substances which relieve pain are called:

a. anesthetics.
b. analgesics.

c. sedatives.
d. hypnotics.

26. In treating addiction to heroin, physicians commonly substitute _____ to alleviate withdrawal pains.

a. meperidine
b. methadone

c. Dilaudid
d. Percodan

27. Cocaine is a sparkling white crystalline powder which is obtained from the leaves of the _____, grown in the South American highlands.

a. poppy plant
b. peyote cactus

c. hemp plant
d. coca shrub

28. The cocaine user most commonly ingests the substance by injection or:

a. by sniffing.
b. by smoking.
c. orally.
d. as a salve.

29. Excessive cocaine use is accompanied by a characteristic deformity commonly called a:

a. deviated septum.
b. eroded septum.
c. "red nose."
d. "rat's nose."

30. Unlike heroin, cocaine is an intense central nervous system _____, affecting the higher brain center to render the user alert, restless, and apparently more energetic.

a. depressant
b. stimulant
c. hallucinogen
d. sedative

31. The continued use of cocaine can develop a strong _____, leading to a profound and dangerous type of abuse.

a. physical dependence
b. psychic dependence
c. tolerance
d. abstinence syndrome

32. Cocaine (cocaine hydrochloride) can be further refined by a method called _____ to produce crack.

a. refining
b. diluting
c. freebasing
d. extracting

33. Crack takes the form of small yellow crystals which are:

a. sniffed.
b. smoked.
c. swallowed.
d. injected.

34. Drug dealers were attracted to crack because it was a substance that was economical, that produced an intense euphoria, and that was:

a. mildly habit forming.
b. inconspicuous to ingest.
c. not addictive.
d. highly addictive.

35. Crack is most commonly sold in:

a. vials.
b. packets.
c. capsules.
d. boxes.

36. A crack _____ is a facility where the drug can be purchased and consumed on the premises.

a. den
b. factory
c. house
d. spot

37. The typical crack smoker is a(n) _____ urban male.

    a. young lower-income   c. older lower-income
    b. young middle-income   d. older middle-income

38. _____ or *cannabis sativa* is the most widely used of the illicit drugs.

    a. Heroin   c. Crack
    b. Cocaine   d. Marihuana

39. *Cannabis sativa* is obtained from the female:

    a. poppy plant.   c. hemp plant.
    b. coca shrub.   d. peyote cactus.

40. Flowers and seed heads exude a resin that contains the highest concentration of active cannabis chemicals. The pure resin is:

    a. marihuana.   c. mescaline.
    b. hashish.   d. psilocybin.

41. Marihuana usually consists of chopped-flowers, seeds, hulls, leaves, and stalks and is imported in the form of a pressed bundle called a _____ because of its 2.2 lb. weight.

    a. key   c. brick
    b. check   d. load

42. Marihuana is usually consumed by:

    a. sniffing.   c. injecting.
    b. smoking.   d. swallowing.

43. A chemical test that is a fairly reliable indication that a substance is marihuana makes use of:

    a. nalorphine.   c. Duquenois reagent.
    b. nalline.   d. luminol.

44. All of the following statements about the effects of marihuana smoking are true except:

    a. It can cause temporary impairment of visual and muscular coordination.
    b. It can impair judgment and memory, and cause anxiety, confusion, or disorientation.
    c. It can incite people to antisocial acts and thus is a cause of crime and violence.
    d. It does not cause severe mental illness.

45. With the continued use of marihuana, the effect on the user will be a greatly increased _____ the drug.

    a. addiction to   c. physical dependence on
    b. tolerance of   d. psychic dependence on

46. Which of the following statements concerning the effects of marihuana smoking are true:

    a. It builds up an addictive need for continued use.
    b. It causes permanent mental impairment.
    c. It leads inevitably to the use of "hard" narcotics and heroin.
    d. None of the above are true.

47 _____ are prescribed by physicians as soporifics or sedatives for the treatment of insomnia, nervousness, and related conditions. They consist of a white powder but are sold in tablet or capsule form under such names as phenobarbital, sodium Amytal, and Seconal.

    a. Amphetamines   c. Opiates
    b. Barbiturates   d. Synthetic Analgesics

48. An overdose of _____ in combination with alcoholic beverages can be fatal and is often used as a method for suicide.

    a. amphetamines   c. Benzedrine
    b. barbiturates   d. cocaine

49. _____ are stimulants that are used to uplift the spirit, dispel fatigue, and impart a sense of great work capacity. They are often sold in the form of colored heart-shaped tables. Benzedrine and Dexedrine are the common trade names.

    a. Amphetamines   c. Opiates
    b. Barbiturates   d. Synthetic Analgesics

50. _____ are drugs used to decrease anxiety and motor activity by depressing the central nervous system.

    a. Analgesics   c. Sedatives
    b. Anesthetics   d. Hypnotics

51. _____ are drugs used to depress the central nervous system to such a degree that it induces a state resembling normal sleep.

    a. Analgesics   c. Sedatives
    b. Anesthetics   d. Hypnotics

52. _____ are commonly prescribed for relief of anxiety, for sedation, and as muscle-relaxants. They include meprobamate (Miltown), chlordiazepoxide (Librium), and diazepam (Valium).

    a. Amphetamines
    b. Barbiturates
    c. Synthetic analgesics
    d. The minor tranquilizers

53. _____ is sold under the trade name Doriden. It is used as a sedative and as a hypnotic, useful in treating insomnia.

    a. Chloral hydrate
    b. Glutethimide
    c. Methaqualone
    d. Methadone

54. _____ is a powerful sedative-hypnotic sold under various trade names such as Sopor and Quaalude. It is used medically for insomnia and for daytime sedation.

    a. Chloral hydrate
    b. Glutethimide
    c. Methaqualone
    d. Methadone

55. _____ can be used criminally in the form of "knockout drops" because it is colorless, odorless, and soluble in water and alcohol. It is sold for medical purposes in tablet or capsule form as a sedative or soporific.

    a. Chloral hydrate
    b. Glutethimide
    c. Methaqualone
    d. Methadone

56. _____ are a group of drugs named for their capacity to cause hallucinatory effects. This group includes several natural chemicals, mescaline and psilocybin, and a number of synthetics, LSD, STP, and DMT.

    a. Opiates
    b. Synthetic analgesics
    c. Hallucinogens
    d. Minor tranquilizers

57 _____ is taken from the spineless peyote cactus in the form of a flower or button which is either eaten or brewed for drinking. This drug has religious and cult associations in northern Mexico and the southwestern United States.

    a. LSD
    b. Mescaline
    c. PCP
    d. Psilocybin.

58. _____ is a substance extracted from Mexican mushrooms. It is obtained in capsules containing either spores or dried ground mushrooms.

    a. LSD
    b. Mescaline
    c. PCP
    d. Psilocybin

59. _____ is the most powerful of the synthetic hallucinogens and widely used for its supposed "mind-expanding" capability. STP and DMT are other well-known synthetic hallucinogens.

    a. LSD   c. PCP
    b. Mescaline   d. Psilocybin

60. _____ or "angel dust" is a white, crystalline substance that can be snorted, swallowed, injected, or smoked. It is a very potent psychoactive drug capable of causing convulsions, violent behavior, and even death. Its chemical name is phencyclidine.

    a. LSD   c. PCP
    b. Mescaline   d. Psilocybin

61. An essential step in the investigation is the establishment of the fact that the substance in question is a prohibited drug. This can be proven by the:

    a. confession of the accused.   c. testimony of the investigator.
    b. confession of the seller.   d. testimony of a chemist.

62. The investigator must prove that the accused's relation to the narcotic was not legally authorized. Possession of a narcotic is presumed to be _____ unless proven otherwise.

    a. legal   c. a neutral act
    b. illegal   d. authorized

63. All of the following are innocent possessions of a drug except:

    a. The drug has been prescribed for the subject by a physician.
    b. The drug has been collected as evidence by a law enforcement officer.
    c. The drug is being held for a friend until he returns from a trip by the subject who is aware that it is an illegal substance.
    d. The subject by mistake picks up a suitcase filled with drugs at the bus terminal.

64. If an illegal drug is found on the subject during a search, the investigator at this time should:

    a. confront the subject with it in order to induce an admission.
    b. pretend it is a legal drug and free the subject so that he can be trailed to the seller.
    c. collect the evidence without comment so as not to alert the subject that he is involved in a narcotics investigation.
    d. immediately inform him that there will be no charges filed against him if he cooperates in naming the seller.

65. If a large quantity of drugs are found in a hiding place, the investigator should:

    a. collect them immediately so that they do not fall into the hands of a minor.
    b. confront the subject with the knowledge of the hiding place and demand an explanation.
    c. arrest the subject for possession of an illegal drug and collect the drugs before he can harm himself by using them.
    d. set up a surveillance in order to show that the drugs in the hiding place are the personal possession of the subject.

66. All of the following evidence can be used to support a charge of using a prohibited drug except:

    a. admissions by the subject and eyewitness testimony on his administration of the drug.
    b. apparatus, such as hypodermic needles and medicine droppers with traces of illegal drugs on them, in the possession of the subject.
    c. testimony that his friends and colleagues used drugs.
    d. medical testimony of the subject's needle marks and withdrawal symptoms.

67. The most reliable indication of addiction is:

    a. a blood test.   c. erratic behavior.
    b. a urine test.   d. the withdrawal symptoms.

68. The chief objective of a narcotics investigation should be the identification and location of:

    a. the subject's drug stash and paraphernalia.
    b. the people who take drugs with the subject.
    c. an eyewitness to the subject's drug use.
    d. the person who sold the drug to the subject.

69. In some states, the mere possession of certain amounts of a prohibited drug is prima facie evidence of _____ illegal drugs.

    a. addiction to   c. using
    b. intent to sell   d. buying

70. In some states, if illegal drugs are found in an automobile, there is a legal presumption of possession for:

    a. all of the occupants.   c. the driver of the vehicle.
    b. the owner of the vehicle.   d. the buyer of the drugs.

71. The identity of the seller of a drug can usually be determined by:

    a. a chemical analysis of the illegal drugs.
    b. the identification of the drug packaging or vials.
    c. surveillance of the user's home.
    d. intensive questioning of the user.

72. In an undercover assignment, ideal evidence of selling illegal drugs would be:

  a. having the investigator buy the drug.
  b. having the investigator's associate make the purchase with the investigator as witness.
  c. having the investigator witness a sale to a user who isn't an associate.
  d. having the seller make an admission acknowledging that his sales are illegal.

73. All of the following are technical aids which would be directly helpful in proving that a drug sale occurred except:

  a. surveillance cameras.
  b. wiretap equipment.
  c. marked money.
  d. tracing powder.

74. When transmitting a substance suspected of being an illegal drug to the laboratory for analysis, the investigator should:

  a. make no suggestions regarding the nature of the substance so that the laboratory analysis is objective.
  b. state his suspicions as to the nature of the substance so that the chemist does not waste time or evidence.
  c. test the substance himself and rely on the laboratory expert only for confirmation.
  d. divide the evidence and send it to several laboratories to be sure of getting a correct analysis.

75. When sending evidentiary material to the laboratory for analysis:

  a. the drugs should be sent in the original container.
  b. the drugs should be sent with the original container but wrapped separately.
  c. the drugs only need be sent.
  d. the drugs should be sent in a separate shipment in case a shipment is lost.

76. When the evidence is in the form of tablets or capsules, it should be _____ by the investigator in the presence of a witness.

  a. only counted
  b. only weighed
  c. both counted and weighed
  d. either counted or weighed

77. The best evidence of recent use of a narcotic is:

  a. contracted pupils.
  b. withdrawal symptoms.
  c. needle scars.
  d. urine and blood analysis.

78. If a person has been using a narcotic, the administration of _____ will cause the pupils to dilate.

  a. Duquinois reagent
  b. methadone
  c. nalorphine (nalline)
  d. luminol

79. All of the following statements about the relationship between narcotics and crime are true except:

    a. Addiction is not a crime under federal or state law.
    b. Heroin addicts, as a group, tend to specialize in violent crime.
    c. Most addicts have a greater tendency than their socioeconomic peers to be delinquent.
    d. A typical heroin addict will tend to drift into a career of small-scale property crimes such as larceny and burglary.

Answers:

1. c	p. 293, 2a.	28. a	p. 306, 9c.	55. a	p. 322, 15d.		
2. a	p. 294, 2b.	29. d	p. 307, 9c.	56. c	p. 323, 16.		
3. b	p. 294, 2c.	30. b	p. 307, 9d.	57. b	p. 323, 16a.		
4. d	p. 294, 2d.	31. b	p. 307, 9f.	58. d	p. 323, 16a.		
5. c	p. 295, 2f.	32. c	p. 309, 10.	59. a	p. 326, 16b.		
6. d	p. 296, 3b.	33. b	p. 309, 10.	60. c	p. 328, 16b.		
7. a	p. 296, 4a.	34. d	p. 309, 10.	61. d	p. 329, 17a.		
8. c	p. 296, 4a.	35. a	p. 310, 10c.	62. b	p. 329, 17b.		
9. d	p. 296, 4a.	36. c	p. 310, 10c.	63. c	p. 329, 17b.		
10. b	p. 296, 4b.	37. a	p. 310, 10c.	64. a	p. 329, 17b.		
11. b	p. 297, 4c.	38. d	p. 310, 11.	65. d	p. 330, 17b.		
12. a	p. 297, 5.	39. c	p. 312, 11a.	66. c	p. 330, 17b.		
13. d	p. 298, 5b.	40. b	p. 312, 11a.	67. d	p. 331, 17b.		
14. c	p. 299, 6.	41. a	p. 312, 11a.	68. d	p. 331, 17b.		
15. a	p. 299, 6a.	42. b	p. 312, 11a.	69. b	p. 331, 17c.		
16. c	p. 299, 6a.	43. c	p. 312, 11b.	70. a	p. 331, 17c.		
17. c	p. 300, 6a.	44. c	p. 313, 11c.	71. d	p. 331, 17c.		
18. a	p. 300, 6a.	45. d	p. 314, 11d.	72. c	p. 332, 17c.		
19. d	p. 301, 6b.	46. d	p. 315, 11e.	73. b	p. 332, 17c.		
20. c	p. 301, 6c.	47. b	p. 318, 13.	74. b	p. 334, 18a.		
21. c	p. 302, 6c.	48. b	p. 319, 13b.	75. a	p. 335, 19a.		
22. b	p. 302, 6c.	49. a	p. 321, 14.	76. c	p. 335, 19b.		
23. c	p. 303, 7c.	50. c	p. 321, 15.	77. d	p. 336, 20b.		
24. c	p. 304, 8.	51. d	p. 322, 15.	78. c	p. 336, 20c.		
25. b	p. 304, 8.	52. d	p. 322, 15a.	79. b	p. 338, 21b.		
26. b	p. 305, 8b.	53. b	p. 322, 15b.				
27. d	p. 305, 9.	54. c	p. 322, 15c.				

Chapter 19
SEX OFFENSES

Questions:

1. An investigation of sex offenses is particularly demanding for the investigator because of:

   a. the lack of physical evidence in these cases.
   b. the complexity of the crimes involved.
   c. the discretion and tact that must be employed.
   d. the dangerousness of the offender.

2. Sex offenses may be divided into two groups. The first, and generally more serious, involves _____ unwilling victims, as in forcible rape and indecent assault.

   a. physical aggression against   c. mental cruelty towards
   b. threatening   d. moral indifference to

3. The second involves _____ acts, such as illicit intercourse.

   a. malicious   c. involuntary
   b. voluntary   d. subversive

4. The elements of proof required to support a conviction of rape are: (1) the accused had sexual intercourse with a certain female; (2) the act was done by force and without her:

   a. knowledge.   c. consent.
   b. objections.   d. understanding.

5. If the sexual intercourse is with a female who is of unsound mind, unconscious, intoxicated, or too young to understand the nature of the act, the accused may be charged with:

   a. rape.   c. indecent assault.
   b. sodomy.   d. carnal knowledge or statutory rape.

6. The act of sexual intercourse with a consenting female below a certain age is

   a. rape.   c. indecent assault.
   b. sodomy.   d. carnal knowledge or statutory rape.

7. _____ , however slight, is sufficient to complete the offense of rape.

   a. Intimate caressing   c. Penetration
   b. Offensive touching   d. Emission

8. In the crime of rape, it is not necessary to prove:

    a. lack of consent.   c. penetration.
    b. physical resistance.   d. emission.

9. Rape _____laws prohibit courtroom inquiry into the prior sexual conduct of the victim.

    a. defense   c. trauma
    b. shield   d. crisis

10. One reason date rape often goes unpunished is that a jury is often reluctant to believe that the victim was raped when she _____ the assailant.

    a. can identify   c. knows
    b. cannot identify   d. is unfamiliar with

11. Rape _____ syndrome is the term that describes characteristic behavior patterns frequently exhibited by rape victims.

    a. defense   c. trauma
    b. shield   d. crisis

12. _____ , the mind's attempt to exclude from consciousness the details of a traumatic event, is an aspect of rape trauma syndrome.

    a. Depression   c. Suppression
    b. Repression   d. Compression

13. In a few jurisdictions, the confidentiality of the relationship of the rape victim and the rape crisis counselor is preserved by considering any statement between them as:

    a. hearsay evidence.   c. admissible.
    b. opinion evidence.   d. privileged communication.

14. In the United States before 1975, a husband could not be charged with raping his wife. This has been called the "marital _____."

    a. exemption   c. privilege
    b. exception   d. objection

15. In Menachen Amir's *Patterns in Forcible Rape*, this offense was found to be an overwhelmingly _____ event in which the victims were mostly _____.

    a. interracial ... white   c. interracial ... black
    b. intraracial ... white   d. intraracial ... black

16. Most rapes are committed _____ on _____.

    a. indoors ... weekdays   c. outdoors ... weekdays
    b. indoors ... weekends   d. outdoors ... weekdays

17. The _____ offender knows that he is sick and typically feels tremendous guilt and shame, and even concern for his victim.

    a. criminal   c. psychiatric
    b. opportunistic   d. serial

18. The _____ offender feels no guilt, has no concern, and does not accept the idea that anything is wrong with him. His action is frequently motivated by contempt and hostility toward females.

    a. criminal   c. psychiatric
    b. opportunistic   d. serial

19. In the absence of signs of physical resistance or physical evidence, the medical examiner may affirm that:

    a. the rape was not accomplished.
    b. the rape cannot be proven to have occurred.
    c. a rape probably occurred.
    d. no conclusion can be reached.

20. In the absence of signs of physical resistance on the part of the victim, _____ takes on a much greater importance in the investigation.

    a. the collection of physical evidence from the victim
    b. the interview with the victim
    c. the acts and demeanor of the victim immediately after the assault
    d. the interrogation of the suspect

21. To process physical evidence properly, physicians in almost every hospital have access to:

    a. crime scene evidence kits.   c. trained sexual assault technicians.
    b. sexual assault evidence kits.   d. forensic laboratory equipment.

22. The two main purposes of collecting physical evidence from the victim of a rape case are: (1) to establish the *corpus delicti*, and (2) to:

    a. verify the victim's interview.
    b. associate the victim with the evidence.
    c. identify the assailant.
    d. verify the suspect's interview.

23. All of the following are kinds of physical evidence frequently collected from the body of the victim except:

    a. fingerprints.   c. dried semen, blood, and saliva stains.
    b. fingernail scrapings.   d. pubic hair and fibers.

24. A _____ involves the placing of evidence on a glass slide for microscopic identification.

    a. swab   c. sample
    b. smear   d. secretion

25. A secretor is one whose ABO blood group can be determined from their saliva or any of their bodily fluids. Approximately _____ percent of the population are secretors.

    a. 98   c. 50
    b. 80   d. 40

26. All of the following physical evidence samples are commonly taken from a suspect for comparison with any physical evidence found on the victim except:

    a. urine and semen.   c. pubic and head hair.
    b. blood and saliva.   d. fingernail scrapings.

27. Clothing is collected from both the victim and the suspect by having the subject disrobe on a _____ and the articles of clothing placed in separate bags.

    a. white table cloth   c. latex plastic sheet
    b. white sheet of paper   d. white tile floor

28. Semen can be described by all of the following adjectives except:

    a. grayish-white.   c. adhesive.
    b. viscous.   d. transparent.

29. If semen stains are not readily visible, the easiest way to locate them is by:

    a. infrared photography.   c. ultraviolet light.
    b. microscopic test.   d. acid phosphatase color test.

30. _____ is used as a screening procedure for determining whether a stain may be semen.

    a. Infrared photography   c. Ultraviolet light
    b. A microscopic test   d. The acid phosphatase color test

31. The finding of _____ through a microscope is considered conclusive evidence that a stain is semen.

    a. spermatozoa or sperm   c. ogliospermia
    b. acid phosphatase   d. aspermia

32. With the increase of vasectomies, _____ , or a complete lack of sperm, is becoming more common.

a. impotence
b. sterility
c. oligospermia
d. aspermia

33. Because rape charges are easily made, it is necessary for the investigator to listen to the victim's story:

a. displaying a healthy scepticism.
b. pretending to accept the story entirely.
c. with close scrutiny, looking for inconsistencies.
d. only after warning her of the consequences of a false report.

34. In prosecutions for sexual offenses such a rape and sodomy, evidence that the victim made complaint a short time thereafter is admissible and is called a(n):

a. spontaneous exclamation.
b. official complaint.
c. fresh report.
d. fresh complaint.

35. To establish lack of consent, it is necessary that the victim resisted at least to the extent of:

a. a stern warning and a loud protest.
b. her ability at the time and under the circumstances.
c. risking her life.
d. struggling after being overcome.

36. All of the following types of physical evidence are commonly found at the crime scene of a sexual assault except:

a. tire and shoe impressions.
b. soil, seeds, and pollen.
c. paint chips and glass particles.
d. clothing and personal belongings.

37. In the neighborhood canvass, particular attention should be paid to whether anyone heard a _____ , which is an utterance made in a state of excitement caused by participation in or observation of an event. This is admissible in court.

a. cry of anguish
b. fresh complaint
c. spontaneous exclamation
d. dying declaration

38. One who stands guard while his friend commits a rape should be charged with:

a. rape.
b. unlawful detainment.
c. carnal knowledge or statutory rape.
d. conspiracy to commit rape.

39. In _____, the victim assents to sexual intercourse but is under sixteen years of age.

    a. rape
    b. carnal knowledge or statutory rape
    c. indecent assault
    d. indecent acts with a child under sixteen

40. If the victim is of unsound mind or very young, the act of sexual intercourse is one of _____ because such a female is considered incapable of consent.

    a. rape
    b. carnal knowledge or statutory rape
    c. indecent assault
    d. indecent acts with a child under sixteen

41. An "assault with intent to commit rape" differs from an "attempt to commit rape" in that it lacks the element of _____ which would have led to the accomplishment of the crime except for some unlooked for interference.

    a. intent   c. an overt act
    b. motive   d. violence

42. An _____ consists of intimate caressing and fondling of a female against her will.

    a. attempt to commit rape   c. indecent assault
    b. indecent act   d. assault with intent to commit rape

43. A(n) _____ involves the taking of any immoral, improper, or indecent liberty with the body of a child of either sex under the age of sixteen.

    a. attempt to commit rape   c. indecent assault
    b. statutory rape   d. indecent act

44. Besides the age of the victim, an "indecent act with a child under the age of sixteen" differs from an "indecent assault" in that the lack of _____ is not an element of the offense.

    a. consent   c. intent
    b. motive   d. physical contact

45. The major difficulty encountered with the investigation of indecent acts with a child usually is:

    a. the inability to obtain parental permission to interview.
    b. the unreliability of the child's account.
    c. the difficulty in identifying the offender.
    d. the lack of interest shown by parents and teachers.

46. _____ is the carnal copulation of human beings in other than the natural manner.

a. Sexual deviance   c. Bestiality
b. Sodomy   d. Fetishism

47 _____ is a form of sodomy consisting of carnal copulation by a human being with an animal.

a. Sadism   c. Bestiality
b. Masochism   d. Fetishism

48. Sodomy can take place in all of the following combinations except:

a. between a male and a female.
b. between two males or between two females.
c. between a human being and an animal.
d. between two animals of different species.

49. _____ must be shown to complete the offense of sodomy.

a. Emission   c. Motive
c. Penetration   d. Intent

50. All of the following statements about the investigation of sodomy cases are true except:

a. Ordinarily a sodomy case develops as an outgrowth of an investigation into homosexuality.
b. The active participant should be interviewed differently from the passive participant.
c. In the early stages of interrogation, euphemisms should be used in describing the offense.
d. The passive participant is less guilty of the offense than the active participant.

51. The best source of physical evidence in a sodomy case would come from:

a. the crime scene.   c. the participants' home or vehicle.
b. the participants' clothing.   d. a medical examination.

52. The sexual attraction for persons of one's own sex is called:

a. heterosexuality.   c. bisexuality.
b. homosexuality.   d. lesbianism.

53. All of the following statements are true concerning homosexuality except:

    a. A male homosexual can invariably be identified by his feminine character-
       istics and mannerisms.
    b. Many homosexuals are married and conduct normal sexual relations with
       their spouse.
    c. The condition of homosexuality is not a crime.
    d. Lesbians are rarely if ever prosecuted in the United States for their sexual
       activities.

54. _____ is a psychiatric term used to refer to any sexual act which constitutes
a departure from the heterosexual act of coitus.

    a. Perversion   c. Sodomy
    b. Homosexual behavior   d. Sexual deviance

55. Indecent exposure is the display of the genitalia to one of the opposite sex
under other than conventionally lawful circumstances. The psychiatric term for
this is:

    a. voyeurism.   c. exhibitionism.
    b. transvestitism.   d. fetishism.

56. The personality of an individual given to indecent exposure is characterized
by:

    a. aggressiveness.   c. indifference.
    b. timidity.   d. anger.

57. The derivation of sexual excitement from viewing the genitalia or naked
body of another is called:

    a. voyeurism.   c. exhibitionism.
    b. transvestitism.   d. fetishism.

58. If a "Peeping Tom" operates from the privacy of his own apartment, he is
usually violating _____ laws.

    a. privacy   c. nuisance
    b. trespassing   d. no

59. A _____ achieves sexual excitement by inflicting physical punishment on
another.
    a. sadist   c. fetishist
    b. masochist   d. transvestite

60. A _____ derives his pleasure by submitting to physical ill treatment at the
hands of another.

    a. sadist   c. fetishist
    b. masochist   d. transvestite

61. A sadist is usually a:

a. male.
b. female.

c. male or a female.
d. bisexual.

62. The recipient of a sadist's attention is usually a:

a. male.
b. female.

c. male or a female.
d. bisexual.

63. _____ involves the use of an object, usually intimate wearing apparel, of a person of the opposite sex to derive sexual satisfaction.

a. Transvestitism
b. Toucherism

c. Tribadism
d. Fetishism

64. _____ is the practice of wearing the clothes of the opposite sex with the erotic desire of simulating attributes thereof.

a. Transvestitism
b. Toucherism

c. Tribadism
d. Fetishism

65. The fetishist is usually a:

a. male.
b. female.

c. male or a female.
d. bisexual.

66. Wearing clothes of the opposite sex by females is for the most part considered:

a. illegal.
b. immoral.

c. socially acceptable.
d. sexually deviant.

67. _____ is a sexual deviance in which excitement is achieved by rubbing against the clothing or anatomical part, usually the buttocks, of someone of the opposite sex.

a. Voyeurism
b. Frottage

c. Toucherism
d. Tribadism

68. _____ is the irresistible impulse to touch the body of another person.

a. Voyeurism
b. Frottage

c. Toucherism
d. Tribadism

69. _____ is a type of sexual relation between two females.

a. Voyeurism
b. Frottage

c. Toucherism
d. Tribadism

70. The frotteur and the toucheur are usually:

    a. male.
    b. female.

    c. male or female.
    d. bisexual.

71. Experts believe that all of the following are among the causes of homosexuality except:

    a. the family background.
    b. a conscious decision.

    c. the cultural environment.
    d. genetics.

72. The well-being of the homosexual in our society would be *best* promoted by:

    a. abolition of sodomy laws.
    b. a more understanding police force.
    c. the recognition that homosexuals are not security risks.
    d. a change in public attitude toward the homosexual.

73. In *Bowers v. Hardwick*, the Supreme Court ruled that private homosexual conduct between consenting adults is _____ by the Constitution.

    a. approved of
    b. protected

    c. not protected
    d. considered an inalienable right

Answers:

1. c	p. 347, 1.	26. a	p. 354, 5.	51. d	p. 367, 19c.		
2. a	p. 347, 1.	27. b	p. 355, 6.	52. b	p. 368, 20.		
3. b	p. 347, 1.	28. d	p. 355, 7.	53. a	p. 368, 21.		
4. c	p. 348, 2.	29. c	p. 355, 7.	54. d	p. 374, 27.		
5. a	p. 348, 2.	30. d	p. 355, 7a.	55. c	p. 375, 28.		
6. d	p. 348, 2.	31. a	p. 356, 7b.	56. b	p. 375, 28.		
7. c	p. 348, 2a.	32. d	p. 356, 7b.	57. a	p. 375, 29..		
8. d	p. 348, 2a.	33. c	p. 356, 8.	58. d	p. 375, 29.		
9. b	p. 349, 2c.	34. d	p. 356, 8a.	59. a	p. 376, 30.		
10. c	p. 349, 2c.	35. b	p. 357, 8b.	60. b	p. 376, 30.		
11. c	p. 350, 2c.	36. c	p. 357, 9.	61. a	p. 376, 30.		
12. b	p. 350, 2c.	37. c	p. 358, 10.	62. c	p. 376, 30.		
13. d	p. 350, 2c.	38. a	p. 359, 11.	63. d	p. 376, 31.		
14. a	p. 350, 2c.	39. b	p. 359, 12.	64. a	p. 376, 32.		
15. d	p. 351, 3.	40. a	p. 359, 12.	65. a	p. 376, 31.		
16. b	p. 351, 3a.	41. c	p. 361, 14.	66. c	p. 376, 32.		
17. c	p. 352, 3b.	42. c	p. 362, 15.	67. b	p. 377, 33.		
18. a	p. 352, 3b.	43. d	p. 362, 16.	68. c	p. 377, 33.		
19. d	p. 352, 4b.	44. a	p. 362, 16.	69. d	p. 377, 34.		
20. c	p. 353, 4b.	45. b	p. 363, 16.	70. a	p. 377, 33.		
21. b	p. 353, 4d.	46. b	p. 364, 18.	71. b	p. 377, 35.		
22. c	p. 353, 4d.	47. c	p. 365, 18.	72. d	p. 379, 35.		
23. a	p. 353, 4d.	48. d	p. 365, 18.	73. c	p. 379, 35.		
24. b	p. 354, 4d.	49. b	p. 365, 18.				
25. b	p. 354, 4d.	50. d	p. 366, 19.				

Chapter 20
LARCENY

Questions:

1. A person who wrongfully takes, obtains, or withholds property in order to *temporarily* deprive its owner of its use or benefit should be found guilty of:

    a. larceny.
    b. robbery.

    c. criminally receiving.
    d. wrongful appropriation.

2. The elements of larceny and the points of proof which must be established by the investigator are the following: (1) that the accused wrongfully *took, obtained, or withheld,* the property described; and all of the following except:

    a. the *intent* to deprive.
    b. the *value* of the property.

    c. the *ownership* of the property.
    d. the *motive* for wanting to deprive.

3. All of the following persons may be guilty of larceny except:

    a. a person rerouting his electric wiring to bypass the meter.
    b. a person enticing an animal by food to leave the owner's property.
    c. a debtor refusing to make payment to a creditor.
    d. a person devoting property to a use not authorized by its owner.

4. If the owner of the property taken cannot be found, the charge of larceny:

    a. must be dropped.
    b. can still be supported by circumstantial evidence.
    c. can still be supported by a confession.
    d. will be difficult to prove.

5. A person obtaining property by a false representation of a fact, such as collecting money by misrepresenting himself as an agent of a creditor, is guilty of:

    a. wrongful appropriation.
    b. larceny.

    c. criminally receiving.
    d. extortion.

6. The intent to steal must be present to constitute larceny. In most cases, it can be established by:

    a. testimony of the owner.
    b. testimony of witnesses.

    c. inference from the circumstances.
    d. the confession of the accused.

7. After a larceny has been accomplished, if the person returns the property:

    a. no crime has been committed.
    b. a crime was committed, but ordinarily the accused is absolved of blame.
    c. it is considered a wrongful appropriation.
    d. he has still committed the crime and should be charged with larceny.

8. The general rule is that the value of property in a larceny is:

   a. the price the owner paid for it.
   b. the market value of the object today.
   c. the market value of the object on the date of the theft.
   d. the price the owner will pay to replace it.

9. A person finds a bicycle in the park with a social security number inscribed on its frame. He drives it away with the intention of keeping it. This person is guilty of:

   a. larceny.   c. wrongful appropriation.
   b. no offense.   d. negligence.

10. A person steals a number of articles from different owners at the same time and place. The value of each article taken separately would support a charge of petty larceny; taken together, grand larceny. The person should be accused of:

   a. a single petty larceny charge.   c. multiple petty larceny charges.
   b. a single grand larceny charge.   d. multiple grand larceny charges.

11. A person steals a number of articles from different owners at different times and places. The value of each article taken separately would support a charge of petty larceny; taken together, grand larceny. The person should be accused of:

   a. a single petty larceny charge.   c. multiple petty larceny charges.
   b. a single grand larceny charge.   d. multiple grand larceny charges.

12. Possession of stolen property by the accused raises the legal presumption that the accused:

   a. acquired the property legitimately.
   b. may have acquired the property legitimately.
   c. may have stolen the property.
   d. stole the property.

13. The fact that the accused absconded at the time of the larceny:

   a. tends to establish his guilt.
   b. by itself is sufficient to support a conviction.
   c. tends not to establish his guilt.
   d. is not significant of guilt or innocence.

14. The most common motive for larceny is:

   a. economic gain.   c. revenge.
   b. kleptomania.   d. malicious mischief.

15. Approximately _____ automobiles are stolen in the United States each year.

 a. two million
 b. one million
 c. two hundred thousand
 d. one hundred thousand

16. The organization set up by insurance companies to assist law enforcement agencies in the recovery of stolen cars and the apprehension of the criminals is the:

 a. Federal Interagency Committee on Auto Theft Prevention.
 b. FBI automotive theft division.
 c. National Auto Theft Bureau.
 d. auto theft detail.

17. A large number of automobile thefts are temporary appropriations that are soon recovered by there owners. The more common types of these offenses include all of the following except:

 a. juveniles out for an evening of joy riding.
 b. professional bank robbers using a stolen car so that it cannot be traced back to them.
 c. thieves disguising a car by changing the VIN and creating a fraudulent registration.
 d. car owners simulating and then reporting a theft in order to cover up a serious accident.

18. The most serious aspect of auto theft is represented by the statistics relating to:

 a. the number of cars stolen.
 b. the dollar loss by the owners.
 c. the rise of insurance rates.
 d. the age of the typical offender.

19. A professional auto thief would rely on any of the following methods of car theft except:

 a. looking for a car with its keys accidentally left in the ignition.
 b. pulling out the ignition cylinder and replacing it with one equipped with a key.
 c. using a tow truck to remove a car.
 d. establishing a connection at a parking garage or restaurant where the key can be copied, and stealing the car later, when it is parked on the street.

20. Automobiles that are stolen are usually identified by means of the:

 a. Vehicle Inspection Number.
 b. Vehicle Registration Number.
 c. license plate.
 d. Vehicle Identification Number.

21. A professional car-theft organization will not only steal the car but also provide a fraudulent:

    a. license plate.   c. registration.
    b. inspection sticker.   d. odometer reading.

22. A "car clout" or "booster" is one who:

    a. cuts up cars into saleable parts.
    b. steals parts and property out of cars.
    c. steals a particular make and model of car for a specific order.
    d. steals cars for the overseas markets.

23. Most of the automobile frauds described in this section involve using a wrecked or dismantled automobile frame to defraud the:

    a. original owner.   c. garage owner.
    b. automobile dealership.   d. insurance company.

24. The method of disguising a heavily-used vehicle to make it look like an almost-new vehicle is called:

    a. Duplicating from Salvage.   c. The "Erector Set" Fraud.
    b. Changing the VIN.   d. The Odometer Rollback Scheme.

25. Which of the following would be suspicious to an auto-theft investigator?

    a. new tags on a new car.   c. old tags on a used car.
    b. new tags on a used car.   d. rusty bolts on an old tag.

26. The new array of auto-theft prevention devices are able to do all of the following except:

    a. delay the thief's entry into the car.
    b. discourage the thief from completing the theft.
    c. prevent the thief from towing it away.
    d. divert the thief to a less well-protected vehicle.

27. In bicycle theft cases, the most important information the investigator should obtain is the _____ of the bicycle.

    a. make and model   c. year of purchase
    b. color   d. serial number

28. There are very few professional pickpockets because:

    a. people don't carry that much money with them anymore.
    b. not many people use public transportation anymore.
    c. of the great skill that is required.
    d. people today are too knowledgeable and alert to have their pockets picked.

29. In the criminal argot, the pickpocket is known as a:

a. cannon.
b. stall.
c. stiff.
d. poke.

30. All of the following statements concerning pickpockets are true except:

a. The purpose served by the pickpocket's confederates is that of actually removing the wallet from the victim's pocket.
b. The *modus operandi* is of great importance in detecting pickpockets.
c. The pickpocket employs the techniques of the professional magician.
d. Distraction of the victim's attention and swiftness of operation are the most important elements of the pickpocket's success.

31. The _____ works in the front of the victim, abstracting money from the most accessible place.

a. fob worker
b. inside worker
c. pants pocket worker
d. lush worker

32. The _____ is able to remove a wallet from a man's side pocket without his knowledge. A "stall" distracts the victim while the pickpocket removes the wallet and passes it to another assistant.

a. fob worker
b. inside worker
c. pants pocket worker
d. lush worker

33. The _____ removes a wallet from the inside pocket of a man's coat, covering his operations with a newspaper.

a. fob worker
b. inside worker
c. pants pocket worker
d. lush worker

34. The _____ operates on trains or busses looking for a perspective victim who is sleeping or unconscious.

a. fob worker
b. inside worker
c. pants pocket worker
d. lush worker

35. A pickpocket operating with assistants will run away if the victim becomes suspicious because:

a. he usually has a long record of arrests and can't afford to be caught.
b. he has the money in his possession and does not want to be caught with evidence on him.
c. he no longer has the money in his possession and so does not fear being caught.
d. if he remains at the scene, the police will probably recognize him.

36. After the pickpocket's assistant receives the wallet or "the poke," he will usually:

    a. run away in the opposite direction away from the pickpocket.
    b. walk away in the opposite direction away from the pickpocket.
    c. walk away in the same direction toward the pickpocket.
    d. remain in the same position.

37. The _____ is a type of "bag stealer" who removes the wallet and change purse from a woman's handbag while it is still suspended from her arm.

    a. bag clipper   c. bag snatcher
    b. bag opener   d. bag dumper

38. The pickpocket is usually identified by the recognition of:

    a. his physical description.   c. his method of operation.
    b. his assistants.   d. his fingerprints on the wallet.

39. In a pickpocket case, after listening to the victim's story, the investigator will:

    a. instruct the victim to go to the same location the following day in an attempt to spot the pickpocket.
    b. have a sketch made from the victim's description and post it near the crime scene.
    c. wait for the pickpocket to start using the victim's credit card and then trace him.
    d. consult the known pickpocket file and show the victim photographs of possible suspects.

40. In _____ , the thieves usually operate in pairs and work in the hotel section of the city.

    a. sneak theft   c. pennyweighting
    b. package theft   d. automobile baggage theft

41. In _____ , the success of the thieves depends upon the carelessness of the agent in guarding or delivering the property.

    a. sneak theft   c. theft by dishonest employees
    b. package theft   d. automobile baggage theft

42. Prevention of _____ is accomplished by careful background investigation and detection usually is the result of intelligent surveillance.

    a. sneak theft   c. theft by dishonest employees
    b. package theft   d. automobile baggage theft

43. _____ is a term used to include a number of forms of petty larceny involving unattended property.

    a. Sneak theft   c. Pennyweighting
    b. Package theft   d. Automobile baggage theft

44. _____ is the name given in this text to the practice of substituting imitation jewelry for real jewelry while pretending to make a purchase.

    a. Sneak theft   c. Shoplifting
    b. Pennyweighting   d. Jewelry theft

45. To defeat hotel thieves, a number of hotels, such as the Algonquin in New York, have installed:

    a. in-room surveillance cameras.
    b. background screening of guests as well as employees.
    c. a computerized locking system with preprogrammed cards to unlock doors.
    d. undercover security personnel disguised as chambermaids.

46. If business desired, they could easily reduce losses due to fraudulent use of credit cards by:

    a. stricter controls on credit card distribution and use.
    b. demanding from the courts longer sentences for credit card theft.
    c. limiting the number of credit cards one person can have.
    d. limiting the number of individual credit card purchases that can be made in one day.

47. Swindling is defined in general as the art of obtaining money or property from another by:

    a. theft.   c. fraud or deceit.
    b. embezzlement.   d. forgery.

48. The distinguishing characteristic of many confidence games (such as Wallet Dropper) is that the victim is knowingly engaging in a _____ act.

    a. dishonest   c. foolish
    b. dangerous   d. criminal

49. All of the following confidence games have as their crucial element the payment of a fee to share in a treasure or money-making scheme except:

    a. The Smack Game.   c. The Sir Francis Drake Swindle.
    b. The Spanish Prisoner.   d. The Money-Making Machine.

50. All of the following swindles have as a crucial element a basically dishonest act done by the victim to defraud someone else except:

    a. The Smack Game.   c. The Money-Making Machine.
    b. Dropping the Wallet.   d. The Sir Francis Drake Swindle.

51. _____ is the fraudulent appropriation of money or goods by a person to whom they are entrusted.

a. Swindling
b. Embezzlement

c. Criminally receiving
d. Loan sharking

52. The money lost through bank robbery is _____ that lost through embezzlement.

a. many times greater than
b. about the same as

c. a little more than
d. a fraction of

53. In embezzlement cases, the criminal usually has a thorough knowledge of:

a. the laws and penalties associated with embezzlement.
b. the various methods of operation used by embezzlers.
c. the financial organization of the company.
d. investigative techniques used to combat embezzlement.

54. To conduct a full investigation of an embezzlement case, the investigator will require the services of an experienced:

a. banker who works for the company.
b. banker who does not work for the company.
c. accountant who works for the company.
d. accountant who does not work for the company.

55. Before proceeding with any embezzlement case, it is very important for the investigator to determine whether:

a. the company has been unfair to its employees.
b. the company will press charges against an employee.
c. the embezzler has returned the missing money.
d. the company president is involved.

56. All of the following are ways that the discovery of a loss by embezzlement usually takes place except:

a. The embezzler suddenly flees his surroundings and moves to another city.
b. An annual audit or an unexpected review of certain accounts uncovers irregularities.
c. A sudden display of prosperity by the embezzler will attract the notice of an informant.
d. An embezzler, after years of creative bookkeeping, will on his own initiative confess to the company president.

57. Before taking any serious action with respect to a suspect in an embezzlement case, the investigator should first satisfy himself that:

a. no one has already returned the money.
b. the suspect has no accomplices.
c. a crime has been committed.
d. the company did not know of the embezzlement.

58. In an embezzlement case, often there is (are) _____ logical suspect(s).

    a. only one   c. a number of
    b. only a few   d. no

59. All of the following are questions that should be asked about an embezzling suspect except:

    a. Does he take his annual vacation?
    b. Does he have any interesting hobbies?
    c. Does he live within his means?
    d. Does he have several bank accounts?

60. Fraudulent intent and appropriation are often established in embezzlement cases by one or all of the following except:

    a. the disposition made of the property, such as depositing it in a bank account.
    b. an extremely complicated record keeping system.
    c. the denial of having received the property.
    d. false entries in documents or ledgers recording the transactions.

61. _____ stolen property is the crime of buying or accepting stolen goods with the intention of converting it to your own use.

    a. Receiving   c. Selling
    b. Illegal possession of   d. Dealing in

62. This crime is difficult to prove because the accused usually hides behind a legitimate business front and the evidence against him is largely circumstantial depending heavily on:

    a. the kind of good being sold.
    b. the price of the goods being sold.
    c. his explanation of how he acquired the goods.
    d. the testimony of thieves.

63. In addition to proving that "the property was stolen," all of the following are elements of the crime of receiving stolen property except:

    a. The property was received by the accused.
    b. The receiver knew that the property was stolen.
    c. The receiver knew who stole the property.
    d. The accused had the intent to convert the property to his own use.

64. Receiving stolen property is often referred to as:

    a. dealing.   c. a sting.
    b. fencing.   d. fronting.

65. In "Operation Sting," the site of the operation set up by the police was selected for its inconvenience with respect to public transportation in order to:

    a. induce the sellers to use their cars.
    b. to avoid charges of entrapment.
    c. to obtain the kind of stolen property too large to carry on a bus.
    d. make it difficult for the sellers to escape.

66. Besides the recovery of stolen property, all of the following are other benefits from "Operation Sting" except:

    a. the apprehension and arrest of burglars.
    b. information on the identity of other fences.
    c. information on the general nature and approximate date of burglary offenses.
    d. the recovery and restitution of stolen money.

67. Most of the persons arrested in "Operation Sting" pleaded guilty to illegal possession of stolen property when confronted with:

    a. the testimony of undercover officers.
    b. the proof that the goods were stolen.
    c. a surveillance videotape of their selling stolen goods.
    d. the list of license plates of cars visiting this location.

68. Loan sharking is the lending of money at exorbitant rates of interest backed ultimately by the threat of _____ in the event the debtor defaults.

    a. foreclosure   c. even higher rates of interest
    b. bankruptcy   d. violence

69. Loan sharking is important because it is considered:

    a. by police to be a grave source of danger to the average businessman.
    b. a threat to legitimate banking.
    c. one of the largest sources of revenue to organized crime.
    d. a difficult crime to prevent and investigate.

70. In the loan sharking business, the interest on the money is known as:

    a. the "poke."   c. "vigorish."
    b. the "score."   d. the "debt."

71. The basic operation of loan sharking can best be described as _____ of distributors or lenders; at each level, higher interest rates are charged.

    a. a pyramid   c. an inverted pyramid
    b. a loose confederation   d. a cooperative partnership

72. The two objectives of a loan shark operation are: (1) the acquisition of money and (2) the:

   a. elimination of competition.
   b. collection of gambling debts.
   c. acquisition of legitimate businesses.
   d. recruitment for organized crime.

73. The preferred victims of the loan shark are:

   a. other organized crime members.
   b. legitimate business and professional men.
   c. businessmen engaged in dishonest activities.
   d. hard-working, blue-collar workers.

74. Loan sharking is a difficult crime to investigate because:

   a. there are usually no witnesses other than the principals.
   b. the danger to the victim is very great.
   c. of the number and complexity of the loan documents.
   d. the customer is usually satisfied with his loan.

75. The documentary evidence in a loan sharking case can best be described as:

   a. simple and clear.
   b. complex and indecipherable.
   c. complete and self-explanatory.
   d. meager and cryptic.

76. The most effective method of investigating loan sharking is by the use of:

   a. a forensic accountant.
   b. a sting operation.
   c. an undercover man.
   d. a fixed-surveillance operation.

Answers:

1. d	p. 383, 1.	27. d	p. 398, 15c.	53. c	p. 411, 19b.
2. d	p. 383, 2.	28. c	p. 399, 16.	54. d	p. 411, 19c.
3. c	p. 384, 3.	29. a	p. 399, 16.	55. b	p. 411, 19c.
4. a	p. 384, 4.	30. a	p. 399, 16a.	56. d	p. 412, 19d.
5. b	p. 384, 5.	31. a	p. 399, 16a.	57. c	p. 412, 19e.
6. c	p. 385, 6.	32. c	p. 400, 16a.	58. a	p. 412, 19f.
7. d	p. 385, 6f.	33. b	p. 400, 16a.	59. b	p. 412, 19f.
8. c	p. 385, 7.	34. d	p. 401, 16a.	60. b	p. 413, 19g.
9. a	p. 386, 8a.	35. c	p. 401, 16a.	61. a	p. 413, 20.
10. b	p. 386, 8b.	36. d	p. 401, 16a.	62. d	p. 414, 20.
11. c	p. 386, 8c.	37. b	p. 401, 16a.	63. c	p. 414, 20.
12. d	p. 386, 8d.	38. c	p. 401, 16b.	64. b	p. 415, 21.
13. a	p. 387, 8e.	39. d	p. 401, 16b.	65. a	p. 415, 21.
14. a	p. 387, 9.	40. d	p. 402, 17a.	66. d	p. 415, 21.
15. b	p. 389, 11.	41. b	p. 402, 17b.	67. c	p. 416, 21.
16. c	p. 389, 11.	42. c	p. 404, 17c.	68. d	p. 416, 22.

17. c	p. 390, 11a.	43. a	p. 405, 17d.	69. c	p. 416, 22.
18. d	p. 390, 11a.	44. b	p. 405, 17e.	70. c	p. 417, 23b.
19. a	p. 391, 11b.	45. c	p. 406, 17f.	71. a	p. 417, 23b.
20. d	p. 392, 11b.	46. a	p. 407, 17g.	72. c	p. 418, 23c.
21. c	p. 393, 11b.	47. c	p. 407, 18.	73. b	p. 419, 25.
22. b	p. 393, 11b.	48. a	p. 407, 18.	74. a	p. 419, 26.
23. d	p. 394, 12.	49. a	p. 408, 18.	75. d	p. 420, 26a.
24. d	p. 395, 12.	50. d	p. 408, 18.	76. c	p. 421, 26b.
25. b	p. 396, 13a.	51. b	p. 410, 19.		
26. c	p. 396, 14.	52. d	p. 411, 19a.		

Chapter 21

BURGLARY

Questions:

1. _____ is the unlawful entering of the building of another with the intent to commit a crime therein.

    a. Trespassing
    b. Burglary
    c. Breaking and entering
    d. Housebreaking

2. Along with breaking and entering, all of the following are elements of the offense of burglary except:

    a. It occurs in the dwelling house of another.
    b. There is an intent to commit a crime therein.
    c. A crime is in fact committed therein.
    d. It occurs in the nighttime.

3. The essence of _____ is the removing or putting aside of some material part of the house on which the dweller relies on as security against intrusion.

    a. breaking
    b. entering
    c. housebreaking
    d. burglary

4. All of the following are instances of breaking except:

    a. opening a closed door.
    b. removing a screen from a window.
    c. walking through a hole in the wall.
    d. a guest in the house forcing an inner door.

5. _____ is the term used to describe the application of physical force to effect entry.

    a. Constructive breaking
    b. Physical breaking
    c. Actual breaking
    d. Housebreaking

6. An example of constructive breaking would be:

   a. forcing a door.
   b. using construction equipment.
   c. using burglary tools.
   d. impersonating a repairman.

7. The insertion of any part of the body into the building constitutes:

   a. breaking.
   b. entry.
   c. constructive breaking.
   d. constructive entry.

8. To support a conviction of two persons for burglary, _____ enter the building.

   a. only one has to
   b. both have to
   c. neither one has to
   d. no one has to

9. With respect to the definition of burglary, all of the following would be considered buildings rather than dwelling houses except:

   a. a grocery store.
   b. an abandoned house.
   c. an abandoned warehouse.
   d. a summer bungalow during winter.

10. All of the following are true statements about burglary and burglary investigation except:

   a. The breaking and entering do not have to occur on the same night.
   b. The crime intended by the burglar on entry does not have to be larceny.
   c. The actual crime intended by the burglar on entry does not have to be possible to complete.
   d. On a burglary stakeout, the investigator should attempt to prevent the crime from happening.

11. The Latin phrase meaning "in the act of committing a crime" is:

   a. *corpus delicti.*
   b. *modus operandi.*
   c. *in flagrante delicto.*
   d. *res gestae.*

12. The locksmith will rely on any of the following methods to open a customer's safe except:

   a. drilling.
   b. burning.
   c. combination deduction.
   d. manipulation.

13. All of the following are indicative of a safeman's level of proficiency except:

   a. choice of method.
   b. precise toolmarks.
   c. quality of equipment.
   d. persistence after failed attempts.

14. The _____ method involves knocking off the dial, driving the spindle back through the locking mechanism, thus releasing the lock.

    a. peel   c. punch
    b. ripping   d. chopping

15. The _____ method involves separating the metal layers on the door and curling back the top layer with a pry bar to expose the lock or bolt.

    a. peel   c. punch
    b. ripping   d. chopping

16. Cutting a hole through the bottom of a safe with a hammer and chisel or an ax is called the _____ method.

    a. peel   c. punch
    b. ripping   d. chopping

17. The blasting method involves the use of _____ to open the safe door.

    a. acetylene   c. nitroglycerine
    b. oxyacetylene   d. a thermal lance

18. The burning method which can produce heat in excess of 7000 degrees and can penetrate any metal surface uses:

    a. acetylene.   c. nitroglycerine.
    b. oxyacetylene.   d. a thermal lance.

19. Perhaps the most effective as well as the most practical method of opening a safe and the one that is used by locksmiths is:

    a. drilling.   c. blasting.
    b. burning.   d. peeling.

20. A _____ is a fiber-optic instrument used to peer inside to examine the contents of a safe.

    a. borescope   c. fluoroscope
    b. stethoscope   d. microscope

21. A _____ can be used to create a circular hole in a safe large enough to reach in and remove its contents.

    a. high-torque drill   c. hacksaw
    b. core drill   d. pry bar

22. _____ is the name given to those safe burglaries where the safeman determines either the combination of the safe or how to open it from the circumstances in the office.

    a. Manipulation   c. Combination deduction
    b. Trial combination   d. Combination surveillance

23. _____ is the art of opening a safe without prior knowledge of the combination using only the senses of sight, hearing, and touch.

    a. Manipulation   c. Combination deduction
    b. Trial combination   d. Combination surveillance

24. All of the following are examples of combination deduction except:

    a. finding the combination number hidden near the safe.
    b. finding the safe on "day-lock" and turning the dial a half turn to open it.
    c. determining the combination by manipulating the dial.
    d. determining the combination through surveillance techniques.

25. A safe manufacturing company may be of help in opening a safe by supplying:

    a. the combination.   c. the master combination.
    b. a trial combination.   d. the universal combination.

26. All of the following are instruments that may be employed in safe-breaking by manipulation except:

    a. a borescope.   c. an audio amplifier.
    b. a stethoscope.   d. a noise filter.

27. The most advanced safes can most accurately be described as being:

    a. "burglarproof."   c. merely fire resistant.
    b. burglary-resistant.   d. impregnable.

28. A loft job usually:

    a. is a crime of opportunity.   c. involves little planning.
    b. is elaborately planned.   d. involves no planning at all.

29. In a loft burglary, entry into the premises usually takes place during:

    a. daylight on a weekday.   c. the night on a weekday.
    b. daylight on a weekend.   d. the night on a weekend.

30. Some loft burglaries involve a "lay-in-mob" which means that the burglars:

    a. hide themselves on the premises during business hours.
    b. hide the stolen articles on the premises.
    c. lay in wait for the night watchman.
    d. break into the premises during business hours.

31. In a loft burglary, the merchandise is usually removed

    a. by automobile.   c. by trailer truck.
    b. by truck.   d. on foot.

32. An apartment house burglar usually selects his target by:

    a. pressing all of the doorbells.
    b. telephoning each apartment.
    c. looking for apartments with darkened windows.
    d. selecting an apartment randomly.

33. An apartment house burglar frequently gains access to the building by ringing the doorbell of a resident _____, opening the front door when "buzzed in" by the resident and, then jamming the locking mechanism.

    a. who is at home   c. whose apartment he will break into.
    b. who is not at home   d. of any apartment a random.

34. For the apartment burglar described as a "door shaker," his modus operandi consists of:

    a. applying pressure to an apartment door until it opens.
    b. knocking on an apartment door to find out if anyone is at home.
    c. trying each door to see if it is unlocked or ajar.
    d. "jimmying" the lock on an apartment door.

35. The suburban and the commuter burglar will determine whether anyone is at home in the premises they intend to break into by:

    a. ringing the doorbell   c. looking through the window.
    b. telephoning the house.   d. keeping the house under surveillance.

36. The commuter burglar is difficult to investigate and apprehend because he:

    a. rarely leaves physical evidence behind.
    b. always takes his burglar tools with him.
    c. often wears gloves when he operates.
    d. rarely returns to the same locality.

37. On arriving at the scene of reported burglary, the first thing an investigator should do is:

   a. protect the crime scene.
   b. search the building for physical evidence.
   c. search the building for the burglar.
   d. try to locate eyewitnesses.

38. The most common clue left at the scene of a safe burglary is:

   a. heelprints on paper.   c. fingerprints on the safe.
   b. fingerprints on paper.   d. clothing.

39. All of the following are places the investigator is likely to find fingerprints at the scene of a burglary except:

   a. window sills.   c. closet doors.
   b. door knobs.   d. bottles and glasses.

40. All of the following are examples of trace evidence frequently found on a burglary suspect except:

   a. glass particles on clothing. c. blood drops on clothing.
   b. paint samples on tools.   d. safe insulation on the shoes.

41. The experienced burglar will _____ the crime scene.

   a. take all of his tools from   c. take only the tools he used from
   b. leave all of his tools at   d. leave only the tools he used at

42. The FBI Laboratory maintains a Petrographic File, one section of which contains samples of and data concerning:

   a. paint chips.   c. fibers from clothing.
   b. glass particles.   d. safe insulation.

Answers:

1. d	p. 429, 2b.	15. a	p. 433, 6a.	29. d	p. 443, 8b.
2. c	p. 429, 3.	16. d	p. 433, 6a.	30. a	p. 443, 8b.
3. a	p. 429, 4a.	17. c	p. 435, 6a.	31. b	p. 443, 8c.
4. c	p. 429, 4a.	18. d	p. 435, 6a.	32. c	p. 444, 9a.
5. c	p. 429, 4a.	19. a	p. 437, 6a.	33. a	p. 444, 9a.
6. d	p. 430, 4a.	20. a	p. 438, 6a.	34. c	p. 444, 9a.
7. b	p. 430, 4a.	21. b	p. 438, 6a.	35. a	p. 444, 10.
8. a	p. 430, 4a.	22. c	p. 438, 6a.	36. d	p. 445, 11a.
9. d	p. 430, 4b.	23. a	p. 438, 6a.	37. c	p. 446, 13.
10. d	p. 431, 4e.	24. c	p. 438, 6a.	38. a	p. 447, 13a.
11. c	p. 431, 4d.	25. b	p. 439, 6a.	39. b	p. 447, 13b.
12. b	p. 432, 6.	26. a	p. 440, 6a.	40. c	p. 448, 13d.
13. d	p. 432, 6a.	27. b	p. 441, 6b.	41. b	p. 449, 13g.
14. c	p. 432, 6a.	28. b	p. 442, 8a.	42. d	p. 450, 13i.

Chapter 22
ROBBERY

Questions:

1. Robbery is:

    a. the taking of someone else's property.
    b. the taking of property from another in his presence and against his will.
    c. the taking of someone else's property after breaking into his home.
    d. all of the above.

2. Robbery is considered a very serious crime because:

    a. it involves the loss of large amounts of money.
    b. it violates one's right to own property.
    c. it involves immediate personal danger to the victim.
    d. it is destructive to the social order.

3. All of the following are elements of the offense of robbery except:

    a. the taking of the property.
    b. that the property was owned by the person.
    c. that the taking was from the person or in the presence of the person.
    d. that the taking was against his will, by force, violence, or putting in fear.

4. A man enters a house and ties the owner up and proceeds to remove all of his valuables from a back room. He has committed:

    a. larceny.
    b. robbery.
    c. criminal possession.
    d. assault.

5. A pickpocket removes a wallet from a person without that person being aware of it. He has committed:

    a. larceny.
    b. robbery.
    c. criminal possession.
    d. assault.

6. A woman enters a bank and hands the teller a note which reads "If you know what is good for you, you will hand over the money in your draw." The woman receives the money and leaves the bank. She has committed:

    a. larceny.
    b. robbery.
    c. extortion.
    d. blackmail.

7. Bank robbery is attractive to highly skilled professional criminals because:

    a. it is safer than other crimes.
    b. banks take little or no precautions to prevent bank robbery.
    c. it is one of the few crimes where the participants can net a large sum of money.
    d. it is easy to recruit other professional criminals to participate.

8. Individual robbers usually enter a bank and hand the teller a note demanding the money in the teller's draw and informing the teller that he is armed with a pistol or an explosive device. They are very often successful because:

   a. robbers are always armed and dangerous.
   b. the teller always believes the threat and acts accordingly.
   c. the teller is instructed by the bank to concede to the robber's wishes.
   d. robbers rarely bluff and hence are dangerous.

9. All of the following statements about robbery are true except:

   a. The methods of operation of individual bank robbers are remarkably similar.
   b. The small branch bank or the savings and loan associations is the preferred target.
   c. Often the day selected for a robbery is one in which a large payroll delivery is expected.
   d. The time of day is selected so that the least number of people are present.

10. All of the following statements about bank robbery are true except:

   a. Most robbers will use some disguise.
   b. Bank robbers rarely carry a gun.
   c. A typical bank robber uses a rented or stolen card to make his getaway and later transfers to his own car.
   d. The typical bank robbery is perpetrated by a pair of criminals.

11. Obtaining information about the layout of the bank and the location and movement of its personnel is called:

   a. casing.   c. surveillance.
   b. planning.   d. intelligence.

12. All of the following statements about professional bank robbers are true except:

   a. Professional robbers select their target carefully often with the help of tips.
   b. Professional robbers carefully plan their bank "jobs", often in minute detail.
   c. Often the bank robber will employ a ruse to gather information concerning the interior of the bank, its operations, and its personnel.
   d. The bank robbers or "heist mob" is usually a group of five or six experienced criminals with a leader or "mastermind."

13. The bank robber who supplies and drives the getaway car and in general is in charge of transportation is called the:

   a. rodman.   c. driver.
   b. wheelman.   d. vehicle man.

14. The person assigned to the task of gathering and transporting the guns is called the:

a. rodman.   c. firearms man.
b. gunman.   d. pieceman.

15. The persons who perform the actual work of the robbery are called:

a. holdupmen.   c. insidemen.
b. robbery men.   d. moneymen.

16. All of the following are true statements describing a professional gang's plan for robbing a bank except:

a. The getaway route is carefully laid out.
b. All of the gang members arrive at the bank in the getaway car.
c. The insidemen occasionally work with masks on their faces.
d. All of the robbers depart in the getaway car and shift to the "front" car.

17. Ideally the behavior of the employees and customers during the robbery should have _____ as its objective.

a. protection of the money   c. the safety of all present
b. apprehension of the robbers   d. remembering the robbers faces

18. As soon as the bank robbers have left, a bank employee should telephone the police giving all of the following information except:

a. that a robbery occurred and the exact time of the robber's departure.
b. the number of robbers and an accurate description of each.
c. the approximate amount of money taken and in what denominations.
d. the make, approximate year, color, style, and license plate of the getaway car and the direction in which it departed.

19. All of the following are major obstacles to the solution of the crime of robbery except:

a. Little or no help is received from the bank and its employees.
b. There are few traces left behind by the criminals.
c. A robbery is of such short duration that the victim has so little time to note the exact appearance of the robber.
d. The violent manner of the robber instills fear and thus inhibits civilian cooperation.

20. The solution of a robbery will most often be reached through:

a. analysis of physical clues.   c. information from criminals.
b. analysis of motive.   d. information from people at the scene.

21. An effective interrogation technique involves accusing a robbery suspect of a homicide that has occurred at a different place but at the same time as when the robbery occurred. This will sometimes lead a suspect to:

    a. confess to the lesser crime of the robbery.
    b. establish an alibi and name his confederates as people who can substantiate it.
    c. confess to the homicide to avoid being charged with the robbery.
    d. explain that he didn't commit the homicide because he was committing the robbery at the time.

22. When interviewing witnesses after a bank robbery, all of the following should be done except:

    a. Each witness should be interviewed separately.
    b. Each witness should be instructed not to discuss the crime with anyone.
    c. Each witness should be shown photographs of bank robbers or the FBI bank robber album to see if they recognize anyone.
    d. Each witness should be permitted to listen to the other witnesses' descriptions without commenting, before giving their own account.

23. All of the following are excellent tracing clues in robbery except:

    a. an abandoned gun.
    b. stolen traveller's checks.
    c. heelprints on the bank floor.
    d. fingerprints in the getaway car.

24. In a robbery case, fingerprints are most often found:

    a. in the getaway car on the rearview mirror.
    b. on the bank counter or other furniture touched by the robbers.
    c. on papers, checks, or currencies handled by the robbers.
    d. on a gun abandoned by the robbers.

25. All of the following are clues that are occasionally found associated with restraining devices or ligatures except:

    a. a characteristic knot made with rope.
    b. a fingerprint on the rope.
    c. an edge match of a piece of adhesive tape with a role found on the suspect.
    d. a fingerprint on the adhesive tape.

26. A clue that is an important part of the modus operandi of the crime of robbery is:

    a. a fingerprint found at the crime scene.
    b. heelprints on the bank floor.
    c. a discarded newspaper or garment.
    d. the manner and content of the criminal's speech.

27. Savings and loan associations are similar to banks except for the fact that:

    a. they have more employees to deal with.
    b. they are weak in structure, permitting a forced entry.
    c. they usually have more money to steal.
    d. they are protected from robbery to a greater degree.

28. Jewelry store robberies usually depend upon the robber initially _____ the owner.

    a. overpowering
    b. intimidating

    c. gaining the confidence of
    d. befriending

29. Robberies of chain stores, restaurants, and pharmacies often take place when they are about to close because at this time:

    a. the store usually has a large sum of money on hand.
    b. the employees are tired and let their guard down.
    c. it is usually dark, so that the robbers can work unobserved.
    d. there are fewer customers to get in the way of the robbers.

30. The investigative technique or equipment that would probably be the most helpful in stopping a series of nighttime robberies of liquor stores, gasoline stations, and delicatessens would be:

    a. an alarm system.
    b. a surveillance camera.

    c. a "plant" or "stakeout."
    d. routine patrols of the area.

31. A mugging may be described as a robbery accompanied by a:

    a. threats.
    b. an assault.

    c. a rape.
    d. a theft.

32. In urban areas, most muggings occur:

    a. indoors.
    b. outdoors.

    c. in buses or subways.
    d. in automobiles.

33. A(n) _____ is usually considered the ideal victim by the mugger.

    a. wealthy person
    b. businessman

    c. woman
    d. intoxicated person

34. Robberies by nonstrangers have a high clearance rate because the offender:

    a. usually commits other offenses in the neighborhood.
    b. is identified and located by the victim.
    c. is identified and located by the police.
    d. will often turn himself in if he thinks he has been recognized.

35. The investigation of a robbery by a stranger requires prompt action in:

   a. interviewing witnesses.
   b. collecting physical evidence.

   c. searching the modus operandi file.
   d. using decoy units.

36. The most successful way of apprehending and convicting muggers is through the use of:

   a. physical evidence.
   b. modus operandi files.

   c. information from criminals.
   d. using decoy units.

37. The _____ robber selects as his victims couples sitting in parked cars in a secluded spot.

   a. house
   b. hitchhiking

   c. lovers' lane
   d. doctor's office

38. A _____ solicits a ride on the highway and then pulls out a gun.

   a. house robber
   b. hitchhiking robber

   c. robber of the elderly
   d. lovers' lane robber

39. In a doctor's office robbery, the criminal tries to arrange an appointment so that he will be:

   a. the first patient of the day.
   b. the last patient of the day.

   c. the last patient before lunch.
   d. the first patient after lunch.

40. In the robbery of a wealthy residence, in which the owner is concealing large sums of money in the house, the investigator should consider _____ as the person who probably tipped off the robber as to the existence of the stash.

   a. a meter reader
   b. a close neighbor

   c. the owner's wife
   d. a servant or former employee

41. The success of robberies of elderly people depend on the use of _____ to open the door.

   a. a ruse
   b. a key

   c. brute force
   d. a celluloid strip

42. The hooker's knockout scam relies on _____ the victim.

   a. overpowering
   b. drugging

   c. hitting the head of
   d. using a gun to threaten

Answers:

1. b	p. 452, 1.	15. c	p. 459, 6d.	29. a	p. 469, 15.
2. c	p. 452, 2.	16. b	p. 460, 6e.	30. c	p. 470, 16.
3. b	p. 453, 2a.	17. c	p. 461, 8a.	31. b	p. 471, 17a.
4. b	p. 454, 2c.	18. c	p. 462, 8b.	32. a	p. 471, 17a.
5. a	p. 454, 2d.	19. a	p. 462, 9a.	33. d	p. 471, 17a.
6. b	p. 454, 2e.	20. c	p. 463, 9a.	34. b	p. 471, 17a.
7. c	p. 455, 3.	21. b	p. 463, 9b.	35. a	p. 472, 17a.
8. c	p. 455, 4a.	22. d	p. 464, 9c.	36. d	p. 472, 17a.
9. a	p. 456, 5.	23. c	p. 464, 10.	37. c	p. 473, 17b.
10. b	p. 457, 5d.	24. a	p. 466, 10b.	38. b	p. 473, 17c.
11. a	p. 458, 6b.	25. b	p. 466, 10c.	39. b	p. 473, 17d.
12. d	p. 459, 6c.	26. d	p. 467, 10f.	40. d	p. 474, 17e.
13. b	p. 459, 6d.	27. b	p. 468, 13.	41. a	p. 474, 17f.
14. a	p. 459, 6d.	28. c	p. 469, 14.	42. b	p. 475, 17g.

Chapter 23

FORGERY

Questions:

1. Forgery, the alteration of documents that impose a financial obligation, dates from the days of:

    a. precivilization bartering transactions.
    b. early civilization with the invention of money.
    c. the merchants who first instituted the procedure of transferring money by means of a piece of paper.
    d. the popular acceptance of the personal check which imposes an obligation on oneself.

2. The forger of extensive knowledge and highly developed skills has become a figure of history primarily because of:

    a. the advances in the detection and apprehension of career criminals.
    b. the inability to obtain the professional equipment anymore.
    c. the universal prevalence of checking accounts and credit cards.
    d. the advances made in copier machines.

3. The prerequisite qualifications for a career in forgery include a degree of clerical skill and elementary business knowledge as well as an exceptional amount of that character trait best described as:

    a. bravery.   c. persistence.
    b. "nerve."   d. fortitude.

4. The _____ Check Passer spends much time in prison with profits barely sufficient to offer a comfortable living.

a. Disguised
b. Roving
c. Successful
d. Habitual

5. The _____ Check Passer has an unusually honest appearance, is professional in his operations, and manages to evade the law for many years.

a. Disguised
b. Roving
c. Successful
d. Habitual

6. The _____ Check Passer is an exceptionally clever criminal who passes several checks in one community and then leaves the jurisdiction.

a. Disguised
b. Roving
c. Successful
d. Habitual

7. The _____ Check Passer escapes arrest for long periods of time by changing his appearance.

a. Disguised
b. Roving
c. Successful
d. Habitual

8. All of the following are steps the criminal will take in order to pass a forged check except:

a. Obtain blank forms either by theft or having facsimiles printed.
b. Equip himself with mechanical devices such as checkwriters, typewriters, and printing equipment to make the checks look authentic.
c. Have a reputable businessman attest to the authenticity of the check when passing it in the bank.
d. Equip himself with supporting documents such as a Social Security card and a driver's license to identify himself to the check casher.

9. Professional criminals are able to obtain official documents such as birth certificates, driver's licenses, and diplomas to sell to people who, for the most part, have no criminal connections. These documents are usually:

a. counterfeit document blanks that are carefully filled in.
b. genuine document blanks that are carefully filled in.
c. genuine documents issued by the official agency.
d. genuine documents originally issued by the official agency to someone else.

10. One successful forger, described in the text, used a method that involved purchasing several hundred dollars worth of merchandise and presenting a forged check for _____ the bill. He would receive change and then avoid taking delivery of the goods.

a. slightly less than
b. significantly less than
c. slightly in excess of
d. significantly in excess of

11. Another forger described in the text, Courtney Taylor, had a successful career passing forged checks through the use of:

    a. stolen blank checks.
    b. genuine office forms.
    c. genuine identification papers.
    d. elaborate credentials.

12. In his _____ scheme, Alexander Thiel would steal checks from the first individual and identification papers from the second. He would then open a bank account in the name of the second person and deposit a check from the account of the first person.

    a. checks in excess of purchase
    b. elaborate credentials
    c. dual signature
    d. fraudulent document

13. In the definition of forgery, a "false writing" is mentioned. "False," as used here, refers to _____ the writing.

    a. the making of
    b. the content of
    c. the facts contained in
    d. the bank referred to in

14. In the definition of forgery, "uttering" a false writing includes all of the following except:

    a. passing.
    b. offering.
    c. making.
    d. putting into circulation.

15. A check bearing the signature of the maker drawn on an account in which he has no credit with the intent to defraud is a(n):

    a. forgery.
    b. bad check.
    c. "raised" check.
    d. embezzlement.

16. A check signed with the name of another and drawn on that persons account with the intent to defraud is a(n):

    a. forgery.
    b. bad check.
    c. "raised" check.
    d. embezzlement.

17. The elements of proof to support forgery include the fact that the accused falsely made, altered, or knowingly uttered the forged instrument and all of the following except:

    a. that the writing was falsely made or altered.
    b. that the writing appears to impose a legal liability on another.
    c. that an actual loss of money or goods has occurred.
    d. that their was an intent to defraud.

18. A "false making" can include all of the following except:

    a. a "raised" check.
    b. a fictitious signature.
    c. the check writer's own signature.
    d. someone's signature made by another.

19. All of the following establish legal liability on another and therefore can be forgeries except:

    a. a parimutuel ticket.
    b. a letter of introduction.
    c. railway ticket.
    d. will.

20. When the forger and the utterer (or passer) are two different people, the defense attorney of the latter will usually claim:

    a. that the checks are not actually forgeries.
    b. that the check was never actually in his possession.
    c. that he presented the check in good faith because he did not know it was a forgery.
    d. that he can't remember what check it was.

21. All of the following may be used to establish that the person who passed the check had the intent to defraud except:

    a. the forged check itself.
    b. the evidence of guilty knowledge.
    c. the existence of other checks passed in this manner.
    d. the existence of a systematic attempt to pass similar checks.

22. Tracing and apprehending the forger is often quite difficult because:

    a. the forger is often prone to violence.
    b. the forger is exceptionally skillful at eluding the police.
    c. most forged checks are never discovered.
    d. a forged check is usually not discovered until long after the forger has departed.

23. All of the following are ways that can lead to the apprehension of the forger except:

    a. having an alert cashier who can detect him in the act.
    b. using a neighborhood canvass to gather information on the forger's whereabouts.
    c. using a "plant" or a stakeout to catch people who steal from mailboxes.
    d. having all of the employees in an establishment become aware of the forger's modus operandi, particularly his "story" and his disguise.

24. All of the following are victims of a forged check except:

    a. the person who presents the check.
    b. the person who cashed the check.
    c. the person whose signature has been forged.
    d. the bank on which the check was drawn.

25. The interview of the person who cashed the check should develop all of the following information except:

    a. a detailed physical description of the check passer.
    b. the manner in which the check was cashed and the story given by the passer.
    c. the possible motives for the check cashier to be in collusion with the forger.
    d. the record of the cashier in regard to cashing checks, especially forged checks.

26. It is important to interview the person whose signature appears on the check early in the investigation because:

    a. he may be in collusion with the forger.
    b. he may remember or become convinced that the signature is his own.
    c. he may deny once again that this is his signature.
    d. he may suggest possible motives of the forger.

27. A representative of the bank should be interviewed to obtain information relating to the proof of the crime. All of the following questions concerning the check should be asked except:

    a. Do you recognize this check?
    b. Is this check invalid?
    c. Does the person whose name appears on the check have an account here?
    d. Has the bank had any similar forged checks?

28. Because many different kinds of forms are used and are generally produced by photocopying, _____ are among the easiest documents to counterfeit or alter.

    a. driver's licenses   c. diplomas
    b. passports   d. birth certificates

29. The questioned check should be safeguarded and protected in a transparent envelope primarily because:

    a. the handwriting on the check may be examined by a document examiner.
    b. there may be latent fingerprints on the check.
    c. the check is part of the *corpus delicti* and hence a valuable piece of evidence.
    d. an investigator is extraordinarily careful in handling all evidence.

30. If the signature has been traced from a model, proof of forgery would lie in the fact that the questioned signature is _____ the authentic signature.

    a. similar to   c. an exact duplicate of
    b. different from   d. totally dissimilar

31. Tracing a signature can be accomplished by illuminating, from underneath glass, a check placed over a genuine signature. It can also be done through the use of:

a. carbon paper.
b. ultraviolet light.
c. a photocopy.
d. infrared light.

32. If a check has been altered or erased, the difference between the original and the additions can be readily detected by the use of:

a. infrared film.
b. a radiograph.
c. strong illumination.
d. an ultraviolet lamp.

33. Defects in rubber stamps, such as mold defects and accidental nicks, are important to the investigator because of the _____ characteristics which are reproduced in each impression.

a. class
b. individual
c. physical
d. unusual

34. A check can sometimes be matched to the checkbook by its:

a. color.
b. paper texture.
c. printing defects.
d. perforations.

35. Exemplars should be obtained from each person whose name appears on the check as well as from the accused for all of the following reasons except:

a. to establish the fact of forgery by the accused.
b. to establish the number of forgeries by the accused.
c. to determine whether an attempt was made to simulate a genuine signature.
d. to verify the genuineness of a check and any endorsement on it.

36. _____ is the FBI's computerized file of professional check passers, containing information on their description, habits, and methods.

a. Checkwriters Standards File
b. Wanted Persons File
c. PROCHEK
d. National Fraudulent Check File

37 _____ is FBI's collection of copies of fraudulent checks written in excess of a specified amount submitted by local police agencies.

a. Checkwriters Standards File
b. Bad Check File
c. PROCHEK
d. National Fraudulent Check File

Answers:

1. c	p. 477, 1.	14. c	p. 484, 5a.	27. a	p. 489, 7c.
2. c	p. 478, 2.	15. b	p. 484, 5a.	28. d	p. 489, 8.
3. b	p. 478, 2a.	16. a	p. 484, 5a.	29. c	p. 490, 9.

4. d	p. 479, 2b.	17. c	p. 484, 5b.	30. c	p. 490, 9c.
5. c	p. 479, 2c.	18. c	p. 485, 5b.	31. a	p. 491, 9c.
6. b	p. 479, 2d.	19. b	p. 485, 5b.	32. d	p. 491, 9d.
7. a	p. 479, 2e.	20. c	p. 486, 5b.	33. b	p. 493, 9f.
8. c	p. 480, 3.	21. a	p. 486, 5b.	34. d	p. 494, 9g.
9. b	p. 481, 3d.	22. d	p. 486, 6.	35. b	p. 494, 10.
10. c	p. 481, 4a.	23. b	p. 486, 6a.	36. c	p. 495, 11b.
11. d	p. 481, 4b.	24. a	p. 487, 7.	37. d	p. 495, 11b.
12. c	p. 483, 4c.	25. c	p. 487, 7a.		
13. a	p. 484, 5a.	26. b	p. 488, 7b.		

Chapter 24

HOMICIDE

Outline:

Homicide
    a. Criminal Homicide
        1) Murder
        2) Manslaughter
            a) Voluntary
            b) Involuntary
    b. Innocent Homicide
        1) Excusable
        2) Justifiable

Questions:

1. _____ is the killing of a human being that is not excusable or justifiable.

    a. Homicide
    b. Criminal homicide
    c. Murder
    d. Manslaughter

2. _____ is the killing of a human being with malice aforethought (premeditation).

    a. Homicide
    b. Criminal homicide
    c. Murder
    d. Manslaughter

3. _____ is the killing of a human being.

    a. Homicide
    b. Criminal homicide
    c. Murder
    d. Manslaughter

4. _____ is the unlawful and felonious killing of a human being without malice aforethought (premeditation).

a. Homicide
b. Criminal homicide

c. Murder
d. Manslaughter

5. To be considered a criminal homicide, the death must have been the result of and occurred within _____ of the act.

a. six months
b. one year

c. a year and a day
d. two years

6. The law presumes all homicides to be:

a. innocent.
b. excusable.

c. murder.
d. manslaughter.

7. _____ is a homicide which does not involve criminal guilt. There are two kinds: excusable and justifiable.

a. Innocent homicide
b. Voluntary homicide

c. Voluntary manslaughter
d. Involuntary manslaughter

8. _____ consists of two kinds: (1) a homicide which is the outcome of an accident while doing a lawful act in a lawful manner; (2) a homicide committed in self-defense.

a. Voluntary manslaughter
b. Involuntary manslaughter

c. Excusable homicide
d. Justifiable homicide

9. _____ is a killing of a human being that is authorized or commanded by the law, such as a soldier killing an enemy on the field of battle.

a. Voluntary manslaughter
b. Involuntary manslaughter

c. Excusable homicide
d. Justifiable homicide

10. In order to excuse a person for killing on the grounds of self-defense, it is required that he must have believed on reasonable grounds that the killing was necessary to preserve his own life or the lives of those whom he might lawfully protect. If the grounds actually exist, the homicide is _____; if the grounds do not actually exist, the homicide is _____.

a. voluntary ... involuntary
b. involuntary ... voluntary

c. excusable ... justifiable
d. justifiable ... excusable

11. A criminal homicide is murder if one of four conditions exist: (1) There is a premeditated design to kill; or any one of the following except:

   a. The accused intended to kill or commit great bodily harm.
   b. The accused killed in the heat of sudden passion caused by adequate provocation.
   c. The accused is engaged in an act that is inherently dangerous.
   d. The accused is engaged in a felony against the person.

12. The term "malice aforethought" or premeditated design to kill, means that the killing must be:

   a. part of a well-laid plan.
   b. methodically carried out.
   c. conceived over a long period.
   d. consciously intended.

13. When a person acts with intent to commit great bodily harm, does an act inherently dangerous, or commits a felony against the person, and someone dies accidentally, that person is:

   a. guilty of murder because a person is presumed to have intended the probable consequences of his actions.
   b. guilty of murder because a person is responsible for the consequences of all of his actions.
   c. not guilty of murder because a person is responsible only for the intended consequences of his actions.
   d. not guilty of murder because the killing as not premeditated.

14. A homicide committed unintentionally or accidentally during a felony against the person constitutes murder. This would include all of the following felonies except:

   a. robbery.
   b. rape.
   c. embezzlement.
   d. burglary.

15. In order to prove the crime of murder, the following elements must be established: (1) the person named or described is dead; (2) the death was the _____ of the accused; and (3) one of the circumstances in question 11 existed.

   a. intention
   b. result of an act
   c. primary purpose
   d. desire

16. A homicide which is neither murder nor innocent homicide is called:

   a. excusable homicide.
   b. justifiable homicide.
   c. criminal homicide.
   d. manslaughter.

17. _____ is an unlawful killing committed in the heat of sudden passion caused by adequate provocation. There is an intent to kill or cause great bodily harm.

   a. Murder
   b. Voluntary manslaughter
   c. Involuntary manslaughter
   d. Justifiable homicide

18. The provocation required for voluntary manslaughter must be sufficient to arouse uncontrollable passion in a _____ man.

    a. patient   c. reasonable
    b. passionate   d. prudent

19. All of the following forms of provocation are considered adequate except:

    a. an unlawful hard blow (battery).
    b. an attempt to commit serious personal injury (assault).
    c. insulting and obscene words.
    d. trespassing at night in a dwelling place.

20. An outrageous act may constitute adequate provocation. All of the following could be considered outrageous acts except:

    a. deliberately colliding with a person's unoccupied parked vehicle.
    b. an adulterous affair with a person's wife or husband.
    c. sexually assaulting a person's daughter.
    d. inflicting serious injury to a person's close relative.

21. To support a voluntary manslaughter charge, the accused must have acted in the heat of passion. It is sufficient if the passion is so extreme that the slayer's action is directed by:

    a. reason.   c. anxiety.
    b. fear.   d. passion.

22. In order to reduce a murder charge to voluntary manslaughter, _____ must be present.

    a. adequate provocation
    b. heat of passion
    c. either adequate provocation or heat of passion
    d. both adequate provocation and heat of passion

23. For an act to be done in the heat of passion, the time lapse between the provocation and the act must be of such a length that a reasonable man could:

    a. cool off.   c. make a plan.
    b. not cool off.   d. think of alternatives.

24. In order for there to be a charge of voluntary manslaughter, it must be shown that the adequate provocation, the heat of passion, and the fatal act:

    a. were causally connected.   c. happened in the proper sequence.
    b. happened in any sequence.   d. were preceded by an intent to kill.

25. _____ is an unlawful homicide committed without an intent to kill or inflict great bodily harm; it is an unlawful killing by culpable negligence.

a. Voluntary homicide
b. Involuntary homicide
c. Voluntary manslaughter
d. Involuntary manslaughter.

26. All of the following are examples of culpable negligence except:

a. conducting target practice at an inhabited house.
b. carelessly shooting into the woods while hunting.
c. making no effort to save a drowning person.
d. leaving poisons and dangerous drugs where they may endanger life.

27. The first element in the proof of a homicide is the establishment of the fact that:

a. The death was the result of an act of the accused.
b. The person named or described is dead.
c. The accused had a premeditated design to kill.
d. The accused intended to kill or inflict great bodily harm.

28. To support a criminal charge, it must be shown that:

a. someone is dead.
b. someone probably died.
c. an identified person is dead.
d. an identified person is probably dead.

29. In a legal sense, death is said to have occurred when the three vital functions have irrevocably ceased. They include all of the following except:

a. cardiac activity.
b. respiration.
c. digestive activity.
d. central nervous system activity.

30. All of the following are signs indicative of death except:

a. cessation of breathing.
b. unconsciousness.
c. absence of heart sounds.
d. loss of flushing of fingernail beds.

31. With the advent of heart transplants and respirators, the cessation of _____ activity has become an acceptable criterion for death.

a. cardiac
b. respiratory
c. digestive
d. brain

32. Identifying the victim is of critical importance because: (1) the identity of the deceased may arouse suspicion in a mysterious death; and (2) it provides _____ for the investigation.

a. additional evidence
b. relatives to contact
c. a focal point
d. more questions

33. The simplest clue to the identity of the victim is provided by his:

    a. fingerprints.
    b. blood group.
    c. physical description.
    d. clothes and possessions.

34. In composing a description of a deceased person, the investigator must remember that skin color tends to _____ after death.

    a. lighten
    b. darken
    c. remain the same
    d. either lighten or darken

35. After death, brown and red hair becomes lighter; while grey and blond hair:

    a. becomes darker.
    b. also becomes lighter.
    c. remains the same color.
    d. loses all color.

36. The best means of identification is by:

    a. fingerprints.
    b. photographs.
    c. dental records.
    d. blood groups.

37. Photographs should be taken of all of the following except:

    a. the whole body.
    b. the hands and feet.
    c. the head, full face and profile.
    d. scars, deformities, and amputations.

38. The apparent age of the deceased can be estimated only roughly from the _____ and the joining of the bones.

    a. teeth
    b. bones
    c. skin
    d. hair

39. Where the corpse is burnt or dismembered, identification by _____ is important.

    a. fingerprints
    b. blood group
    c. physical description
    d. dental records

40. The investigation of homicide is one of the most exacting tasks confronting the investigator. Not only is the event of the utmost gravity but also it is:

    a. a common occurrence.
    b. a complex crime.
    c. an unpleasant experience.
    d. methodical work.

41. All of the following aspects of criminal homicide make it extremely complex except:

    a. the motives and methods of the criminal.
    b. the variety of physical evidence presented.
    c. the objective of the investigator.
    d. the coordination of the efforts of the experts involved.

42. Most important of all, the investigator brings to the investigation the invaluable ingredients of good judgement, which will enable him to establish causal relations between the various elements that are discovered, and _____, which will aid in reconstructing the crime.

a. imagination
b. perseverance

c. inquisitiveness
d. objectivity

43. On receiving notification of a possible homicide, the investigator should at once:

a. begin the investigation with a sense of urgency.
b. attempt to find out exactly what happened.
c. resort to methodical procedure by first recording the receipt of the information.
d. hurry to the crime scene to protect the physical evidence.

44. The first step in the investigation is the recording of:

a. the victim's name and address.
b. details about the receipt of the information.
c. the name of the investigator in charge.
d. the nature and location of the incident.

45. Bloodstains of a suspect found at the crime scene can establish _____ his association with the crime.

a. the possibility of
b. the probability of

c. with a high degree of probability
d. with certainty.

46. Blood can be positively identified with an individual using:

a. genetic markers.
b. DNA analysis.

c. blood grouping.
d. the precipitin test.

47. Preliminary field or screening tests are used on bloodstains:

a. because other substances, such as lipstick or rust, appear similar to blood.
b. to confirm that the stain is positively blood.
c. to positively identify the assailant.
d. to positively identify the victim.

48. In the preliminary field tests for blood, such as the benzidine test, if the color appears, it means the substance tested:

a. is blood.
b. is not blood.

c. could be blood.
d. is probably not blood.

49. In the preliminary field tests for blood, if the color does not appear, the substance being tested:

    a. is blood.
    b. is not blood.
    c. could be blood.
    d. is probably not blood.

50. The _____ test is applied by aerosol spray and is useful for detecting minute traces of blood while searching large areas, such as walls or carpeting.

    a. benzidine
    b. luminol
    c. precipitin
    d. Teichmann or hemin crystal

51. The most common confirmatory procedure for determining whether a stain is definitely blood is the _____ test.

    a. benzidine
    b. luminol
    c. precipitin
    d. Teichmann or hemin crystal

52. The _____ reaction distinguishes between the blood of a human being and that of an animal.

    a. benzidine
    b. luminol
    c. precipitin
    d. Teichmann or hemin crystal

53. In ABO blood grouping, blood is tested with known serums containing anti-A and anti-B _____ to see if clumping occurs.

    a. antigens
    b. antibodies
    c. agglutination
    d. enzymes

54. _____ blood, which has neither A nor B antigens, can have both anti-A and anti-B antibodies present without agglutination.

    a. A
    b. B
    c. AB
    d. O

55. Because they have many inheritable variations, some enzymes and proteins can be grouped and are called:

    a. blood groups.
    b. genetic markers.
    c. polymorphisms.
    d. nucleotides.

56. For each form of enzyme and protein, statistics are kept to determine its _____ in human blood.

    a. presence
    b. absence
    c. relative frequency
    d. stability

57. Enzymes and proteins are located and separated by a technique called:

    a. grouping.
    b. polymorphism.
    c. agglutination.
    d. electrophoresis.

58. _____ has the same DNA as anyone else.

    a. Hardly anyone
    b. No one
    c. Any twin
    d. Only an identical twin

59. DNA analysis is also commonly called all of the following except:

    a. DNA grouping.
    b. DNA fingerprinting.
    c. DNA typing.
    d. DNA profiling.

60. DNA is found in the chromosomes of _____ in the human body.

    a. every cell
    b. every blood cell
    c. every cell with a nucleus
    d. only blood and tissue cells

61. In DNA analysis, a radioactive probe will combine with a complementary sequence of nucleotides making it radioactive and hence detectable. It will appear as black bands on a white background on the developed film called a(n):

    a. multi-locus probe.
    b. Southern blotting.
    c. hybridization.
    d. autoradiograph.

62. DNA analysis is especially important in sexual assault cases because:

    a. it requires only a small amount of body fluid.
    b. it can differentiate sources of mixes stains.
    c. dried or old stains can be analyzed.
    d. DNA band patterns can be computerized.

63. In 1992 in *U.S. v. Jakobetz*, the U.S. Court of Appeals ruled that DNA evidence was admissible in criminal trials. To determine the admissibility of this scientific evidence, the court used:

    a. the relevancy standard.
    b. the *Frye* standard.
    c. the general acceptance standard.
    d. judicial notice.

64. Secretors are individuals whose blood group can be determined by an analysis of their:

    a. blood.
    b. tissue.
    c. body fluids.
    d. DNA.

65. All of the following statements about secretors are true except:

    a. Approximately 80 percent of the population are secretors.
    b. A secretor may change to a nonsecretor during his life.
    c. A secretor's body fluid group will always be identical with his blood group.
    d. Perspiration on an abandoned shirt may be sufficient to determine the blood group of the owner.

66. When examining a weapon for blood, the laboratory expert will pay particular attention to cracks in wooden handles looking for:

a. stains.
b. seepage.

c. splatter.
d. smears.

67. The average body of 154 pounds contains approximately _____ pints of blood.

a. 32 3/4
b. 22 3/4

c. 12 3/4
d. 7 3/4

68. If a dead body is found with an amount of blood next to it that is less than what one would expect to find, one may conclude that:

a. the victim died suddenly.
b. the victim was a slow bleeder.
c. the crime was committed elsewhere.
d. the blood must still be in the body.

69. When blood is exposed to air, under normal conditions clotting will be complete in ten to twenty minutes and the blood will change in color from red to:

a. black.
b. dark red.

c. purple.
d. dark brown.

70. All of the following statements concerning the drying of bloodstains are true except:

a. High temperature, wind, and sunlight increase the speed of drying.
b. Increased humidity will slow the drying.
c. Bloodstains dry faster on smooth and nonabsorbent surfaces.
d. The smaller the stain, the longer it will take to dry.

71. A study of the shape and size of a stain of blood on the floor can indicate:

a. the age of the blood and the rate of its decomposition.
b. the direction and distance of its fall.
c. the amount of blood lost.
d. the source of the blood.

72. Blood drops falling vertically are characterized by a(n) _____ stain.

a. round
b. elongated

c. oval or tear-shaped
d. irregular-shaped

73. Blood drops falling at an angle other than 90 degrees are characterized by a(n) _____ stain.

a. round
b. elongated

c. oval or tear-shaped
d. irregular-shaped

74. All of these recommendations for collecting hair and fiber evidence should be followed except:

   a. Hair and fibers from different locations at the crime scene should be placed in separate containers.
   b. Hair and fibers should be wrapped in a druggist fold and placed in a pill box.
   c. Hair specimens for comparison purposes should be collected from only one area of the suspect's scalp.
   d. When hair is attached to an object, the whole object should be forwarded to the laboratory.

75. Shoe and tire impressions should be:

   a. noted and sketched only.
   b. developed and lifted.
   c. photographed and then casted.
   d. casted and then photographed.

76. In the investigation of homicides involving shooting, the deceased's clothing can be important in determining all of the following except:

   a. the number of shots fired.
   b. the approximate angle of fire.
   c. whether the firearm was discharged from a distance.
   d. the entrance and exit holes of the bullet.

77. In homicides involving a violent struggle, fingerprinting of the deceased should be postponed until the medical examiner:

   a. removes the clothes.
   b. collects hair and fibers.
   c. removes the gags and ligatures.
   d. takes fingernail scrapings.

78. The primary purpose of the postmortem examination is to determine the:

   a. identity of the deceased.
   b. cause of death.
   c. motive of the killer.
   d. circumstances of the death.

79. The postmortem examination includes all of the procedures in the investigation surrounding certain types of death that will be carried out by any one of the following except:

   a. the investigator.
   b. the medical examiner.
   c. the coroner.
   d. the pathologist.

80. The branch of medicine called _____ is the study of abnormal changes in bodily tissues or functions caused by diseases, poisons, or other bodily affections.

   a. histology
   b. pathology
   c. serology
   d. toxicology

81. As a general rule, a postmortem examination including an autopsy should be performed in:

    a. every death.
    b. every death where there is a suspicion of homicide (including suicide).
    c. only deaths where the cause is unknown.
    d. only sudden, unexpected, or accidental deaths.

82. If a postmortem examination is necessary, a preliminary examination by a qualified physician will take place at:

    a. the physician's office.   c. the scene of the death.
    b. the mortuary.   d. the hospital only.

83. An autopsy is performed when the cause of death is doubtful or if _____ is involved.

    a. an accidental cause   c. negligence
    b. criminal violence   d. a sudden cause

84. All of the following are titles given to physicians who perform autopsies except:

    a. medical examiner.   c. coroner.
    b. pathologist.   d. toxicologist.

85. A simple procedure that may be overlooked by the investigator but is vital to the chain of evidence is the identification of the _____ to the medical examiner.

    a. the body   c. the witness
    b. the investigator   d. murder weapon

86. The identification of the body to the medical examiner should be made by:

    a. a relative or close friend of the victim.
    b. an attending physician.
    c. the first law enforcement agent at the scene.
    d. the first law enforcement agent having jurisdiction at the scene.

87. The investigator's role at the autopsy is to:

    a. work with the physician in preparing the autopsy report.
    b. give the physician insight and direction in what to look for.
    c. determine whether the medicolegal purposes (evidence collection, body identification) of the autopsy are being served.
    d. to be an objective, detached observer so as not to influence the findings.

88. An autopsy protocol is:

    a. a list of those who can legally authorize an autopsy.
    b. the order of rank of the physicians involved in the autopsy.
    c. the method of performing the autopsy.
    d. the record of the findings of the autopsy.

89. Authorization for an autopsy may be made by all of the following except:

    a. the consent of the person entitled to the custody of the body.
    b. the request of the investigator.
    c. the coroner or medical examiner.
    d. the will of the deceased.

90. An autopsy _____ a privileged communication. The next of kin _____ own the dead body.

    a. is ... can   c. is ... cannot
    b. is not ... can   d. is not ... cannot

91. In a homicide investigation, the findings of the autopsy may provide all of the following information except:

    a. the probable cause, manner, and time of death.
    b. the time elapsed between receiving the wound and death.
    c. evidence of why the homicide was committed.
    d. evidence of substance abuse and sexual assault.

92. All of the following are changes that take place in the body soon after death except:

    a. temperature change and change in the rate of cooling.
    b. postmortem lividity and rigor mortis.
    c. teeth and skeletal changes.
    d. putrefaction.

93. The changes that take place in the body after death can provide information on all of the following points except:

    a. the exact cause of death.
    b. the time of death.
    c. alterations in the position of the body after death.
    d. whether the death was a suicide or murder.

94. The rate of cooling of a body depends upon all of the following except:

    a. the temperature of the air.
    b. the time of the last meal.
    c. whether the body is clothed.
    d. the size, weight, and age of the body.

95. _____ is the dark blue discoloration that is observable on the parts of the body which are nearest the ground, caused by the blood settling under its own weight.

   a. Postmortem lividity   c. Cadaveric spasm
   b. Asphyxia   d. Rigor mortis

96. Lividity must be differentiated from:

   a. wounds.   c. bruises.
   b. cuts.   d. swellings.

97. _____ is the stiffening of the body after death caused by chemical changes in the muscle tissue.

   a. Postmortem lividity   c. Cadaveric spasm
   b. Asphyxia   d. Rigor mortis

98. _____ is the stiffening occurring immediately after a death in which there is a severe injury to the central nervous system or there was great tension at the moment of death. It is characterized by a tenacious grasp.

   a. Postmortem lividity   c. Cadaveric spasm
   b. Asphyxia   d. Rigor mortis

99. Rigor mortis should begin within _____ hours after death and end within _____ hours of death.

   a. 2 ... 10   c. 10 ... 36
   b. 4 ... 12   d. 24 ... 48

100. It is a strong indication of suicide if the body is found with:

   a. the hand clutching a weapon.
   b. the weapon held loosely by the hand.
   c. the weapon is lying near the body.
   d. the weapon is anywhere in the room.

101. Putrefaction, which is perceived as bloating, skin discoloration, and blistering, is influenced in its development mainly by:

   a. the body's size and weight.
   b. the temperature of the environment.
   c. the ground on which the body rests.
   d. whether the body is clothed.

102. Activities performed or not performed by the deceased may be indicative of the time of death. All of the following conditions would suggest the time of death except:

    a. the light switch, whether on or off.
    b. books on the table, whether opened or closed.
    c. mail in the mailbox, whether collected or not.
    d. meal preparation, whether completed or not.

103. If the meal time of the deceased is known, the stomach contents of the deceased may indicate an approximate time of death primarily by:

    a. the position of the meal in the stomach.
    b. the size of the meal.
    c. the kinds of foods eaten.
    d. the number of meals eaten that day.

104. An entomologist may make an estimate of the time of death by determining the _____ of the maggots on the body.

    a. species   c. age
    b. number   d. size

105. Asphyxia or _____ is a suspension of breathing due to a deficiency of oxygen in the red blood cells.

    a. strangulation   c. smothering
    b. choking   d. suffocation

106. Besides drowning, choking, smothering, and hanging, asphyxia may also be caused by all of the following except:

    a. pneumonia.   c. electrocution.
    b. carbon monoxide poisoning.   d. a severe wound.

107. The postmortem appearance of an asphyxia victim is characterized by:

    a. lividity.   c. cadaveric spasm.
    b. swelling.   d. rigor mortis.

108. In hanging deaths, there may be several causes, the most common of which is:

    a. asphyxia.   c. cutting off the blood to the brain.
    b. inhibition of the heart.   d. fracture of the spine.

109. A characteristic of a hanging death is a _____ on the neck.

    a. rope burn   c. swelling
    b. deep groove   d. deep cut

110. The most common reason for a hanging is:

    a. an accident.   c. murder.
    b. suicide.   d. sexual asphyxia.

111. Sexual asphyxia, a kind of hanging involving bizarre sexual practices, is usually a(n):

    a. accident.   c. murder.
    b. suicide.   d. death by natural causes.

112. A drowning victim has the characteristic appearance of a fine foam around the mouth and the body is usually _____ in color.

    a. pale   c. purple
    b. dark   d. red

113. Indications that a person truly drowned rather than having been killed and dumped in the water include all of the following except the:

    a. swelling of the lungs.   c. presence of serious wounds.
    b. signs of asphyxia.   d. nature of the water in the stomach.

114. A submerged body will usually:

    a. stay submerged.
    b. rise again because of gases.
    c. either rise or sink depending on water current.
    d. stay submerged if the victim was wearing heavy clothes.

115. A situation in which a criminal uses fire as a lethal agent or to conceal a homicide could be described as:

    a. accidental fire and accidental death.
    b. accidental fire and intended death.
    c. arson and accidental death.
    d. arson and intended death.

116. Because of the combination of fire and death, the establishment of _____ is the most important step in investigating this type of homicide.

    a. the cause of the fire   c. the approximate time of the fire
    b. the cause of death   d. the approximate time of death

117. Besides being directly exposed to flames, all of the following are common causes of death in a burning building except:

    a. exposure to gases.   c. electrocution from loose wires.
    b. falling beams and masonry.   d. falls while attempting to escape.

118. The exposure of a dead body to fire sometimes results in the so-called pugilistic posture, in which the arms and wrists are flexed in a boxer's pose. This indicates _____ life was present during the fire.

a. probably
b. definitely

c. definitely no
d. no determination whether

119. Lightning and electrocution deaths are commonly due to a marked change in the strength and rhythm of the heartbeat, which is called a :

a. heart attack.
b. stroke.

c. fibrillation.
d. blockage.

120. In a death from lightning, sometimes a characteristic superficial burn may be observed in a _____ -shaped markings.

a. treelike
b. smudgelike

c. circular or oval
d. arrowhead

121. In deaths caused by electric shock, at the point of contact:

a. burn marks are always present.
b. burn marks are never present.
c. there will be some mark apparent.
d. often no marks are apparent.

122. For the purposes of investigation, wounds may be classified according to the instruments used in their production. All of the following are classifications except:

a. cutting or stabbing wounds (sharp point).
b. wounds caused by instruments with no blades (blunt force).
c. crushing wounds as in motor vehicle crashes.
d. gunshot wounds.

123. The primary causes of death of people with stab wounds include all of the following except:

a. shock.
b. pneumonia.

c. hemorrhaging or bleeding.
d. injury to a vital organ.

124. Although rare, accidental deaths by stabbing occur in:

a. hunting accidents.
b. kitchen accidents.

c. falling situations.
d. sporting activities.

125. A common indication of suicide is the existence of superficial cuts, approximately one inch long at the point of origin of the wound, made by testing the razor on the skin. These are called _____ marks.

a. suicide
b. hesitation

c. determination
d. indecision

126. The part of the body most frequently attacked in a suicide by a razor or a knife is the:

a. throat.
b. left wrist.
c. left chest.
d. femoral artery.

127. All of the following are indications that a stabbing is suicide except:

a. the knife held in the right hand.
b. the knife or razor clenched in the dead person's hand.
c. an effort by the dead person to leave the location of the stabbing.
d. the existence of hesitation marks.

128. A wound in the back is usually indicative:

a. of suicide.
b. of homicide.
c. of accidental death.
d. that no determination can be made.

129. The largest category of homicide that the investigator has to deal with are those deaths caused by the application of direct violence or:

a. cutting or stabbing.
b. blunt force.
c. gunshot.
d. crushing force.

130. All of the following injuries involve the use of blunt force except:

a. clubbing over the head.
b. kicking in the stomach.
c. spearing in the stomach.
d. hurling to the ground.

131. All of the following types of cases usually involve blunt force except:

a. suicide.
b. assault.
c. motor vehicle homicide.
d. negligent homicide.

132. In approximately 45 percent of the fatal motor vehicle accidents, the cause of death is an injury to the:

a. chest.
b. head.
c. neck.
d. spine.

133. A suicide death may be contrived to look like an accident or murder most commonly for the purpose of:

a. preserving the reputation of the deceased.
b. punishing relatives by creating suspicion and feelings of guilt.
c. defrauding insurance companies.
d. placing blame on someone the deceased disliked.

134. All of the following are indications that a death due to gunshot wounds is suicidal except:

a. the area of the wound is readily accessible.
b. the gun was fired not more than a few feet from the body.
c. a total absence of preparation for the event.
d. the gun held clenched in the hand.

135. When a gun is fired at a distance of rom 2 to 18 inches, smoke and powder are deposited on the skin resulting in what is called:

a. scorching.
b. smearing.

c. smudging.
d. tattooing.

136. When a gun is fired, unburnt powder and particles of molten metal are discharged and imbedded in the lower layers of the skin. This effect is called:

a. scorching.
b. smearing.

c. smudging.
d. tattooing.

137. A _____ is a substance when introduced into the body in small quantities causes a harmful or deadly effect.

a. drug
b. contaminant

c. poison
d. additive

138. Poisonous materials in _____ quantities are usually found in _____ cases.

a. small ... murder
b. large ... murder

c. small ... negligent homicide
d. large ... robbery and assault

139. The most commonly occurring poison in murder cases, which is extremely effective in small doses, is:

a. arsenic.
b. antimony.

c. mercury.
d. lead.

140. Taken in minute quantities, _____ is a deadly poison that causes the face to turn blue and the mouth to be contracted in a fixed grin—the *risus sardonicus.*

a. opium
b. belladonna

c. arsenic
d. strychnine

141. As a popular method of suicide, excessive doses of _____ result in a profound coma and subsequent death. It is commonly prescribed as a soporific.

a. barbiturate
b. morphine

c. belladonna
d. strychnine

142. A widely used soporific, _____ is the active ingredient of the so-called "Mickey Finn."

    a. opium
    b. morphine

    c. belladonna
    d. chloral hydrate

143. The most common cause of death from chemical asphyxiation is _____, a colorless, odorless, and tasteless gas. Deaths are almost always accidental or suicidal. The skin of a victim is characterized by a cherry red color.

    a. hydrogen sulphide
    b. phosgene

    c. carbon monoxide
    d. carbon dioxide

144. In suspected poisoning cases, the investigator should collect all of the following except:

    a. prepackaged cereals.
    b. all medicines.

    c. all alcoholic beverage bottles.
    d. all insecticides.

145. The most common method of administering poison is:

    a. serving it with food.
    b. by hyperdermic needle.

    c. mixing it in an alcoholic drink.
    d. substituting pills with poison ones.

146. In poisoning homicide cases, it is necessary to establish all of the following points of proof except:

    a. that the accused had access to the poison.
    b. that the accused had access to the victim.
    c. that the accused would benefit from the death of the victim.
    d. that the accused knew it was a poisonous substance.

147. _____ is the science which deals with poisons, their effects and antidotes, and recognition.

    a. Histology
    b. Pathology

    c. Serology
    d. Toxicology

148. Suicide and attempted suicide are generally considered:

    a. a medical issue only.
    b. illegal and punishable.

    c. a right protected by the Constitution.
    d. legal in most jurisdictions.

149. All of the following statements about suicide are true except:

    a. The cause of death is the best indicator in determining whether the case is one of suicide.
    b. Any part of the body that is accessible to the suicide is accessible to the murderer.
    c. A combination of motives is indicative of suicide.
    d. Severe wounds in great numbers is always indicative of murder.

150. All of the following statements about suicide are true except:

    a. A suicide will always select the least painful way to die.
    b. A female suicide will tend to avoid purposely disfiguring her face.
    c. A suicide will tend to push away his clothing so that the weapon may be in direct contact with the body.
    d. In drawing a conclusion of suicide, the combination of wounds must not be physically impossible.

151. The motive for suicide usually involves anxiety over:

    a. love.
    b. marital harmony.
    c. work and finances.
    d. loss of a close friend or relative.

152. The clearest expression of motive and intent is usually found in the:

    a. statements from close relatives.
    b. financial and insurance records of the deceased.
    c. occupational and psychological records of the deceased.
    d. suicide note.

153. Distinguishing between death by accident, natural causes, and suicide is often important:

    a. to comfort the relatives only.
    b. for insurance purposes.
    c. to allay suspicions of wrong doing.
    d. to satisfy the investigator's professional interest.

154. In a homicide investigation where the body displays marks of violence, the investigator may rule out the possibility of death from:

    a. suicide.
    b. accident.
    c. natural causes.
    d. none of the above.

155. The vital question of the identity of the perpetrator will be answered ordinarily by:

    a. interviewing witnesses.
    b. interrogating suspects.
    c. examination of physical evidence.
    d. consultation with experts.

156. Witnesses may be classified according to the type of testimony that they may be expected to give. Besides eyewitness and expert testimony, it would include testimony to all of the following except the:

    a. circumstances of the crime.
    b. motive for the fatal act.
    c. criminal history of the accused.
    d. flight subsequent to the slaying.

157. In gathering evidence about the circumstances of the crime, it is useful to categorize physical evidence according to the information it can provide. _____ evidence shows that the accused was linked to the crime scene or with the fatal act (an article of clothing left at the crime scene).

    a. *Corpus delicti*   c. Identifying
    b. Associative   d. Tracing

158. _____ evidence helps to locate the suspect (credit card receipts).

    a. *Corpus delicti*   c. Identifying
    b. Associative   d. Tracing

159. _____ evidence tends to identify the person who caused the death (a fingerprint at the crime scene).

    a. *Corpus delicti*   c. Identifying
    b. Associative   d. Tracing

160. _____ evidence tends to show that the crime has been committed (a dead body with a gunshot wound).

    a. *Corpus delicti*   c. Identifying
    b. Associative   d. Tracing

161. In a homicide investigation where a gun is found, it is very important to identify the _____ of the gun.

    a. manufacturer   c. owner
    b. seller   d. sales receipt

162. The National Firearms Tracing Center was established and is run by the:

    a. ATF.   c. FBI.
    b. DEA.   d. IRS.

163. If the theft of a gun has previously been reported, the National Crime Information Center's stolen gun file may provide the identity of the:

    a. thief.   c. person who received the gun.
    b. owner.   d. person using the gun.

164. It is _____ for the prosecution to prove a motive in a homicide.

    a. necessary   c. sometimes necessary
    b. not necessary   d. sometimes not necessary

165. The absence of the suspect from his home and haunts can be interpreted as _____, which is a sign of guilt.

    a. reckless behavior   c. flight
    b. irresponsibility   d. negligence

166. All of the following suggestions concerning the interviewing of eyewitnesses should be followed except:

    a. The investigator must be patient and exhaustive in interviewing the eyewitnesses.
    b. The witness should be directed to tell his story so that it follows a recognizable pattern.
    c. The investigator should mentally evaluate the witness according to his moral and intellectual character.
    d. The investigator should mentally evaluate the physical condition of the witness with respect to the reliability of his senses and his ability to attend a trial.

167. More than half of all homicides are committed on _____. Most homicides are committed during _____ hours.

    a. weekdays ... daylight
    b. weekdays ... nighttime
    c. weekends ... daylight
    d. weekends ... nighttime

168. More than _____ percent of all murders are committed with firearms.

    a. 20
    b. 45
    c. 65
    d. 90

169. Less than _____ percent of all murders are accomplished with cutting instruments.

    a. 50
    b. 20
    c. 40
    d. 10

170. _____ of the homicide cases involve alcohol as a factor, with the assailant or the victim, or both, drinking heavily.

    a. A majority
    b. Less than 1/2
    c. Less than 1/4
    d. Only a few

171. _____ commit more than three-fourths of the homicides. _____ comprise more than three-fourths of the victims.

    a. Males ... Males
    b. Males ... Females
    c. Females ... Males
    d. Females ... Females

172. Generally, whites murder _____ and blacks murder _____.

    a. whites ... whites
    b. whites ... blacks
    c. blacks ... whites
    d. blacks ... blacks

173. In about _____ of the cases, the victim knows his assailant.

    a. 90 percent
    b. three-quarters
    c. one-quarter
    d. 10 percent

174. In about _____ of the cases, the victim is a member of the family.

   a. 90 percent
   b. three-quarters
   c. one-quarter
   d. 10 percent

175. All of the following statements concerning murder are true except:

   a. A significant number of murders are attributable to quarrels over a woman.
   b. Where a male kills a female, the victim is usually his wife or girlfriend.
   c. A quarrel over property is a common cause of homicide.
   d. A quarrel that is trivial in nature is rarely a cause of homicide.

176. Infanticide, the slaying of a newborn infant, is concerned only with the period from the time of birth until the time when:

   a. the baby is one month old.
   b. the baby is six months old.
   c. the birth is reported to authorities.
   d. a physician examines the body.

177. All of the following are common causes of infant death except:

   a. Sudden Infant Death Syndrome.
   b. bacterial and viral infection.
   c. birth defects or birth injuries.
   d. accidental smothering.

Answers:

1. b	p. 498, 2a.	60. c	p. 518, 26a.	119. c	p. 549, 66.
2. c	p. 498, 2a.	61. d	p. 519, 26a.	120. a	p. 549, 66.
3. a	p. 498, 2a.	62. b	p. 520, 26c.	121. d	p. 550, 67a.
4. d	p. 498, 2a.	63. a	p. 520, 26d.	122. c	p. 550, 68.
5. c	p. 498, 2a.	64. c	p. 521, 27a.	123. b	p. 551, 69b.
6. c	p. 498, 2a.	65. b	p. 521, 27a.	124. c	p. 552, 69d.
7. a	p. 498, 2b.	66. b	p. 523, 28f.	125. b	p. 552, 69d.
8. c	p. 498, 2b.	67. c	p. 524, 29a.	126. a	p. 552, 69d.
9. d	p. 499, 2b.	68. c	p. 524, 29a.	127. c	p. 552, 69d.
10. d	p. 498, 2b.	69. d	p. 525, 29b.	128. b	p. 553, 69d.
11. b	p. 499, 3.	70. d	p. 525, 29c.	129. b	p. 553, 70.
12. d	p. 499, 4.	71. b	p. 525, 29d.	130. c	p. 553, 70.
13. a	p. 499, 5.	72. a	p. 525, 29d.	131. a	p. 554, 70.
14. c	p. 500, 7.	73. c	p. 525, 29d.	132. b	p. 554, 70.
15. b	p. 500, 8.	74. c	p. 527, 31.	133. c	p. 557, 73b.
16. d	p. 501, 9.	75. c	p. 528, 32.	134. c	p. 558, 73b.
17. b	p. 501, 10.	76. a	p. 529, 34a.	135. c	p. 558, 73b.
18. c	p. 502, 10.	77. d	p. 530, 36.	136. d	p. 558, 73b.
19. c	p. 502, 10a.	78. b	p. 531, 37.	137. c	p. 560, 75.
20. a	p. 502, 10a.	79. a	p. 531, 37.	138. a	p. 560, 75.
21. d	p. 502, 10b.	80. b	p. 531, 38.	139. a	p. 562, 76b.
22. d	p. 502, 10b.	81. b	p. 532, 40.	140. d	p. 563, 76c.
23. b	p. 502, 10c.	82. c	p. 532, 40.	141. a	p. 564, 76c.

24. a	p. 503, 10d.	83. b	p. 532, 40.	142. d	p. 564, 76c.		
25. d	p. 503, 11.	84. d	p. 533, 41.	143. c	p. 565, 76d.		
26. c	p. 503, 11a.	85. a	p. 534, 43.	144. a	p. 570, 78d.		
27. b	p. 504, 12.	86. d	p. 534, 43.	145. c	p. 570, 78e.		
28. a	p. 504, 12.	87. c	p. 535, 44.	146. c	p. 570, 80.		
29. c	p. 505, 13a.	88. d	p. 535, 46.	147. d	p. 572, 82.		
30. b	p. 505, 13b.	89. b	p. 536, 47a.	148. b	p. 576, 85.		
31. d	p. 505, 13d.	90. d	p. 536, 47b.	149. d	p. 578, 87c.		
32. c	p. 506, 14.	91. c	p. 537, 48.	150. a	p. 579, 87e.		
33. d	p. 506, 14.	92. c	p. 537, 49.	151. c	p. 581, 89a.		
34. b	p. 507, 14b.	93. a	p. 537, 49.	152. d	p. 581, 89b.		
35. a	p. 508, 14b.	94. b	p. 538, 50.	153. b	p. 583, 91.		
36. a	p. 508, 14b.	95. a	p. 538, 51.	154. d	p. 583, 91a.		
37. b	p. 508, 14b.	96. c	p. 538, 52.	155. a	p. 585, 92.		
38. a	p. 508, 14b.	97. d	p. 539, 52.	156. c	p. 585, 92b.		
39. d	p. 509, 14b.	98. c	p. 539, 52d	157. b	p. 586, 93a.		
40. b	p. 510, 15.	99. c	p. 539, 52c.	158. d	p. 586, 93a.		
41. c	p. 510, 15.	100. a	p. 539, 52d.	159. c	p. 586, 93a.		
42. a	p. 511, 15.	101. b	p. 540, 53.	160. a	p. 586, 93a.		
43. c	p. 511, 16.	102. b	p. 540, 54.	161. c	p. 587, 93a.		
44. b	p. 511, 16.	103. a	p. 541, 55a.	162. a	p. 587, 93a.		
45. d	p. 512, 18.	104. c	p. 542, 57a.	163. b	p. 587, 93a.		
46. b	p. 513, 20.	105. d	p. 542, 59.	164. b	p. 588, 94.		
47. a	p. 513, 21.	106. c	p. 543, 59a.	165. c	p. 589, 95.		
48. c	p. 514, 22.	107. a	p. 543, 59b.	166. b	p. 589, 96.		
49. b	p. 514, 22.	108. a	p. 543, 60a.	167. d	p. 591, 100a.		
50. b	p. 514, 21c.	109. b	p. 544, 60b.	168. c	p. 591, 100c.		
51. d	p. 515, 22a.	110. b	p. 544, 60c.	169. b	p. 591, 100c.		
52. c	p. 515, 23.	111. a	p. 544, 60c.	170. a	p. 591, 100d.		
53. b	p. 516, 24.	112. a	p. 545, 61a.	171. a	p. 592, 101a.		
54. d	p. 516, 24.	113. c	p. 545, 61b.	172. b	p. 592, 101b.		
55. b	p. 516, 25.	114. b	p. 545, 61c.	173. b	p. 592, 101c.		
56. c	p. 516, 25.	115. d	p. 546, 62d.	174. c	p. 592, 101c.		
57. d	p. 517, 25.	116. b	p. 547, 63.	175. d	p. 593, 101d.		
58. d	p. 517, 26.	117. c	p. 547, 63a	176. c	p. 593, 102.		
59. a	p. 517, 26a.	118. d	p. 548, 65b.	177. d	p. 596, 105c.		

Chapter 25

ASSAULT

Questions:

1. A tactic used by some police departments that is often effective in controlling domestic violence is:

    a. trying to placate the participants.
    b. giving a stern warning to the violent spouse.
    c. making an arrest, if an assault is witnessed.
    d. dropping charges when requested by the victim.

2. In ordinary conversation, "He was a victim of an assault" means, in legal terms, that he was a victim of:

    a. assault only.   c. both assault and battery.
    b. battery only.   d. either assault or battery.

3. The willful attempt or immediate threat to do physical harm to another is the legal definition of:

    a. assault.   c. attempted assault.
    b. battery.   d. attempted battery.

4. The unlawful application of force to another is the legal definition of:

    a. assault.   c. intentional bodily injury.
    b. battery.   d. culpable negligence.

5. An example of battery is:

    a. tapping someone on the shoulder to attract their attention.
    b. seizing a person to prevent them from falling.
    c. hitting a person in self-defense.
    d. touching a person offensively.

6. All of the following statements are true except:

    a. Assaults are committed without physical contact.
    b. Every assault involves a battery.
    c. Battery may be looked upon as a completion of an assault.
    d. Every battery involves an assault.

7. A simple assault is an assault unaccompanied by _____ factors.

    a. harmful   c. aggravating
    b. intentional   d. annoying

8. A felony is a crime of a serious nature that is usually punishable by a prison term of:

    a. more than one year.   c. less than six months.
    b. less than one year.   d. a life sentence.

9. In order to make an arrest for a misdemeanor, the law enforcement officer is generally required to have an arrest warrant or to have:

    a. probable cause to believe that an offense has occurred.
    b. information from a reliable source.
    c. witnessed the infraction.
    d. orders from his supervisor.

10. The serious attendant circumstances which make an assault an aggravated assault may include all of the following except:

    a. the causing of severe bodily harm.
    b. past instances of aggravated assault.
    c. the use of a dangerous weapon.
    d. the intent to commit a serious crime.

11. To make an arrest for a felony, a police officer is generally required to have an arrest warrant or to have:

    a. "probable cause" to believe that the offense has occurred.
    b. information from reliable sources.
    c. witnessed the infraction.
    d. orders from his superior.

12. In some jurisdictions, the categories of simple and aggravated assault has been replaced by _____ of assault.

    a. types   c. classes
    b. kinds   d. degrees

13. All of the following are kinds of aggravated assault except:

    a. assault with a dangerous weapon.
    b. assault with depraved indifference to human life.
    c. assault in which grievous harm is intentionally inflicted.
    d. assault with intent to commit other offenses.

14. Assault is the immediate threat or attempt to do harm to another. The major difference between an immediate threat and an attempt is in the _____ the victim.

    a. the injury to   c. the suddenness of the assault on
    b. the awareness of   d. the actual threat to

15. All of the following may be considered assaults except: **A** points with intent to shoot:

    a. an unloaded gun at **B** who is unaware of the act.
    b. an unloaded gun at **B** who is aware of the act.
    c. a loaded gun at **B** who is unaware of the act.
    d. a loaded gun at **B** who is unaware of the act.

16. Which one of the following is an assault?

    a. **A** picks up a stone in case he wants to throw it at **B**.
    b. **A**, with a bat in his hand, says to **B**, "Next time I am going to hit you!"
    c. **A** says to **B**, "Give me your wallet now or I'll hit you!"
    d. **A** telephones **B**, "I'm coming right over to hit you!"

17. All of the following may be assaults except:

    a. **A** demands his money back now or he will knock **B** down.
    b. **A** fails to restrain his attack dog when he confronts B.
    c. **A** fires what he thinks is a loaded gun at **B** while **B** isn't looking, but, unbeknownst to **A**, the cartridge could not possibly fire because it was defective.
    d. **A** telephones **B**, "I'm coming right over to hit you!"

18. In order to constitute an assault, there must be _____ to inflict the injury.

    a. only a desire   c. an apparent present ability
    b. a present ability   d. a detailed plan

19. In assault with a dangerous weapon, the weapon may be:

    a. only objects that are actual weapons such as guns and knives.
    b. only actual weapons used in a manner that will cause bodily injury.
    c. any object.
    d. any object used in a manner that will cause serious bodily harm.

20. To constitute an offense of aggravated assault with a dangerous weapon, it is _____ serious bodily harm has actually been inflicted.

    a. necessary that   c. necessary that at least some
    b. not necessary   d. an element of the offense that

21. If **A** assaults **B** with the intention of robbing **B** but is interrupted before he can take or demand **B**'s property, the offense committed is:

    a. robbery.   c. assault with intent to commit robbery.
    b. attempted robbery.   d. a simple assault.

22. The major difference between an "assault with intent to commit a crime" and an "attempted crime" is that the former often lacks the _____ that is an essential element of the latter charge.

a. intent
b. motive

c. overt act
d. premeditation

23. An aggravated assault investigation is quite similar in technique to a _____ investigation.

a. homicide
b. burglary

c. arson
d. robbery

Answers:

1. c	p. 614, 1.	9. c	p. 616, 3a.	17. d	p. 618, 4d.
2. c	p. 615, 2a.	10. b	p. 616, 3b.	18. c	p. 618, 4d.
3. a	p. 615, 2a.	11. a	p. 616, 3b.	19. d	p. 618, 5.
4. b	p. 615, 2b.	12. d	p. 617, 3b.	20. b	p. 619, 5.
5. d	p. 616, 2c.	13. b	p. 617, 3b.	21. c	p. 620, 7.
6. b	p. 616, 2c.	14. b	p. 617, 4b.	22. c	p. 620, 7.
7. c	p. 616, 3a.	15. a	p. 617, 4b.	23. a	p. 620, 8.
8. a	p. 616, 3a.	16. c	p. 618, 4b.		

Chapter 26

CRIMINAL EXPLOSIONS

Questions:

1. In an explosion investigation, the initial action of the investigator will include all of the following except:

a. An attempt is made to determine the nature and cause of the explosion.
b. Witnesses are detained, identified, and interviewed.
c. The crime scene is cleared as much as possible of wreckage and debris.
d. The crime scene is placed under safeguard.

2. An explosive characterized by a low-frequency sound and an absence of relatively severe damage in the area of the explosion is caused by:

a. a low explosive.
b. a high explosive.

c. dynamite.
d. nitroglycerine.

3. All of the following are low explosives except:

a. gunpowder.
b. gasoline.

c. carbon monoxide.
d. nitroglycerine.

4. An explosion characterized by a high-frequency sound and a point of origin of severe damage from which objects are blown outward is caused by:

a. a low explosive.
b. a high explosive.
c. gunpowder.
d. gasoline.

5. All of the following are high explosives except:

a. dynamite.
b. nitroglycerine.
c. gasoline.
d. plastic explosives.

6. Criminal explosions present many of the difficulties usually associated with ____ , paramount among which is the partial or total destruction of evidence tending to establish a *corpus delicti.*

a. arson
c. burglary
c. sabotage
d. narcotics violations

7. Documentation of a crime scene involving an explosion should be unusually painstaking primarily because:

a. the crime is often quite serious.
b. the extent of the crime scene can be so great that the investigator can become confused.
c. of the difficulty in determining what articles and areas are part of the crime scene.
d. of the significance of the pattern of strewn objects and the importance of tracing this pattern to the point of origin.

8. In documenting the crime scene, special emphasis should be placed on all of the following activities except:

a. photography.
b. sketching.
c. taking notes.
d. surveillance.

9. In searching the crime scene of an explosion, if the point of origin can be located, the ____ method can be used effectively.

a. grid
b. zone
c. spiral
d. double grid

10. In the search of the crime scene, the search team will be looking for clues that will establish all of the following except:

a. that an explosive device was used.
b. that there was an intent to cause injury to a person or object.
c. that someone had a motive for setting an explosive device.
d. the identity of the perpetrator or evidence that links him to the scene.

11. The medical examiner can usually help in determining all of the following except:

    a. the cause and manner of death.
    b. whether the explosion was accidental or deliberate.
    c. the time of death, whether before or after the explosion.
    d. the identity of the deceased.

12. When examining the electrical and telephone systems for the source of the electrical energy needed for detonation, a safety expert or an electrician is required not only because of the complexity of the investigative problem but also:

    a. to prevent the investigator from setting off a second explosion.
    b. to witness the fact that the investigator did not tamper with the system.
    c. to turn off the telephone or the electrical system if necessary.
    d. because of the need for expert testimony in the event of a trial.

13. One of the characteristics of crimes involving explosions, which make them difficult to investigate, is that often the bomber is:

    a. a hardened professional criminal.
    b. not a criminal by record or inclination.
    c. is a member of organized crime.
    d. is ruthless with no concern for the public welfare.

14. All of the following are common types of bombers who are not professional criminals except:

    a. someone faking his own death for insurance purposes.
    b. someone with a personal grievance.
    c. a jealous suitor or a deceived husband.
    d. a political agitator or a self-styled patriot.

15. Crimes involving persons who are not professional criminals are usually difficult to solve because:

    a. they are usually more intelligent than the professional criminal.
    b. they are usually more secretive than the professional criminal.
    c. there are no established sources of information.
    d. there are many more nonprofessionals than professionals.

16. When investigating a bombing by a person who is not a professional criminal, attention should be placed on the circumstances surrounding the case, especially on suspects with:

    a. personal grievances.   c. financial distress.
    b. psychological conditions.   d. criminal tendencies.

17. All of the following questions will *ordinarily* form the basis of a successful bombing investigation except:

    a. Who or what was the *target?*
    b. Who had the *opportunity* and what was the *motive?*
    c. What explosive material (*means*) and what technique (*modus operandi*) was used?
    d. Who else was involved (*accomplices*) and how can they be located (tracing)?

18. On first receiving a bomb threat, the person receiving the phone call should ask and record the answer to all of the following questions except:

    a. When is the bomb set to explode and where is it?
    b. What kind of bomb is it and what does it look like?
    c. When will you set off the next bomb?
    d. Why did you place the bomb?

19. An offense has been committed if it can be established that an explosion took place _____ or criminal negligence.

    a. by accident
    b. through criminal intent
    c. with a motive
    d. by an illegal means

20. In deciding whether an offense has been committed, the most helpful factor is the determination of the _____ explosion.

    a. type of
    b. target of the
    c. time of the
    d. witnesses to the

21. If the explosion is directed against a person, the device will often be such that an act of _____ is required to detonate the explosive.

    a. the victim
    b. the perpetrator
    c. an accomplice
    d. an uninvolved third party

22. In a bombing designed to effect the death of a particular person and there appears to be no apparent motive, the investigator should first consider the possibility of:

    a. a conspiracy.
    b. an accidental explosion.
    c. mistaken identity.
    d. a random act of violence.

23. Because the construction of an explosive device requires preparation, labor, and the handling of materials, _____ is very likely to be found on the suspect's person or in his home, place of work , and vehicle.

    a. a receipt for equipment
    b. a diagram
    c. a tool
    d. trace evidence

24. If professional explosives were used in a bombing, the investigator would look for any of the following except:

   a. filaments, handmade squibs, ammonium nitrate.
   b. dynamite and nitroglycerine.
   c. gun cotton, black powder, or smokeless powder.
   d. blasting caps, fuses, and primacord.

25. Miliary explosives are manufactured in two basic forms: sheet explosives and _____ (also called composition).

   a. sticks of dynamite
   b. solid explosives
   c. liquid explosives
   d. plastic explosives

26. The most common as well as the most powerful of the military explosives is:

   a. RDX.
   b. PETN.
   c. nitroglycerine.
   d. dynamite.

27. Tools found in the suspect's home may be significant to the investigation because:

   a. it shows that the suspect had the ability to build a bomb.
   b. receipts may provide the source of the tools.
   c. trace evidence on the tools may link them to the bomb.
   d. fingerprints on the tools may show that the suspect had previous convictions.

28. The investigator will examine a suspect's vehicle for evidence not only relating to the presence of explosives but also to associate the suspect's vehicle with:

   a. the suspect.
   b. the scene of the explosion.
   c. the suspect's driving at the time of the explosion.
   d. the suspect's associates or accomplices.

29. In determining the source of explosives, it is more common for the suspect to have obtained them:

   a. by legitimate purchase.
   b. by local theft.
   c. through organized crime.
   d. on the black market.

30. Among the more common motives for bombing include all of the following except:

   a. financial gain and insurance fraud.
   b. sabotage and concealment of crimes.
   c. enjoyment and sexual satisfaction from explosives.
   d. revenge and hatred.

31. In interviewing witnesses to determine the motive for a bombing, it is important to explore the relationships between people suspected of being in the area of the explosion and the:

    a. victim.
    b. suspect.
    c. witness.
    d. insurer.

32. Unlike the saboteur or someone fraudulently collecting insurance, the terrorist often will _____ his enterprise.

    a. disguise
    b. not disguise
    c. repudiate
    d. abandon

33. If it was necessary to gain entry by force in order to plant the bomb, the investigator should be alert for the typical evidence associated with the offense of:

    a. arson.
    b. robbery.
    c. burglary.
    d. insurance fraud.

34. All of the following are kinds of physical evidence that are sometimes found after a bomb explosion that can link the perpetrator to the bombing except:

    a. fragments of the packing, wrapping, and binding, to show common origin with material in the perpetrator's possession.
    b. small pieces of paper with writing to be matched with the writing in the possession of the perpetrator.
    c. edges of stamps, paper, and cardboard to match with edges on material in the perpetrator's possession.
    d. fingerprints on paper to be matched with the perpetrator's.

35. The laws relating to the transportation, manufacture, sale, and storage of explosives become the essence of the offense when:

    a. when the bomb is shipped over state lines.
    b. when the bomb does not explode.
    c. there is no intent to injure or damage property.
    d. the bomb is made from manufactured explosives.

36. If there is a warning of a bomb on board an airplane or in a public building the most practical and effective police response would be to:

    a. cancel the flight or close the building.
    b. call in a bomb-detecting dog team to search the premises.
    c. detain all people at the airport or on the premises fitting the profile of a bomber.
    d. ignore the threat because the majority of these warnings are false.

Answers:

1. c	p. 624, 2.	13. b	p. 629, 5.	25. d	p. 633, 7b.
2. a	p. 624, 3a.	14. a	p. 629, 5.	26. a	p. 633, 7b.
3. d	p. 624, 3a.	15. c	p. 630, 5.	27. c	p. 633, 7b.
4. b	p. 624, 3b.	16. a	p. 630, 5.	28. b	p. 633, 7c.
5. c	p. 624, 3b.	17. d	p. 630, 5e.	29. b	p. 634, 7d.
6. a	p. 625, 4.	18. c	p. 630, 5f.	30. c	p. 634, 8a.
7. d	p. 626, 4b.	19. b	p. 631, 6.	31. a	p. 635, 8d.
8. d	p. 626, 4b.	20. b	p. 631, 6.	32. b	p. 635, 8d.
9. c	p. 627, 4c.	21. a	p. 631, 6.	33. c	p. 636, 9.
10. c	p. 627, 4c.	22. c	p. 631, 6.	34. d	p. 637, 9d.
11. b	p. 628, 4d.	23. d	p. 632, 7.	35. c	p. 637, 10.
12. d	p. 629, 4e.	24. a	p. 632, 7b.	36. b	p. 638, 11.

Chapter 27

RULES OF EVIDENCE

Questions:

1. The term _____ includes all the means by which an alleged fact is established or disproved.

    a. testimony
    b. admissibility

    c. evidence
    d. law

2. The laws of evidence are the rules governing its _____ in court.

    a. relevance
    b. significance

    c. irrelevance
    d. admissibility

3. The rules of evidence are designed to _____ types of information that tend to be irrelevant or to confuse the issues.

    a. accept
    b. screen out

    c. consider
    d. infer

4. An eyewitness account of a criminal act is _____ evidence.

    a. direct
    b. circumstantial

    c. real
    d. material

5. A fact or circumstance from which one may infer another fact at issue is called _____ evidence.

   a. direct   c. real
   b. circumstantial   d. material

6. The essence of direct evidence is:

   a. probability.   c. immediate experience.
   b. inference.   d. relevance.

7. The essence of circumstantial evidence is:

   a. probability.   c. immediate experience.
   b. inference.   d. relevance.

8. **A** hears a shot and sees **B** emerge from a room with a gun in his hand and finds **C**'s body on the floor. **A**'s testimony would be _____ evidence.

   a. direct   c. real
   b. circumstantial   d. immaterial

9. **A** sees **B** shoot **C**. **A**'s testimony would be _____ evidence.

   a. direct   c. real
   b. circumstantial   d. immaterial

10. _____ evidence is the name given to tangible objects, such as guns, fingerprints, and bloodstains, introduced at a trial to prove a fact at issue.

   a. Admissible   c. Relevant
   b. Material   d. Real

11. When the evidence tends to prove a fact that is a significant issue in the case, it is:

   a. circumstantial.   c. relevant.
   b. direct.   d. material.

12. If evidence is immaterial, it:

   a. is not related to an issue.
   b. does not truly reflect the facts.
   c. does not affect an issue significantly.
   d. does not involve real evidence.

13. When evidence tends to prove the truth of a fact related to an issue, it is:

   a. circumstantial.   c. relevant.
   b. direct.   d. material.

14. If evidence is irrelevant, it:

   a. it is not related to an issue.
   b. does not truly reflect the facts.
   c. does not affect an issue significantly.
   d. does not involve real evidence.

15. Evidence to be admissible must be significant and related to an issue, in other words:

   a. direct and circumstantial.   c. competent and admissible.
   b. material and relevant.   d. important and relative.

16. A(n) _____ witness is one who is eligible to testify.

   a. intelligent   c. relevant
   b. significant   d. competent.

17. In legal terms, the ability to see, recall, and relate is called:

   a. cognitive awareness.   c. mental competency.
   b. perceptual intelligence.   d. perception.

18. In legal terms, the understanding of the importance and consequence of telling the truth is called moral:

   a. development.   c. intelligence.
   b. competency.   d. perception.

19. _____ is the discrediting of a witness.

   a. Impeachment   c. Judicial notice
   b. A presumption   d. Burden of proof

20. As a general rule, the court will not require proof of matters of general knowledge, such as historical and geographical facts. This is called:

   a. impeachment.   c. judicial notice.
   b. a presumption.   d. burden of proof.

21. In criminal cases, the burden of proof means that the prosecution has the task of proving the accused guilty:

   a. by showing probable cause.   c. with a preponderance of evidence.
   b. beyond any doubt.   d. beyond a reasonable doubt.

22. _____ is a justifiable inference which shifts the burden to the opposing party to establish contradictory facts.

   a. Hearsay evidence   c. A presumption
   b. An opinion   d. Circumstantial evidence

23. _____ is considered final and not to be overcome by contradictory evidence.

a. A conclusive presumption   c. A rebuttable presumption
b. An expert opinion   d. Judicial notice

24. _____ is a justifiable inference that can be overcome by proof of its falsity.

a. A conclusive presumption   c. A rebuttable presumption
b. An expert opinion   d. Judicial notice

25. All of the following are rebuttable presumptions except:

a. Everyone is presumed to be innocent.
b. Everyone is presumed to know the law.
c. Everyone is presumed to be sane.
d. Everyone intends the natural consequences of his actions.

26. The function of the rules of exclusion is to limit the evidence a witness may present to those things of which he has:

a. direct, sensory knowledge.   c. formed an opinion about.
b. read and studied.   d. heard from reliable sources.

27. Aside from several exceptions, the general rule is that opinion evidence _____ admissible in a trial.

a. can be   c. is for the most part
b. is not   d. is always

28. The layman may express an opinion on matters of common observation such as all of the following except:

a. physical properties such as color, weight, and size.
b. estimates of a person's age.
c. the emotional state of a person.
d. the medical condition of a person.

29. Before an expert can render an opinion in court about a technical matter in his specialty, he must first demonstrate to the court his:

a. knowledge.   c. qualifications.
b. experience.   d. good character.

30. Aside from several exceptions, the general rule states that testimony concerning a person's character and reputation _____ be introduced for the purpose of raising an inference of guilt.

a. can   c. for the most part can
b. cannot   d. can always

31. The defendant may introduce evidence of his own good character and reputation to show:

    a. the probability of his innocence.
    b. that he deserves a second chance.
    c. that he has many fine qualities.
    d. that often good people make mistakes.

32. As an exception to the general rule, previous acts or crimes of the accused may be introduced in evidence if they tend to show that the defendant:

    a. is the type of person who would commit this crime.
    b. is a career criminal who might have committed this crime.
    c. would have committed this crime if given the opportunity.
    d. actually committed this crime.

33. The prosecution may introduce a defendant's previous crimes as evidence for the present crime by showing:

    a. that it is very difficult for a criminal like the defendant to reform.
    b. that the present crime is part of a pattern of previous crimes.
    c. that he is the type of person who would commit this crime.
    d. that he probably has committed a number of crimes.

34. Hearsay evidence is derived from what the witness _____ the crime in question:

    a. heard himself at   c. personally experienced at
    b. was told by others about   d. theorized about

35. Hearsay evidence is excluded for all of the following reasons except:

    a. The author of the statement is not present and under oath.
    b. The defendant is not given the right to confront his accuser.
    c. A witness will usually distort or misrepresent any information that he does not obtain directly.
    d. There is a possibility of error in the passage of information from one person to another.

36. All of the following are exceptions to the hearsay rule except:

    a. a confession.
    b. an interrogation statement.
    c. a failure to deny an accusation before apprehension.
    d. a dying declaration.

37. In order for a dying declaration to be admissible, all of the following conditions must exist except:

    a. The victim's statement must be concerned with the circumstances of the injury and the identity of the person who caused it.
    b. The victim must believe he is dying.
    c. The victim must in fact have died.
    d. The victim must have sworn under oath to the truth of his statement.

38. _____ is an utterance concerning the circumstances of a startling event by an individual in a condition of excitement, shock, or surprise.

    a. A spontaneous exclamation   c. *Res gestae*
    b. A dying declaration   d. Fresh complaint

39. The term *res gestae* literally means: "things which _____."

    a. happened   c. were thought
    b. were said   d. were implied

40. A spontaneous exclamation is admissible when made by:

    a. a victim.   c. a witness.
    b. a suspect.   d. anyone of the above.

41. A fresh complaint is a statement made within a reasonable time after a sexual offense by the:

    a. victim.   c. witness.
    b. suspect.   d. any of the above.

42. All of the following are exceptions to the rule prohibiting hearsay evidence except:

    a. dying declaration.   c. opinion evidence.
    b. spontaneous exclamation.   d. documentary evidence.

43. The "best evidence" rule, which governs the admissibity of documents as evidence, requires that where available _____ of a document should be submitted.

    a. an original   c. either an original or a copy
    b. a copy   d. both an original and a copy.

44. Under exceptional circumstances when the original is unavailable, copies, carbons, and duplicates may be admissible as:

    a. an official record.   c. a deposition.
    b. secondary evidence.   d. not the "best evidence."

45. The testimony of a witness, who will be unable to attend court at the time of trial, may be formally reduced to writing and is ordinarily admissible. This is called a:

    a. testimonial utterance.   c. deposition.
    b. *res gestae.*   d. privileged communication.

46. Information obtained in certain confidential relationships that will ordinarily not be received in evidence is called a:

    a. testimonial utterance.   c. deposition.
    b. *res gestae.*   d. privileged communication.

47. All of the following are examples of privileged communication except:

    a. informants reporting to public officers.
    b. transcripts of interrogations.
    c. deliberations of a grand jury.
    d. diplomatic correspondence.

48. All of the following relationships are privileged except:

    a. husband and wife.   c. clergyman and penitent.
    b. attorney and client.   d. parent and child.

49. The Fifth Amendment privilege against self-incrimination prohibits compelling a person to give the following type of evidence:

    a. verbal and other communications in which knowledge of a matter is expressed.
    b. the utterance of any words for any reason even for a voiceprint.
    c. personal evidence such as trying on clothes or participating in a lineup.
    d. scientific tests in which samples of blood, urine, saliva, or breath are taken.

50. Evidence that involves the intervention of the mind is considered _____ evidence, and hence, its compulsion is prohibited.

    a. physical evidence   c. testimonial evidence
    b. psychological evidence   d. nontestimonial evidence

51. Entrapment is the act of a police officer in inducing a person to commit a crime _____ by him for the purpose of prosecuting him.

    a. previously attempted   c. contemplated
    b. not previously attempted   d. not contemplated

52. Entrapping a subject into committing a crime is:

    a. sometimes necessary.   c. sometimes legal.
    b. just bad police work.   d. illegal.

53. All of the following activities of an undercover investigator are legal except:

    a. employing a "decoy" to be a victim of a crime.
    b. supplying an opportunity to commit a crime.
    c. arranging transportation to and from a crime.
    d. pretending to fall in with the criminal's plan.

54. Before a conviction can be sustained, the prosecution must establish the *corpus delicti*, which means that:

    a. a body has been identified in a homicide case.
    b. a defendant has been charged with a crime.
    c. at least some law has been broken.
    d. the crime was committed.

55. All of the following rules concerning the *corpus delicti* are true except:

    a. A confession can be used to establish it.
    b. It must be sustained before there can be a conviction.
    c. It does not have to be proven beyond a reasonable doubt.
    d. Confessions of co-accused may be used to establish it.

Answers:

1. c	p. 643, 1.	20. c	p. 646, 7.	39. a	p. 652, 13c.
2. d	p. 643, 2.	21. d	p. 646, 8.	40. d	p. 652, 13c.
3. b	p. 644, 2.	22. c	p. 646, 9.	41. a	p. 653, 13c.
4. a	p. 644, 3a.	23. a	p. 646, 9a.	42. c	p. 653, 13c.
5. b	p. 644, 3b.	24. c	p. 646, 9b.	43. a	p. 653, 13c.
6. c	p. 644, 3b.	25. b	p. 646, 9b.	44. b	p. 653, 13c.
7. b	p. 644, 3b.	26. a	p. 647, 10b.	45. c	p. 654, 13c.
8. b	p. 644, 3b.	27. b	p. 648, 11.	46. d	p. 655, 14.
9. a	p. 644, 3b.	28. d	p. 648, 11b.	47. b	p. 655, 14a.
10. d	p. 644, 3c.	29. c	p. 649, 11b.	48. d	p. 655, 14b.
11. d	p. 645, 4a.	30. b	p. 649, 12.	49. a	p. 656, 15.
12. c	p. 645, 4a.	31. a	p. 650, 12a.	50. c	p. 656, 15.
13. c	p. 645, 4b.	32. d	p. 650, 12b.	51. d	p. 656, 16.
14. a	p. 645, 4b.	33. b	p. 650, 12b.	52. d	p. 656, 16.
15. b	p. 645, 4.	34. b	p. 651, 13a.	53. c	p. 657, 16.
16. d	p. 645, 5.	35. c	p. 651, 13b.	54. d	p. 657, 17.
17. c	p. 645, 5.	36. b	p. 651, 13c.	55. a	p. 657, 17.
18. b	p. 645, 5.	37. d	p. 652, 13c.		
19. a	p. 645, 6.	38. a	p. 652, 13c.		

Chapter 28

TESTIMONY IN COURT

Questions:

1. The effectiveness of the evidence as well as the reputation of the investigator rests in great part on:

a. his accumulation of facts.
b. his use of his notebook.
c. his courtroom performance.
d. the substance of his testimony.

2. To become a proficient witness, the investigator must *first* have knowledge of:

a. courtroom personnel.
b. the rules of evidence.
c. courtroom procedure.
d. the details of his own case.

3. The investigator should also know all of the following except:

a. the jurisdiction of the various courts.
b. the functions of the court personnel.
c. the terms and operations of the court.
d. the dates and times when court is in session.

4. Prior to testifying in court, the investigator should recall the significant data of the case *primarily* by reviewing:

a. his notes.
b. the report of investigation.
c. previous courtroom testimony.
d. all evidence reports.

5. When testifying in court, the investigator ideally should consult his notebook:

a. not at all.
b. only for details.
c. for all important facts.
d. only when his facts are challenged.

6. The testimony of the investigator should be given in all of the following ways except:

a. slowly.
b. distinctly.
c. audibly.
d. eagerly.

7. The investigator's narration of events should be designed to present:

a. every detail of the case.
b. the elements of proof.
c. interesting personal experiences.
d. the unsavory nature of the defendant.

8. In giving his testimony, the investigator should display:

a. a sincere interest in convicting the accused.
b. his disapproval of the crime and the criminal.
c. a sincere interest in accuracy and truth of statement.
d. a spirited defense of the evidence he is presenting.

9. To win over the judge and jury to a belief in his honesty and integrity, the investigator should be guided by all of the following rules except:

a. Make known all biases and prejudices in an honest manner.
b. Tell only what is known from personal knowledge to be the truth.
c. Give the impression of telling the truth.
d. Maintain an attitude of respect at all times.

10. To win over the judge and jury to a belief in his honesty and integrity, the investigator should be guided by all of the following rules except:

a. Answer the questioned asked in a responsive manner.
b. Maintain emotional composure at all times.
c. Speak in natural unaffected tones.
d. Answer each question as completely as possible.

11. An expert witness deals with:

a. facts.
b. opinions.
c. personal experience.
d. common knowledge.

12. Before an expert witness may express an opinion on a state of fact within his specialty, it must be established that:

a. what he is saying is true.
b. his statements are consistent with his previous testimony.
c. he is honest.
d. he is an expert in his specialty.

13. The investigator may be asked to testify about events from common experience such as any of the following except:

a. the length of time required to go from one place to another.
b. the cause of a victim's death.
c. the results of firing a given weapon.
d. the nature and audibility of a sound.

14. The investigator can prove facts like those mentioned in the previous question by appealing to:

a. experimentation.
b. common experience.
c. educated guesswork.
d. common sense.

15. The most serious consequence of having someone not fully qualified testifying in scientific matters is that:

a. inaccurate information may go into testimony.
b. the witness may be embarrassed.
c. the success of the case may be jeopardized.
d. other expert witnesses may boycott the trial.

16. Among the subjects most often mastered by the investigator, and on which he may be called to testify as an expert witness, are all of the following except:

a. casting.
b. photography.

c. developing latent fingerprints.
d. handwriting analysis.

Answers:

1. c	p. 660, 1.	7. b	p. 663, 4.	13. b	p. 666, 5b.
2. b	p. 661, 2.	8. c	p. 663, 4.	14. a	p. 666, 5c.
3. d	p. 662, 2b.	9. a	p. 663, 4.	15. c	p. 666, 5d.
4. a	p. 662, 3.	10. d	p. 665, 4d.	16. d	p. 667, 5e.
5. b	p. 663, 3.	11. b	p. 665, 5a.		
6. d	p. 663, 4.	12. d	p. 666, 5a.		

Chapter 29

OBSERVATION AND DESCRIPTION

Question:

1. The investigator must ultimately rely on _____ for a comprehensive and significant representation of the crime scene.

a. his own observations
b. photographs and sketches

c. the descriptions by others
d. the reports of investigation

2. Although the eye is the most fruitful source of information, it is often unreliable because the observer:

a. has no control of his eyesight.
b. tends to fill in the gaps left by inadequate observation.
c. tends to concentrate on his eyesight to the neglect of the other senses.
d. tends to imagine that he sees things that are not there.

3. Approximately 85 percent of our sensual knowledge comes from sight while 13 percent comes from:

a. smell.
b. touch.

c. taste.
d. hearing.

4. For investigative purposes, all of the following are stages in the process of observation except:

a. perception.
b. attention.

c. imagination.
d. report.

5. In the first stage of observation, called _____, the observer becomes aware of a phenomenon or of being in the presence of a fact.

    a. perception   c. understanding
    b. attention   d. report

6. Recognition of the significance of a fact is termed:

    a. perception.   c. intelligence.
    b. attention.   d. recognition.

7. All of the following are important contributory factors in understanding a fact to which attention has been drawn except:

    a. intelligence.   c. experience and occupation.
    b. educational background.   d. enthusiasm.

8. In the second stage of observation called perception, the observer not only apprehends a phenomenon but also _____ it.

    a. attends to   c. understands
    b. communicates   d. reports

9. In the third stage of observation called _____, the observer becomes aware of the significance of a fact and identifies it.

    a. understanding   c. identification
    b. communication   d. report

10. The first important classification system for physical identification of people in custody was based on:

    a. fingerprints.   c. verbal descriptions.
    b. body measurements.   d. age and weight.

11. Alphonse Bertillon (1853-1914) was connected with the introduction of all of the following except:

    a. anthropometry.   c. Paris Bureau of Identification.
    b. *portrait parlé*.   d. *modus operandi* files.

12. The system of measuring physical features for identification is called:

    a. anthropometry or *bertillonage*.   c. *portrait parlé*.
    b. physical description.   d. *modus operandi*.

13. The systematic procedure for verbal description is called:

    a. anthropometry or *bertillonage*.   c. *portrait parlé*.
    b. physical description.   d. *modus operandi*.

14. In order to fully identify a person by name, the investigator should obtain:

    a. his full name only.
    b. his full name and aliases.
    c. his full name and nicknames.
    d. all his names, aliases, and nicknames.

15. All of the following numbers are important for identifying persons except the:

    a. Social Security number.
    b. Military serial number.
    c. Fingerprint classification number.
    d. Insurance identification number.

16. In describing the physical features, often an exceptionally useful item is:

    a. religious background.
    b. national origin.
    c. military record.
    d. occupational background.

17. In identifying a person, a description of all of the following physical habits are very important except:

    a. the manner of walk.
    b. the sound of the voice.
    c. the manner of working.
    d. speech characteristics.

18. In characterizing an individual, the most important personal habit usually is:

    a. his standard of dress.
    b. his sports activities.
    c. the establishments he frequents.
    d. his hobbies and entertainments.

19. In a verbal description, all of the following characteristics are very helpful in creating a mental picture except:

    a. personality type.
    b. apparent social status.
    c. a comparison with a celebrity.
    d. a comparison with a personal friend.

20. The principle belief underlying voice identification is that:

    a. all voices have a similarity that can be demonstrated.
    b. people have the ability to consciously alter their voice.
    c. each individual can be uniquely associated with his voice.
    d. loudness and rapidity of speech distinguishes each voice.

21. Voice identification will often be important evidence in all of the following types of cases except:

    a. burglaries.
    b. bomb threats.
    c. kidnappings.
    d. extortion.

22. Voice identification uses the electronic recording of the energy output of the subject's voice in producing a specific word. The result is properly called:

    a. a voicegraph.
    b. a voiceprint.
    c. sound spectrogram.
    d. a voice pattern.

23. Voice identification is successful because it confines itself to those characteristics of voice that are:

    a. easily changed.   c. not easily changed.
    b. under conscious control.   d. not under conscious control.

24. U.S. state appeals court have found that voiceprint analysis is a(n)
_____ means of personal identification.

    a. infallible   c. unreliable
    b. reliable   d. worthless

25. An important means of recovering stolen property are:

    a. criminal profiles.   c. *modus operandi* files.
    b. expert systems.   d. lost and stolen property files.

26. Stolen property tends to circulate in the local area in the possession of new
buyers and second-hand dealers because the thieves tend to _____ stolen property.

    a. abandon   c. resort to haphazard sales of
    b. return   d. give away

27. Lost and stolen property records may be filed together because:

    a. there are not enough cases of each to justify separate files.
    b. stolen property is, in a sense, lost property.
    c. it is always more convenient in searching for a missing object.
    d. it is often not known whether an article has been lost or stolen.

28. Property is primarily filed according to the _____of article, in other words,
what the article is.

    a. kind   c. material
    b. physical appearance   d. brand name

29. The most important element for identifying expensive manufactured prod-
ucts is the:

    a. physical description.   c. model number.
    b. brand name.   d. serial number.

30. In describing lost or stolen jewelry, besides the kind, number, and size of the
stones, it is also important to provide the:

    a. probable value.   c. shape and cut of the stones.
    b. year it was bought.   d. name of the jeweler who sold it.

31. An excellent means of facilitating the recovery of stolen valuables is to have these items engraved beforehand with the _____ and registered with the police.

    a. owner's name and address
    b. owner's phone number.

    c. serial number of the product
    d. owner's Social Security number

32. A summary of the habits, techniques, and peculiarities of behavior of a criminal is often referred to as:

    a. the *modus operandi.*
    b. the physical description.

    c. the criminal profile.
    d. *portrait parlé.*

33. MO files are maintained for all of the following reasons except:

    a. to associate a group of crimes with a single perpetrator.
    b. to predict a possible next target for a criminal.
    c. to understand why the criminal commits his crime.
    d. to recognize a perpetrator from characteristics of his criminal activity.

34. The MO file is most effective in crimes involving personal contact between the criminal and the victim. Therefore, it should be *least* effective against:

    a. robbery.
    b. burglary.

    c. confidence games.
    d. forgery.

35. All of the following were significant elements in the MO file arrangement devised by Atcherly except the:

    a. nature of the stolen property in crimes involving larceny.
    b. verbal description of the criminal.
    c. fingerprint and blood evidence from the crime scene.
    d. personal mannerisms and speech characteristics.

36. A description of the personality and behavioral traits of a perpetrator (derived from a study of the behavioral traits of other criminals who have committed the same offense and the details of the crime scene) is called:

    a. the *modus operandi.*
    b. artificial intelligence.

    c. the *portrait parlé.*
    d. the criminal profile.

37. The details of the crime that are considered in criminal profiling are primarily those that express:

    a. the attitude of the victim.
    b. the greed of the perpetrator.

    c. the lack of concern for the law.
    d. the personality of the perpetrator.

38. Crimes that lend themselves to profiling are those in which there is extensive contact by the perpetrator with the crime scene and the victim, and those in which the act itself indicates:

    a. a lack of concern for the victim.
    b. a psychological disorder.
    c. that the perpetrator is violent.
    d. a long history of criminal behavior.

39. All of the following criminal activities might be suitable for personality profiling except:

    a. sexual homicide.   c. contract killings.
    b. pyromania.   d. mutilation.

40. Of the following criminal activities, which one is most likely to be suitable for profiling the perpetrator?

    a. assault   c. loan sharking
    b. robbery   d. torture

41. The personality profiling through the analysis of the messages from anonymous letter writers and threatening telephone callers is called _____ analysis.

    a. psycholinguistic   c. letter pattern
    b. psychological   d. message pattern

42. When profiling an anonymous letter writer, the investigator is least concerned with:

    a. the word usage and linguistic patterns.
    b. the actual message being communicated.
    c. the personality and background of the author.
    d. the frame of mind of the author.

43. After analyzing the crime scene of a sexual homicide and finding it "disorganized," the investigator would conclude that the perpetrator would probably display many of the personality characteristics of _____ murderers.

    a. organized   c. either organized or disorganized
    b. disorganized   d. both organized and disorganized

44. A computer program designed to solve problems by simulating human intelligence is called a(n) _____ system.

    a. computer intelligence   c. expert
    b. intelligence simulating   d. intelligence

45. In a system using "artificial intelligence," retiring detectives can preserve much of their knowledge and experience in the form of:

a. aphorisms.
b. maxims.
c. instructive generalities.
d. "if...then" rules.

46. The purpose of an expert system in criminal investigation, is to analyze clues left at the crime scene, using a system of rules and detailed criminal histories, in order to:

a. determine if a crime has been committed.
b. give direction to the investigation.
c. obtain a list of possible suspects.
d. observe patterns of criminal behavior.

47. All of the following are necessary elements in an expert system except:

a. clues found at the scene.
b. details of the motives of the suspects.
c. details of the criminal histories of the suspects.
d. a collection of "if...then" rules from experienced detectives.

Answers:

1. a	p. 671, 1.	17. c	p. 674, 5l.	33. c	p. 682, 14.		
2. b	p. 671, 2.	18. a	p. 674, 5i.	34. b	p. 682, 14.		
3. d	p. 672, 2.	19. d	p. 675, 6a.	35. c	p. 683, 15.		
4. c	p. 672, 3.	20. c	p. 676, 7.	36. d	p. 684, 16a.		
5. b	p. 672, 3a.	21. a	p. 677, 7.	37. d	p. 684, 16b.		
6. a	p. 672, 3b.	22. b	p. 677, 7.	38. b	p. 684, 16c.		
7. d	p. 672, 3b.	23. d	p. 677, 7.	39. c	p. 685, 16c.		
8. c	p. 672, 3b.	24. c	p. 678, 7.	40. d	p. 685, 16c.		
9. d	p. 672, 3c.	25. d	p. 679, 8.	41. a	p. 685, 16e.		
10. b	p. 673, 4.	26. c	p. 679, 8.	42. b	p. 685, 16e.		
11. d	p. 673, 4.	27. d	p. 679, 9.	43. b	p. 686, 16f.		
12. a	p. 673, 4.	28. a	p. 680, 10.	44. c	p. 687, 17.		
13. c	p. 673, 4.	29. d	p. 680, 10.	45. d	p. 687, 17.		
14. d	p. 673, 5.	30. c	p. 680, 11c.	46. c	p. 687, 17.		
15. d	p. 673, 5.	31. d	p. 681, 12.	47. b	p. 687, 17.		
16. b	p. 674, 5f.	32. a	p. 682, 13.				

Chapter 30

IDENTIFICATION BY WITNESSES

Questions:

1. All of the following are methods recommended for identifying an unknown criminal from the observation of an eyewitness except:

    a. the *portrait parlé* or written description.
    b. the use of the photographic files of known criminals or Rogues Gallery.
    c. the automated fingerprint identification system (AFIS).
    d. the use of an artist.

2. The selection of photographs from the Known Criminals File for viewing by a witness would be suggested primarily by the _____ of the crime.

    a. *modus operandi*   c. recency
    b. seriousness   d. motive

3. When using an artist to portray the composite features of a face described by eyewitnesses, the investigator may do all of these preliminary steps except:

    a. separate the witnesses so that they cannot confer with each other.
    b. obtain a written description from each witness.
    c. from the written descriptions, attempt to establish a common denominator for each of the features of the unknown criminal.
    d. confront the witnesses when there are discrepancies in their descriptions.

4. When drawing a composite picture of the face of the suspect from the witnesses' description of each individual feature, the artist should:

    a. make only a final sketch, ignoring any differences of opinion.
    b. make several preliminary sketches which can be examined, selected, and corrected by each individual witness.
    c. consider only written descriptions by the witnesses.
    d. give equal weight to each witness description.

5. _____ consists of a variety of facial features that can be systematically composed into a single face in response to the direction of the witness.

    a. Miracode   c. An identification kit
    b. Videotape identification   d. A computer sketch

6. _____ consists of an eyewitness viewing of a prerecorded sequence of actions, profiles, and spoken words by individual lineup participants in order to identify a suspect.

    a. Miracode   c. An identification kit
    b. Videotape identification   d. A computer sketch

7. _____ uses a cassette cartridge of microfilm into which has been coded twenty-five characteristics of recently arrested criminals.

a. Miracode
b. Videotape identification

c. An identification kit
d. A computer sketch

8. _____ system can store up to 100,000 different facial features which can be combined to form a facial composition in response to a standardized witness interview.

a. Miracode
b. Videotape identification

c. An identification kit
d. A computer sketch

9. All of the following are advantages of computer generated sketches except:

a. The operator needs no artistic ability.
b. Redrawing or correcting the sketch can be done in seconds.
c. Witnesses need not be accurate in remembering details.
d. Multiple copies can be printed quickly for circulation.

10. An eyewitness identification will often be of critical importance to a criminal investigation where:

a. there are number of suspects.
b. there is an absence of suspects.
c. there is plenty of other evidence.
d. there is an absence of other evidence.

11. The three important methods of eyewitness identification include all of the following except:

a. lineup.
b. showup.

c. computer sketch.
d. photographic identification.

12. A _____ , or single suspect confrontation, is used in emergency situations such as when the victim is dying.

a. lineup
b. showup

c. computer sketch
d. photographic identification

13. A _____ is the customary means of police identification in which the suspect of a crime is exhibited with a number of other participants so that a witness can identify him.

a. lineup
b. showup

c. computer sketch
d. photographic identification

14. A _____ is often employed when a suspect is not in custody.

a. lineup
b. showup

c. computer sketch
d. photographic identification

15. In order to eliminate the power of suggestion as a factor in identification, a lineup is made of participants of _____ appearance.

    a. similar   c. unusual
    b. dissimilar   d. distinctive

16. A lineup may be dispensed with in all of the following situations except:

    a. when there is other incriminating evidence and the eyewitness recollection is weak.
    b. when there is very little other evidence and the eyewitness recollection is strong.
    c. when the witness knows the suspect and recognizes him during the offense.
    d. when the witness does not know the suspect and the eyewitness recollection is weak.

17. To conduct a lineup, a group of at least _____ persons, including the suspect, should be assembled.

    a. four   c. eight
    b. six   d. ten

18. All of the following statements concerning the conduct of a lineup are true except:

    a. The persons participating in the lineup should have the same general appearance.
    b. A two-way mirror which would permit the witnesses to view the lineup unobserved is desirable.
    c. The witness should announce out loud, clearly and distinctly, when an identification has been made.
    d. The suspect should be permitted to select his own position in the lineup.

19. All of the following statements concerning the conduct of a lineup are true except:

    a. If there is more than one witness, they should make their identification separately without conferring with each other.
    b. The suspect has the right to refuse to participate in a lineup.
    c. A suspect's request for legal counsel should be honored even though it is not necessary to do so.
    d. Color photographs of the front and the profile of lineup participants should be taken.

20. In 1967, the Supreme Court in _____ ruled that a suspect is entitled to a lawyer at a lineup because it is a critical stage of the prosecution.

    a. *Miranda v. Arizona*   c. *Kirby v. Illinois*
    b. *U.S. v. Wade*   d. *Schmerber v. California*

21. In 1972, the Supreme Court in _____ ruled that only a suspect who has been indicted is entitled to have a lawyer present at a lineup.

    a. *Miranda v. Arizona*   c. *Kirby v. Illinois*
    b. *U.S. v. Wade*   d. *Schmerber v. California*

22. All of the following are situations in which a showup, or a single suspect confrontation, may be necessary except:

    a. There are not enough similar-looking people to form a lineup.
    b. There are a number of suspects and only one person committed the crime.
    c. The victim is dying.
    d. The suspect decides he prefers a showup to participating in a lineup.

23. Unless there is a state law to the contrary, a suspect _____ have the right to legal representation at a showup.

    a. does   c. may waive
    b. does not   d. may not waive

24. All of the following are recommended procedures for a showup except:

    a. If possible the suspect should appear in handcuffs.
    b. When confronting the suspect, the witness should be asked "Is this the person?"
    c. The investigator should not comment on the identification in the presence of the suspect or witness.
    d. A written report of the procedure should be made.

25. All of the following are circumstances in which a photographic identification is commonly used except:

    a. when a suspect is not in custody.
    b. where there is a surveillance photograph of the suspect but no knowledge of who he is.
    c. where the witness lives at too great a distance from where the suspect is being held.
    d. when the witness has failed to pick the suspect out of a lineup.

26. For a photographic identification, at least _____ photographs, including that of the suspect, should be used.

    a. four   c. eight
    b. six   d. ten

27. Each photograph should resemble the general appearance of the suspect and should be someone who is:

    a. of known identity.   c. a known suspect.
    b. of unknown identity.   d. an unknown suspect.

28. All of the following are proper procedures for conducting a photographic identification except:

    a. If the witness recognizes the suspect, he should initial the back of the photograph.
    b. If the witness fails to identify the suspect in the first set of pictures, the suspect's photograph should be placed in a second group of pictures and the identification process repeated.
    c. The suspect need not be informed that the identification is taking place.
    d. The investigator should not inform the witness whether or not the suspect's photograph is actually among the pictures displayed.

29. The suspect _____ the right to have a lawyer present at the photographic identification.

    a. does have
    b. does not have
    c. may waive
    d. may not waive

30. The _____ Amendment guarantees that: "No person...shall be compelled in any criminal case to be a witness against himself."

    a. First
    b. Fourth
    c. Fifth
    d. Sixth

31. No one is required to give testimonial evidence against himself. Testimonial evidence involves:

    a. writing for identification.
    b. speaking for identification.
    c. blood or breath samples.
    d. conscious communication.

32. All of the following are examples of testimonial evidence except:

    a. admissions.
    b. confessions.
    c. handwriting exemplars.
    d. sworn statements.

33. In _____ , the Supreme Court held that the taking of a blood sample, for chemical analysis to show intoxication, did not violate the defendant's right against self-incrimination.

    a. *Schmerber v. California*
    b. *Gilbert v. California*
    c. *U.S. v. Wade*
    d. *Kirby v. Illinois*

34. In _____ the Supreme Court ruled that the taking of handwriting exemplars from a suspect and their use against him does not violate the privilege against self-incrimination.

    a. *Schmerber v. California*
    b. *Gilbert v. California*
    c. *U.S. v. Wade*
    d. *Kirby v. Illinois*

35. All of the following evidence is considered to be nontestimonial evidence that a suspect may be compelled to give except:

    a. fingerprints and blood samples.
    b. handwriting and voice exemplars.
    c. lineup and showup participation.
    d. admissions and confessions.

36. A suspect _____ constitutional right to refuse to provide nontestimonial evidence.

    a. does have a   c. may waive his
    b. does not have a   d. may not waive his

Answers:

1. c	p. 692, 3.	13. a	p. 697, 4a.	25. d	p. 701, 4c.
2. a	p. 692, 3b.	14. d	p. 697, 4a.	26. b	p. 702, 4c.
3. d	p. 693, 3d.	15. a	p. 697, 4a.	27. a	p. 702, 4c.
4. b	p. 694, 3d.	16. b	p. 697, 4a.	28. b	p. 702, 4c.
5. c	p. 694, 3e.	17. b	p. 697, 4a.	29. b	p. 702, 4c.
6. b	p. 694, 3f.	18. c	p. 698, 4a.	30. c	p. 702, 5.
7. a	p. 695, 3f.	19. b	p. 699, 4a.	31. d	p. 702, 5.
8. d	p. 695, 3f.	20. b	p. 700, 4a.	32. c	p. 702, 5.
9. c	p. 695, 3f.	21. c	p. 700, 4a.	33. a	p. 703, 5a.
10. d	p. 696, 4a.	22. d	p. 700, 4b.	34. b	p. 703, 5b.
11. c	p. 696, 4a.	23. b	p. 701, 4b.	35. d	p. 704, 5b.
12. b	p. 697, 4a.	24. a	p. 701, 4b.	36. b	p. 704, 6.

Chapter 31

FINGERPRINTS AND THE MECHANICS OF RECORDING

Questions:

1. To establish a positive identification, there _____ points of agreement between the ridge characteristics of two fingerprints.

    a. must be a minimum number of
    b. is no minimum number of
    c. must be twelve
    d. must be more than twelve

2. At present, the most successful method of identifying a person is through:

a. physical description.
b. physical measurement.
c. fingerprint classification.
d. photography.

3. All of the following are the major qualities of an effective identification system such as fingerprint classification except:

a. permanence.
b. intricacy.
c. universality.
d. unicity.

4. Ridge patterns of fingerprints are present at birth and:

a. last throughout a person's life.
b. can be changed by cuts and burns.
c. can be changed by surgical grafting.
d. can never be totally destroyed.

5. Empirically, fingerprints are said to be unique because no two people have been found that have _____ pattern(s) in common.

a. all ten fingerprints
b. even one fingerprint
c. more than one fingerprint
d. a number of fingerprint

6. Theoretically, it is _____ that two people share a common fingerprint pattern.

a. highly probable
b. highly improbable
c. probable
d. impossible

7. Fingerprints are usually _____ to record.

a. easy
b. difficult
c. easy only for a trained professional
d. difficult even for a professional

8. For a fingerprint classification system to be effective, not only must the classifying process be relatively simple, but also each person must be able to be classified:

a. as a member of a small group.
b. as a member of a large group.
c. as having almost a unique position.
d. in several different ways.

9. Because all objects are collections of molecules whose number and position can never exactly be reproduced, a basic principle of criminal investigation follows that:

a. All objects are essentially alike.
b. Objects are rarely, if ever, alike.
c. Two objects may sometimes be alike.
d. No two objects are alike.

10. A fingerprint pattern is a configuration of ridges and intervening:

    a. pores.   c. lines.
    b. perspiration ducts.   d. valleys or depressions.

11. The essential equipment for rolling fingerprints consists of all of the following except:

    a. a tube of ink.   c. a spoon or other curved surface.
    b. a rubber roller.   d. a slab of glass.

12. When fingerprinting a subject, the rubber roller is used for:

    a. rolling fingers on the glass and then onto the card.
    b. removing excess ink from the slab.
    c. spreading the ink evenly over the slab.
    d. rolling the fingerprint onto the card.

13. All of the following are appropriate procedures and precautions for taking fingerprints except:

    a. A standard fingerprint card from the FBI or other law enforcement agency should be used.
    b. An appropriate amount of ink should be spread evenly over the slab.
    c. The subject should clean his hands of perspiration, grease, and dirt.
    d. The subject should control the rolling process completely.

14. The key to successful rolling is to follow all of the rules below except:

    a. Roll the little finger first.   c. Roll with even pressure.
    b. Roll the fingers smoothly.   d. Roll with the fingers relaxed.

15. Space is provided on the fingerprint card for taking the four fingerprints simultaneously without rolling:

    a. in case one of the rolled prints is illegible.
    b. as a check on the sequence in which the rolled prints are taken.
    c. for additional information for fingerprint classification.
    d. because this method is often more reliable than rolling prints.

16. All of the following are valid reasons for the rejection of a set of fingerprints except:

    a. Either too much or insufficient ink was used.
    b. The entire first joint of the finger has been entirely inked and rolled.
    c. The impressions are blurred or smudged from moisture or a foreign substance on the finger.
    d. The hands were reversed or the impressions were not recorded in the correct sequence.

17. Before forwarding the recorded fingerprints to the identification bureau, the experienced investigator should examine them critically to determine:

    a. if they can be classified.
    b. if they can be duplicated.
    c. the classification himself.
    d. whether he recognizes them from a previous case.

18. All of the following statements are true except:

    a. Both the soles of the feet and the palms of the hands bear a permanent and relatively complex set of ridges and lines.
    b. Latent sole and palm prints found at the scene of the crime may be used to place the suspect at the scene.
    c. There is no generally accepted system of classification for sole and palm prints.
    d. Identification by sole and palm prints have not been accepted in court.

19. With infant footprints, both ridge areas and _____ are commonly used for identification.

    a. flexure lines   c. toe prints
    b. valleys or depressions   d. pores

20. All of the following statements about footprints are true except:

    a. The maintenance of adequate footprint records at the hospital is important for infant identification.
    b. Instruction in footprinting should stress the importance of using a limited quantity of ink and of applying the correct pressure.
    c. Identification by ridge areas has a greater validity than identification by flexure lines.
    d. There are two kinds of flexure lines: one group of lines disappear after about seven months; and the other group of lines are permanent.

21. A relatively invisible print made with the bare foot and found at the crime scene is called a latent:

    a. footprint.   c. sole print.
    b. sole impression.   d. foot impression.

22. Latent sole prints are usually found at the crime scene on all of the following surfaces except _____ floors.

    a. tile bathroom   c. polished wood
    b. carpeted   d. papers on the

23. After developing a latent sole print at the scene of the crime, the investigator should then _____ it.

a. photograph
b. lift

c. collect
d. cast

24. As a general principle, the action taken by the investigator in fingerprinting a deceased person should depend on:

a. Whether *rigor mortis* has set in.
b. the length of time the person has been dead.
c. whether the person has been immersed in water.
d. the fragility of the skin.

25. In fingerprinting a deceased person, the effect of rolling the finger can be achieved by pressing the finger against a:

a. spatula.
b. plate.

c. spoon.
d. card.

26. If the fingers of the deceased person are wrinkled from immersion in water, fingerprint collecting can best be accomplished:

a. only through photography.
b. by surgical removal of the skin.
c. by filling the fingers through water by means of a hypodermic needle.
d. by pressing the fingers firmly against a spoon to remove the wrinkles.

27. When the deceased person is in an advanced state of decomposition, the investigator collecting fingerprints should generally restrict his activity to:

a. photographing the ridge area.
b. inking and rolling the print.

c. surgical removal of the skin.
d. the dusting-tape method.

Answers:

1. b	p. 708, 1.	10. d	p. 710, 2.	19. a	p. 714, 4a.
2. c	p. 708, 1.	11. c	p. 710, 3a.	20. c	p. 714, 4a.
3. b	p. 708, 1.	12. c	p. 710, 3a.	21. c	p. 715, 4d.
4. a	p. 708, 1a.	13. d	p. 711, 3d.	22. b	p. 715, 4d.
5. b	p. 708, 1c.	14. a	p. 711, 3d.	23. a	p. 715, 4d.
6. b	p. 708, 1c.	15. b	p. 711, 3d.	24. d	p. 716, 5.
7. a	p. 709, 1d.	16. b	p. 712, 3e.	25. c	p. 716, 5a.
8. c	p. 709, 1e.	17. a	p. 713, 3f.	26. c	p. 717, 5a.
9. d	p. 709, 2.	18. d	p. 714, 4.	27. a	p. 717, 5b.

Chapter 32
LATENT FINGERPRINTS

Questions:

1. Each of the following is a class of fingerprints found at the crime scene except:

    a. visible.   c. invisible.
    b. latent.   d. plastic.

2. _____ fingerprints are "hidden" or relatively invisible and must be developed by a special method.

    a. Visible   c. Invisible
    b. Latent   d. Plastic

3. _____ fingerprints are impressions, depressed below the original surface and found on such objects as soap, butter, and putty.

    a. Visible   c. Invisible
    b. Latent   d. Plastic

4. _____ fingerprints are left by fingers covered with a colored material such as paint, blood, grease, and ink.

    a. Visible   c. Invisible
    b. Latent   d. Plastic

5. When searching an indoor crime scene for fingerprints, special attention should be given to all of the following except:

    a. the type of crime and the modus operandi of the culprit.
    b. smooth, hard, glossy surfaces and objects.
    c. points of entrance and departure.
    d. rough, soft, and absorbent surfaces and objects.

6. Latent fingerprints of value for comparison are not frequently found at the crime scene primarily because:

    a. most criminals wear gloves.
    b. of the delicate nature of the fingerprints.
    c. there are not enough receptive surfaces for fingerprints in most rooms.
    d. most fingerprints are deliberately wiped away by the criminal.

7. In order for a finger to deposit a clear print onto a surface, all of the following conditions must exist except:

    a. There must be a surface that can retain the print.
    b. The finger must have some moisture or perspiration on it.
    c. The finger must not slip or move.
    d. The finger must exert great pressure when touching the surface.

8. Even though finding a fingerprint may be unlikely, the investigator should make the effort to search because:

    a. persistent effort is invariably successful.
    b. of the great value of a fingerprint as evidence.
    c. chance plays an important part in an investigation.
    d. there are always useful fingerprints at the crime scene.

9. All of the following are helpful techniques for discovering latent fingerprints at the crime scene except:

    a. rubbing a surface gently with a cloth to reveal underlying fingerprints.
    b. holding a flashlight at an acute angle to reveal hidden prints.
    c. visually examining a surface from different angles to reveal prints.
    d. breathing on a surface to cause fingerprints to become visible.

10. Converting a latent fingerprint into a visible image is called:

    a. photography.   c. brushing.
    b. developing.   d. fuming.

11. Besides the traditional powder techniques of developing fingerprints, other recommended methods include all of the following except:

    a. vapor (fuming).   c. radiation.
    b. liquid (immersion).   d. laser light.

12. When developing fingerprints on a dark background, a _____ powder should be used.

    a. black   c. fluorescent
    b. white or grey   d. ferromagnetic

13. When developing fingerprints on a multicolored background, a _____ powder is recommended.

    a. black   c. fluorescent
    b. white or grey   d. ferromagnetic

14. A fingerprint on a white or light-colored surface can be developed with a _____ powder.

    a. black   c. fluorescent
    b. white or grey   d. ferromagnetic

15. All of the following rules concerning the application of powder by brush should be followed except:

    a. One brush should not be used with different colors.
    b. The brush should be pushed directly into the bottle to obtain powder.
    c. Powder should be applied sparingly.
    d. More powder should be added gradually when needed.

16. Of the following methods of developing fingerprints by powder, _____ is the simplest and most effective.

    a. brushing   c. Magna-Brush
    b. rolling or sifting   d. aerosol spraying

17. The _____ method of developing fingerprints by powder can be used to process large areas.

    a. brushing   c. Magna-Brush
    b. rolling or sifting   d. aerosol spraying

18. The method of developing fingerprints on paper that uses a magnet to move the powder across the paper is the _____ method.

    a. brushing   c. Magna-Brush
    b. rolling or sifting   d. aerosol spraying

19. The method of developing fingerprints on paper, which involves tilting the paper back and forth to spread the powder is:

    a. brushing.   c. Magna-Brush.
    b. rolling or sifting.   d. aerosol spraying.

20. Developing a fingerprint by exposing it to a chemical vapor is called:

    a. chemical development.   c. immersion.
    b. fuming.   d. laser detection.

21. All of the following types of chemical development are especially effective with fingerprints on paper except:

    a. iodine vapor.   c. silver nitrate.
    b. cyanoacrylate (Super Glue).   d. ninhydrin.

22. The _____ method is a fuming technique which is excellent for developing fingerprints on porous surfaces such as paper and cardboard.

    a. silver nitrate   c. ninhydrin
    b. iodine   d. cyanoacrylate (Super Glue)

23. The _____ method is a fuming technique that is effective for developing fingerprints on nonporous surfaces such as glass, metal, tin foil, leather and is especially useful for plastics and plastic bags.

    a. silver nitrate   c. ninhydrin
    b. iodine   d. cyanoacrylate (Super Glue)

24. The _____ method is an immersion techniques used to develop fingerprints on paper that converts the sodium chloride content of the latent print into a photosensitive substance which darkens on exposure to light.

    a. silver nitrate   c. ninhydrin
    b. laser light   d. fluorescent light

25. The _____ method is a chemical development technique which is useful in developing old fingerprints on paper; _____ reacts with the amino acids in the fingerprints turning them pink. It is often sprayed on documents.

    a. Super Glue   c. iodine
    b. fluorescent powder   d. ninhydrin

26. The _____ method causes fingerprint residues to become luminescent and is especially useful for difficult surfaces like styrofoam, cloth, and skin.

    a. Super Glue   c. laser
    b. fluorescent powder   d. silver nitrate

27. The _____ method is nondestructive, that is, it does not alter the evidence and thus can be used prior to all of the other methods.

    a. Super Glue   c. laser
    b. fluorescent powder   d. silver nitrate

28. A _____ camera has a fixed focus; it is used to copy fingerprints on flat surfaces.

    a. fingerprint   c. Speed Graphic
    b. Polaroid   d. 35mm

29. When photographing under difficult conditions, with a _____ camera you will be able to tell at once whether you have captured the important details.

    a. fingerprint   c. Speed Graphic
    b. Polaroid   d. 35mm

30. A fingerprint camera produces a copy of a fingerprint:

    a. at an enlarged size.   c. with a wide-angle view.
    b. at a smaller size.   d. at a natural size.

31. Polaroid now produces a _____ film which eliminates the need for taking duplicate pictures with another camera.

    a. "positive only"   c. "positive-negative"
    b. "negative only"   d. digital

32. All of the following are proper recommendations and procedures for the removal and transportation of objects bearing fingerprints except:

   a. Gloves may be worn.
   b. Articles should be touched only on those places least likely to have latent prints.
   c. Objects should be wrapped in a handkerchief and small objects placed in a paper bag.
   d. Cellophane sheets and envelopes may be used for protecting papers.

33. An object bearing a developed latent fingerprint:

   a. should be photographed only in the laboratory.
   b. need not be photographed if it can be transported.
   c. should have the latent print photographed with a fingerprint camera only.
   d. should have the latent print photographed with a fingerprint camera and with another camera to show the relationship of the object to its surroundings.

34. In an important criminal case where a fingerprint is found on the surface of a large object, it is advisable to:

   a. collect the object leaving the fingerprint on the surface.
   b. extensively photograph the print but not collect it.
   c. photograph the print and collect it by "lifting" it.
   d. "lift" the print with transparent tape.

35. If the scene of a crime is a room and a suspicious fingerprint is found in it, fingerprints should be recorded of all the persons who entered this room, prior to the commission of the crime, for the primary purpose of:

   a. implicating them in the crime.
   b. exonerating them from all involvement in the crime.
   c. eliminating any of their fingerprints found there from further examination.
   d. running their fingerprints through the identification system to see if they have a police record.

36. The physical removal of a latent fingerprint from its original surface is called:

   a. brushing.   c. fuming.
   b. rolling.   d. lifting.

37. All of the following statements about lifting a fingerprint are true except:

   a. Air bubbles under the lifting material may leave a blank spot in the lifted impression.
   b. A fingerprint found at the crime scene should be lifted whenever possible.
   c. The admissibility of a lifted impression in court may be objected to on the grounds that the evidence has been tampered with.
   d. When lifting a fingerprint usually only one attempt is possible.

38. A fingerprint may be lifted with an adhesive-backed rubber lifter or with:

a. transparent tape.   c. duct tape.
b. Super Glue.   d. adhesive tape.

39. When printing or enlarging a photograph of a lifted impression obtained by a rubber lifter, it is necessary for the negative to be _____ in order to obtain a true picture of the fingerprint.

a. right-side up   c. reversed
b. upside down   d. left as is

Answers:

1. c	p. 719, 1.	14. a	p. 722, 3a.	27. c	p. 727, 3c.
2. b	p. 719, 1a.	15. b	p. 722, 3a.	28. a	p. 727, 3d.
3. d	p. 719, 1b.	16. a	p. 722, 3a.	29. b	p. 727, 3d.
4. a	p. 719, 1c.	17. d	p. 723, 3a.	30. d	p. 727, 3d.
5. d	p. 719, 2.	18. c	p. 723, 3a.	31. c	p. 727, 3d.
6. b	p. 720, 2a.	19. b	p. 723, 3a.	32. c	p. 728, 4.
7. d	p. 720, 2a.	20. b	p. 724, 3b.	33. d	p. 729, 4g.
8. b	p. 720, 2a.	21. b	p. 724, 3b.	34. a	p. 729, 4j.
9. a	p. 721, 2b.	22. b	p. 724, 3b.	35. c	p. 729, 5.
10. b	p. 721, 3.	23. d	p. 725, 3b.	36. d	p. 730, 6.
11. c	p. 722, 3.	24. a	p. 725, 3b.	37. b	p. 730, 6a.
12. b	p. 722, 3a.	25. d	p. 726, 3b.	38. a	p. 730, 6b.
13. c	p. 722, 3a.	26. c	p. 726, 3c.	39. c	p. 731, 6b.

Chapter 33

CLASSIFICATION OF FINGERPRINTS

Questions:

1. The basic elements of the Henry System of fingerprint classification are the:

a. ridges.   c. type lines.
b. pattern areas.   d. bifurcations.

2. A line that splits into two and each one continues separately is called a(n):

a. ending ridge.   c. inclosure or island.
b. fork or bifurcation.   d. spur or hook.

3. A ridge line that splits into two and then rejoins forming an enclosed pocket is called a(n):

a. fork or bifurcation.
b. spur or hook.
c. ending ridge.
d. inclosure or island.

4. A ridge line that stops is called a(n):

a. dot.
b. ending ridge.
c. spur.
d. bridge.

5. A ridge line of minute length is called a(n):

a. point.
b. dot.
c. ending ridge.
d. bridge.

6. A _____ is a ridge line that connects one ridge to another.

a. spur or hook
b. trifurcation
c. double bifurcation
d. bridge

7. A ridge line that divides into three is called a:

a. bifurcation.
b. double bifurcation.
c. trifurcation.
d. bridge.

8. That part of the fingerprint that contains the ridges necessary to determine the classification is called the:

a. type lines.
b. core.
c. delta.
d. pattern area.

9. The innermost ridges which start as parallel lines, diverge, and bound the pattern area are called the:

a. type lines.
b. core.
c. delta.
d. center of divergence.

10. The imaginary point at which the type line diverge is called the:

a. core.
b. delta.
c. center of divergence.
d. shoulders.

11. The first fork or bifurcation nearest the center of divergence is called the:

a. core.
b. delta.
c. type lines.
d. shoulders.

12. The _____ is the approximate center of the pattern located on or within the innermost looping ridge.

    a. core
    b. delta
    c. center of divergence
    d. shoulders

13. All of the following are basic fingerprint groups except:

    a. arches.
    b. loops.
    c. whorls.
    d. accidentals.

14. A(n) _____ is a series of ridges that enter from one side of the pattern and flow without interruption to the other side with a slight rise in the center.

    a. tented arch
    b. plain arch
    c. ulnar loop
    d. radial loop

15. A(n) _____ is a series of ridges that flow from one side of the pattern to the other with a sharp rise in the center.

    a. tented arch
    b. plain arch
    c. ulnar loop
    d. radial loop

16. A(n) _____ is formed by one or more ridges entering one side of the pattern, curving around the core, and terminating on the same side at which they entered.

    a. arch
    b. loop
    c. whorl
    d. double loop

17. In a(n) _____ loop, the ridges flow in the direction of the thumb of the hand.

    a. inner
    b. outer
    c. ulnar
    d. radial

18. In a(n) _____ loop, the ridges flow in the direction of the little finger of the hand.

    a. inner
    b. outer
    c. ulnar
    d. radial

19. In order to classify loops according to the direction of the flow of ridges, it is necessary to know:

    a. the number of loops in each hand.
    b. the ridge count of the loop.
    c. which hand the impression came from.
    d. whether the subject is right- or left-handed.

20. A(n) _____ is a pattern in which one or more ridges revolve around the core.

a. whorl
b. arch

c. radial loop
d. ulnar loop

21. All whorls have two or more:

a. pattern areas.
b. cores.

c. deltas.
d. loops.

22. A _____, which resembles an ordinary loop, has a ridge which forms a circular pocket in the center of the pattern.

a. plain whorl
b. central pocket loop

c. double loop
d. lateral pocket loop

23. A(n) _____ consists of two separate but not necessarily unconnected loop formations.

a. ulnar loop
b. central pocket loop

c. accidental
d. double loop

24. The FBI no longer distinguishes between twinned loops and lateral pocket loops. Both forms are considered part of a single classification, the:

a. ulnar loop.
b. central pocket loop.

c. accidental.
d. double loop.

25. The _____ derives its name from the unusual formation of the ridge pattern which does not conform to any of the rules that apply to the other patterns.

a. plain whorl
b. central pocket loop

c. accidental
d. double loop

26. Marking the pattern symbol below each pattern on a fingerprint card is called:

a. blocking out.
b. ridge counting.

c. fingerprint classification.
d. primary classification.

27. A slanted line in the direction of the pattern is the symbol for a:

a. radial loop.
b. ulnar loop.

c. tented arch.
d. whorl.

28. In blocking out, the appropriate capital letter is placed under _____ for all patterns except the ulnar loop.

a. the thumb
b. the index finger

c. the little finger
d. all of the fingers

29. In blocking out, the appropriate small letter is placed under _____ for all patterns except the ulnar loop.

    a. the thumb
    b. the index finger

    c. all the fingers except the thumb
    d. all the fingers except the index

30. The classification of _____ depends largely on ridge counting.

    a. arches and loops
    b. loops and whorls

    c. arches and whorls
    d. whorls only

31. In classifying _____ , the ridge count is the number of ridges counted on an imaginary straight line drawn from the delta to the core.

    a. arches
    b. loops

    c. whorls
    d. whorls and loops

32. In classifying _____, a ridge count is made between a tracing line connecting the two deltas and the right delta. Depending on the position of the ridges in relation to the delta and the number of ridges counted will determine if it is inner, meeting, or outer.

    a. arches
    b. loops

    c. whorls
    d. whorls and loops

33. In determining the _____ classification, numerical values are assigned to each finger which is counted only when the finger is a whorl.

    a. final
    b. secondary

    c. sub-secondary
    d. primary

34. The _____ classification is the assignment of letters to the fingers. It takes the form of a fraction with the letters representing the right hand as the numerator and the letters representing the left hand as the denominator.

    a. final
    b. secondary

    c. sub-secondary
    d. primary

35. In a _____ classification, only loops and whorls on the three middle fingers are considered and are classified by ridge counting.

    a. final
    b. secondary

    c. sub-secondary
    d. primary

36. The _____ classification is a number indicating a ridge count on the little finger.

    a. final
    b. secondary

    c. sub-secondary
    d. primary

37. In the National Crime Information Center's fingerprint classification (NCIC FPC) system, each finger is represented by _____ characters.

 a. one   c. three
 b. two   d. four

38. An automated fingerprint identification system (AFIS) consists of two technological instruments: 1) a scanning machine which translates the images of a fingerprint into a _____; and 2) a computer.

 a. fingerprint pattern   c. Henry System subgroup
 b. numerical code   d. collection of minutiae

39. Minutiae are the points at which _____ lines end or split.

 a. type   c. ridge
 b. tracing   d. diverging

40. The AFIS scanning machine will record all of the following information concerning the minutiae of a fingerprint except:

 a. the *type* of minutiae, that is whether it is on a split or ending ridge line.
 b. the *position* of the minutiae with respect to a landmark such as the core and its direction with respect to the fingerprint pattern.
 c. the *ridge count* between each minutia and its four closest neighbors.
 d. The *pattern* group of which it is a part such as arches, loops, or whorls.

41. The AFIS scanning machine has the ability to process up to 100 minutiae for each fingerprint, although it can make an identification using as little as _____ minutiae.

 a. 2   c. 30
 b. 8   d. 40

42. The AFIS computer compares the numerical code of the "questioned" print with the _____ of the "known" prints on file.

 a. fingerprint patterns   c. Henry System subgroups
 b. numerical codes   d. minutiae

43. At the end of an AFIS search, the computer will list and rank, in probable order, the _____ most closely resemble the "questioned" print.

 a. individual fingerprints that
 b. numerical codes of the fingerprints that
 c. the names of the persons whose fingerprints
 d. fingerprint patterns that

44. In an AFIS search, _____ will make a decision on a possible match.

 a. the computer   c. a technician
 b. the investigator   d. a fingerprint expert

Answers:

1. a	p. 734, 2.	16. b	p. 740, 6.	31. b	p. 744, 8b.
2. b	p. 735, 2.	17. d	p. 740, 6a.	32. c	p. 745, 8b.
3. d	p. 735, 2.	18. c	p. 741, 6b.	33. d	p. 747, 9.
4. b	p. 735, 2.	19. c	p. 741, 6b.	34. b	p. 748, 10.
5. b	p. 735, 2.	20. a	p. 741, 7a.	35. c	p. 749, 11.
6. d	p. 735, 2.	21. c	p. 741, 7a.	36. a	p. 749, 12.
7. c	p. 735, 2.	22. b	p. 741, 7b.	37. b	p. 752, 15.
8. d	p. 736, 3a.	23. d	p. 741, 7c.	38. b	p. 756, 16.
9. a	p. 736, 3b.	24. d	p. 742, 7c.	39. c	p. 756, 16a.
10. c	p. 736, 3c.	25. c	p. 742, 7d.	40. d	p. 756, 16a.
11. b	p. 736, 3c.	26. a	p. 742, 8a.	41. b	p. 757, 16a.
12. a	p. 736, 3d.	27. b	p. 743, 8a.	42. b	p. 757, 16b.
13. d	p. 739, 4.	28. b	p. 743, 8a.	43. c	p. 757, 16b.
14. b	p. 739, 5a.	29. d	p. 743, 8a.	44. c	p. 757, 16b.
15. a	p. 739, 5b.	30. b	p. 743, 8b.		

Chapter 34

LAUNDRY AND DRY CLEANER MARKS

Questions:

1. An article of clothing with a laundry or dry cleaning mark found at the scene of the crime is important evidence because:

    a. it associates the owner of the garment with the crime scene.
    b. it indicates that the owner of the garment committed the crime.
    c. it associates the owner with this garment and perhaps other similar garments.
    d. it means that the person who committed the crime was concerned about his appearance.

2. Laundries and dry cleaners mark or tag the clothing they process:

    a. to help the customer in case he loses an article of clothing.
    b. to provide a means for police to identify an article of clothing.
    c. to make sure that the right garment is returned to each customer.
    d. to keep track of how much business each customer provides.

3. Clothing as a clue is often important in all of the following types of police cases except:

    a. crimes of violence such as murder, rape, assault, and robbery.
    b. buying and selling crimes such as narcotics and firearms violations.
    c. incidents involving unidentified persons and dead bodies.
    d. wanted person incidents involving tracing the whereabouts of a fugitive.

4. The line number is used by:

    a. the wholesaler to designate a particular retail store.
    b. the retailer to designate a particular wholesaler.
    c. the retailer to identify a particular customer.
    d. the wholesaler to identify a particular customer.

5. The name given to the number used to designate a particular customer is called the:

    a. line number.   c. customer's receipt number.
    b. customer identification number.   d. retail number.

6. If a laundry or dry cleaning mark or tag has been traced to a particular retailer, it is important because he will:

    a. have other clothes processed for the customer.
    b. be able to recognize the customer by sight.
    c. be able to confirm that it is a customer's receipt number.
    d. often be able to supply the name and address of the customer.

Answers:

    1. a   p. 760, 2.   3. b   p. 760, 4.   5. c   p. 761, 5b.
    2. c   p. 760, 3.   4. a   p. 761, 5a.   6. d   p. 761, 5b.

Chapter 35

CASTING

Questions:

1. Casting is a method of _____ of the objects that were used to make the impressions left at the crime scene.

    a. reproducing the outer surface   c. constructing a model
    b. making an exact replica   d. recording all of the fine details

2. The comparison of a cast of an impression from the crime scene with an object that is suspected of making the impression will help to establish that:

    a. the person who committed the crime was at the scene.
    b. the impression was actually found at the crime scene.
    c. the object, and hence its owner, was at the crime scene.
    d. the owner of the object is the person who committed the crime.

3. All of the following are conveniently reproduced by casting except:

a. shoe and tire impressions.　　c. bite marks.
b. fingerprints.　　　　　　　　 d. tool marks.

4. Both _____ and casting play an important part in the accurate recording of an impression.

a. taking notes　　　　　　c. photography
b. sketching　　　　　　　 d. verbal description

5. A cast will reproduce the _____ area of an impression, the part which gets the most wear and often has the most identifying characteristics.

a. indented　　　　c. curved
b. raised　　　　　 d. flat

6. All of the following are commonly used casting materials except:

a. plaster of paris.　　　　　c. silicone rubber.
b. class 1 dental stone.　　　 d. cyanoacrylate (Super Glue).

7. In order to represent the true size of the impression in a photograph, the investigator should:

a. measure the impression and make a note of it.
b. measure the cast of the impression and make a note of it.
c. write the true measurement on a photographic print.
d. place a ruler in the field of view.

8. If the receiving surface of the impression is a soft substance such as dust, sand, or flour, the investigator should:

a. only photograph it.
b. cast it according to the usual method.
c. spray it first with a quick-drying fixative and then cast it.
d. apply several coats of a spray wax such as "snow print wax" before casting it.

9. After the cast has been permitted to harden for approximately thirty minutes, at this time:

a. all extraneous material found in the impression should be removed.
b. it should be reinforced by laying on pieces of fine mesh wire or light, flat pieces of wood.
c. the date, case number, and initials of the investigator can be scratched on the upper surface for identification.
d. it should be washed and lightly brushed in water to remove adhering debris.

10. Casts should be made of a tool mark when:

    a. the mark displays many fine details suitable for casting.
    b. a good casting material such as silicone rubber is available.
    c. the investigator believes that a high quality reproduction will be the result.
    d. it is impractical to remove the impression to the laboratory for examination.

Answers:

1. a	p. 766, 1.	5. b	p. 766, 1.	9. c	p. 768, 2f.		
2. c	p. 766, 1.	6. d	p. 767, 2.	10. d	p. 768, 3.		
3. b	p. 766, 1.	7. d	p. 767, 2a.				
4. c	p. 766, 1.	8. c	p. 767, 2b.				

Chapter 36

VARIOUS IMPRESSIONS

Questions:

1. The evidential value of impressions made by a shoe, hand tool, or other article is based on the theory that:

    a. all physical objects are alike.
    b. two physical objects may be identical.
    c. no two physical objects are alike.
    d. most physical objects are alike.

2. There are two types of characteristics associated with an impression. First, there are the _____ characteristics which identify the kind, make, or model of the object that produced the impression.

    a. class   c. general
    b. group   d. ordinary

3. Second, there are the _____ characteristics which serve to identify the specific object that caused the impression.

    a. distinctive   c. specific
    b. individual   d. extraordinary

4. A _____ would be a class characteristic found on a tire.

    a. surface nick or cut   c. wear pattern
    b. a flat tire repair   d. tread pattern

5. The _____ would be an individual characteristic of a shoe.

a. size
b. shape

c. wear pattern
d. tread pattern

6. When dealing with a number of consecutive footprints, besides searching for individual characteristics of the prints, the investigator should attempt to discern from these prints:

a. the exact number made.
b. a distinctive walking pattern.

c. the distance that was walked.
d. the time of day of the walk.

7. The _____ deforms the surface, while the _____ merely deposits a layer of dust, liquid, mud, or perspiration on it.

a. foot impression...footprint
b. footprint...foot impression

c. shoe print...footprint
d. shoe impression...foot impression

8. A shoe print is found most often at the scene of a(n):

a. robbery.
b. arson.

c. home burglary.
d. office burglary.

9. A shoe print found on any surface should first be:

a. cast.
b. developed.

c. photographed.
d. lifted.

10. Surface footprints made with bare feet are called:

a. foot impressions.
b. bare footprints.

c. heel prints.
d. sole prints.

11. Often the prints made with bare feet can be developed by the usual methods used in connection with:

a. foot impressions.
b. shoe prints.

c. tire impressions.
d. latent fingerprints.

12. Palm prints are quite frequently discovered at a crime scene, particularly in _____ cases.

a. arson
b. burglary

c. homicide
d. robbery

13. The friction ridges of the palms and fingers contain an additional means of identification; each ridge is dotted by pores which differ in all of the following except:

a. color.
b. position.

c. size.
d. shape.

14. In a situation where a suspect's fingerprints are available for comparison and only a partial latent fingerprint has been developed, a study of the pore pattern can be used when there are not enough corresponding _____ characteristics to compare.

    a. delta
    b. flexure line
    c. type line
    d. friction ridge

15. Poroscopy is rarely used because:

    a. comparing friction ridges is a more accurate identification method.
    b. there are too many visible pore patterns, hence it is too confusing.
    c. the outline of pores are usually not clearly visible and are often too delicate and easily destroyed.
    d. pore patterns can't be developed with powder or fuming methods.

16. Earprints found at the crime scene are usually on:

    a. pillows.
    b. head phones.
    c. telephone receivers.
    d. outside doors and windows.

17. Latent earprints are usually developed with:

    a. fingerprint powders.
    b. fuming techniques.
    c. ninhydrin.
    d. Super Glue.

18. After developing a latent earprint, the next step is to:

    a. classify it.
    b. lift it.
    c. compare it to a suspect's earprint.
    d. photograph it.

19. In taking comparison earprints, the investigator should:

    a. press the ear firmly on the card.
    b. press the ear lightly on the card.
    c. attempt to duplicate the amount of pressure of the original earprint.
    d. use whatever pressure makes the clearest print.

20. Earprints found on a door may be useful to the investigator _____ of the suspect.

    a. to estimate the height
    b. to estimate the weight
    c. to estimate the head size
    d. only for the positive identification

21. All of the following statements concerning earprints are true except:

    a. Earprints are an excellent means of positive identification.
    b. No two ears have been found to be identical.
    c. Earprint structure patterns are unique and remain constant throughout life.
    d. Earprints of twins, triplets, and quadruplets have been found to be identical.

22. All of the following statements concerning car movement and tire impressions are true except:

    a. In cars going forward in a straight line, only the front tire tracks will be visible.
    b. Oil drops on hard surfaces will taper in the direction of travel.
    c. Tire impressions in important cases should be measured, photographed, and cast.
    d. The FBI maintains a collection of photographs of tire tread patterns.

23. When a metal instrument is applied to a relatively hard surface, it leaves behind what investigator's call a:

    a. tool print.   c. tool impression.
    b. tool mark.   d. tool pattern.

24. If a metal instrument, which has manufacturing defects or has been ground, sharpened, or used extensively, is applied to a soft metal, it will probably leave _____ characteristics.

    a. both class and individual   c. only individual
    b. only class   d. no identifiable

25. When the defects of the tool are sufficient in number and are reflected in the impression, it is possible for the laboratory expert to conclude:

    a. only that certain tools could not have made the impression.
    b. only that a certain type of tool made the impression.
    c. that a particular tool made this particular impression.
    d. nothing certain about the origin of the impression.

26. Tool mark evidence can be useful for all of the following purposes except:

    a. to identify the type of tool.
    b. to identify the individual tool.
    c. to identify the store in which the tool was purchased.
    d. to link other crimes to the tool and establish a common modus operandi.

27. Two of the most common types of tool marks are: one in which the tool is pressed into a surface; and the other in which the tool _____ the surface.

    a. hits or bangs   c. stabs or punctures
    b. crushes   d. is drawn across

28. Tool marks are usually found in _____ investigations.

    a. burglary   c. narcotics
    b. homicide   d. robbery

29. All of the following are reasons that should seriously affect the decision whether to remove property bearing a tool mark except:

a. the importance of the case.
b. the probative significance of the tool impression.
c. the portability, size, and value of the property being moved.
d. the wishes of the employees of the building.

30. All of the following statements concerning the collection of tool mark evidence are true except:

a. The item removed as evidence should be marked with the investigator's initials and the date.
b. Before the tool mark is disturbed or altered by casting or removal, it should be photographed.
c. Two types of photographs are required: one showing tool marks together with the background for identification and location; and a close-up photograph to show minute details.
d. A cast of the tool mark should be made whether or not the investigator decides to remove the original evidence.

31. A cast of a tool mark in a door can be satisfactorily accomplished with:

a. modeling clay.
b. plaster of paris.
c. dental stone.
d. Super Glue.

32. Chemical etching is a method used by investigators to _____ serial numbers on metal objects that have been filed away.

a. inscribe
b. stamp
c. restore
d. remove

33. The investigator uses chemical etching methods in order to:

a. identify the file marks on the surface of an object.
b. establish ownership of a stolen object.
c. identify the manufacturer of an object.
d. identify the person who stole the object.

34. After metal has been stamped with a serial number, the compressed metal below the surface compared with the surrounding metal will:

a. remain fundamentally the same in molecular structure.
b. have a visibly altered appearance.
c. react differently in a chemical reaction.
d. react similarly in a chemical reaction.

35. Chemical etching causes the serial numbers that have been filed or ground away to become faintly visible in the presence of an "etching solution" which is usually a(n):

    a. concentrated acid or base.   c. organic solvent.
    b. dilute acid or base.   d. inorganic solvent.

36. During chemical etching, it is important to photograph the numbers immediately as they appear because:

    a. of evidence requirements.
    b. of the danger of prolonged exposure to chemicals.
    c. of the difficult photography involved.
    d. the numbers may disappear.

37. To halt the chemical reaction after etching, add:

    a. more acid or base.   c. organic solvents.
    b. water.   d. inorganic solvents.

38. All of the following are natural characteristics of teeth which can be used for identification except:

    a. size.   c. spacing.
    b. shape.   d. wear.

39. All of the following are acquired characteristics which can be used for identification except:

    a. breaking.   c. loss.
    b. direction of growth.   d. fillings.

40. A dentist trained in the recovery and analysis of dental evidence is called a forensic:

    a. odontologist.   c. periodontist.
    b. anthropologist.   d. orthodontist.

41. After comparing a bite mark with an exemplar and finding only one unexplained discrepancy, an expert would conclude that:

    a. the bite mark was consistent with the exemplar.
    b. the bite mark and the exemplar could have been made by the same teeth.
    c. the teeth should be compared again.
    d. the bite mark and the exemplar were of different origin.

42. In bite mark analysis, a positive identification is _____ made.

    a. often   c. rarely
    b. sometimes   d. never

43. Photographing a bite mark requires two different kinds of shots: (1) a close-up of at least one-to-one size; and (2) a _____ shot.

   a. wide-angle
   b. telephoto
   c. reenactment
   d. location or orientation

44. The primary reason that a cast will often be made of a bite mark is that:

   a. a cast records fine details sometimes missed by a photograph.
   b. a bite mark is frequently made on a perishable object and needs to be preserved.
   c. the cast is a tangible object and hence more convincing as evidence.
   d. the cast is a back-up in case the photographer overexposes or otherwise destroys the film.

45. Bite marks appear in a variety of forms including the characteristic doughnut and _____ patterns.

   a. single-horseshoe
   b. double-horseshoe
   c. circular
   d. semicircular

46. In homicide and assault cases where the investigator believes biting was involved, the suspect should be checked primarily for:

   a. broken teeth.
   b. accidental bites made on himself.
   c. defensive bites made by the victim.
   d. old bite marks from previous encounters.

47. Bite marks occur frequently in all of the following situations except:

   a. robbery attempts.
   b. child abuse.
   c. sexual assaults or homicides.
   d. as defensive wounds in non-sexual assaults and homicides.

48. In sexual assault cases, biting is often followed by a sucking of the skin which sometimes results in a _____ which is the accumulation of blood in the tissues following a rupture of the blood vessel.

   a. hemorrhage
   b. abscess
   c. tumor
   d. hematoma

49. Because the color and appearance of bite marks change with the passage of time, bite marks, on both live and deceased victims, should be photographed at intervals over a period of:

   a. a few hours.
   b. one day.
   c. two days.
   d. five days.

50. In order to avoid distortion when photographing on a curved surface, it is essential to position the camera _____ to the bite mark.

a. perpendicular
b. parallel

c. at an oblique angle
d. at an acute angle

51. Because the shape and appearance of the bite mark will sometimes change, when photographing a bite mark on a living victim, it is helpful to have him:

a. take the position he was in at the time of the bite.
b. stand.
c. sit.
d. lie down.

52. By examining the _____ from a bite wound, it is possible to determine the blood type and the secretor status of the assailant as well as make a positive identification of him through DNA analysis.

a. loose skin
b. blood

c. saliva
d. teeth marks

Answers:

1. c	p. 770, 1.	19. c	p. 775, 7b.	37. b	p. 783, 10e.		
2. a	p. 770, 1.	20. a	p. 775, 7c.	38. d	p. 784, 11.		
3. b	p. 770, 1.	21. d	p. 776, 7c.	39. b	p. 784, 11.		
4. d	p. 770, 1.	22. a	p. 776, 7.	40. a	p. 784, 11.		
5. c	p. 770, 1.	23. b	p. 776, 8.	41. d	p. 784, 11.		
6. b	p. 771, 2b.	24. a	p. 778, 8.	42. c	p. 784, 11.		
7. a	p. 771, 3.	25. c	p. 778, 8.	43. d	p. 784, 11a.		
8. d	p. 771, 3.	26. c	p. 778, 8a.	44. a	p. 785, 11a.		
9. c	p. 772, 3.	27. d	p. 778, 8b.	45. b	p. 785, 11b.		
10. d	p. 772, 4.	28. a	p. 779, 8c.	46. c	p. 785, 11b.		
11. d	p. 772, 4.	29. d	p. 779, 8c.	47. a	p. 785, 11b.		
12. b	p. 773, 5.	30. d	p. 780, 8e.	48. d	p. 786, 11b.		
13. a	p. 773, 6.	31. a	p. 780, 8e.	49. d	p. 786, 11b.		
14. d	p. 773, 6a.	32. c	p. 781, 10.	50. a	p. 786, 11b.		
15. c	p. 774, 6a.	33. b	p. 782, 10a.	51. a	p. 786, 11b.		
16. d	p. 775, 7a.	34. c	p. 782, 10b.	52. c	p. 786, 11b.		
17. a	p. 775, 7a.	35. b	p. 782, 10b.				
18. d	p. 775, 7a.	36. d	p. 783, 10e.				

Chapter 37
BROKEN GLASS

Questions:

1. All of the following are ingredients of glass except:

   a. silica sand (silicon dioxide). c. salt (sodium chloride).
   b. soda ash (sodium carbonate). d. limestone (calcium carbonate).

2. Because of its thickness, the _____ glass used in store windows is especially resistant to breakage.

   a. window c. tempered
   b. plate d. safety

3. _____ glass, used on the rear and side windows of automobiles, will fragment into thousands of tiny cubes when broken.

   a. Window c. Tempered
   b. Plate d. Safety

4. _____ glass , used on windshields, consists of two panes of window glass separated by a thin sheet of transparent adhesive plastic.

   a. Flat c. Tempered
   b. Plate d. Safety

5. _____ glass is a heat- and corrosion-resistant form used in headlight lamps, laboratory vessels, and pyrex cookware.

   a. Soda-lime-silica c. Borosilicate
   b. Laminated d. Lead

6. When a large amount of glass is found on the floor inside of the broken window of a burned-out building indicates:

   a. that the window was broken from the outside.
   b. that the window was broken from the inside.
   c. that fire created a vacuum drawing the glass inwards.
   d. nothing definite concerning the direction from which the window was broken.

7. Because glass will withstand more bending then stretching, it will break:

   a. first on the side of impact.
   b. first on the side opposite the point of impact.
   c. on both sides simultaneously.
   d. first on the side of concentric fractures.

8. The spoke-like cracks in glass emanating from the area of impact are called:

    a. radial fractures.
    b. concentric fractures.

    c. rib marks.
    d. spiral fractures.

9. _____ are the secondary cracks which open on the side of impact due to forces working in the opposite direction of the initial blow.

    a. Radial fractures
    b. Concentric fractures

    c. Rib marks
    d. Conchoidal striations

10. Because radial cracks occur prior to concentric ones, all of the concentric lines:

    a. will cross radial lines at both ends.
    b. will cross a radial line at one end.
    c. are stopped when they meet radial lines at both ends.
    d. will be stopped when they meet radial lines at one end.

11. _____are the curved lines of stress that are faintly visible on a piece of broken glass that run almost parallel to one surface and then curve to become nearly perpendicular to the opposite surface.

    a. Concentric fractures
    b. Spiral fractures

    c. Rib marks
    d. Hackle marks

12. From a single isolated piece of broken glass, the investigator _____reliably determine the direction of impact.

    a. can
    b. cannot
    c. can only if the rib marks are perpendicular to one side
    d. can only if the rib marks are parallel to one side

13. When reassembling a window in order to determine the direction of impact, the first consideration is to identify the inside and the outside surfaces. The second consideration is to identify:

    a. radial and concentric fractures.
    b. rib marks.
    c. the physical fit of the pieces.
    d. the position of the pieces with respect to the inside and outside of the window.

14. Radial fractures have rib marks that are:

    a. parallel to the side of impact.
    b. parallel to the side opposite the side of impact.
    c. perpendicular to the side of impact.
    d. perpendicular to the side opposite the side of impact.

15. The 4R rule states that _____ on _____ are at _____ to _____.

    a. radial cracks...rib marks...the reverse side...right angles
    b. radial cracks...rib marks...right angles...the reverse side
    c. rib marks...radial cracks...right angles...the reverse side
    d. rib marks...radial cracks...the reverse side...right angles

16. Concentric fractures have rib marks that are:

    a. parallel to the side of impact.
    b. parallel to the side opposite the side of impact.
    c. perpendicular to the side of impact.
    d. perpendicular to the side opposite the side of impact.

17. All of the following do not readily lend themselves to glass fracture examination to determine the side of impact except:

    a. window glass broken with a hammer.
    b. window glass after breaking that falls on a hard surface and breaks again.
    c. tempered glass that will "dice" on impact.
    d. window glass broken by heat, wind, or explosion that does not have a point of impact.

18. Glass broken by the intense heat of fire will:

    a. have rib marks perpendicular to the source of the fire.
    b. have rib marks perpendicular to the side opposite the source of the fire.
    c. have no rib marks.
    d. fall outward from the building.

19. On safety glass, the impact side:

    a. is the side that bends inward.
    b. is the side that bends outward.
    c. is the side that does not bend.
    d. cannot readily be determined.

20. _____ marks are irregular lines found on the impact edge of glass that is broken with great force, formed when two glass surfaces scrape against each other.

    a. Tension   c. Rib
    b. Stress   d. Hackle

21. When a bullet penetrates glass, it leaves a:

    a. smaller, saucer-shaped entrance hole and a larger, clean-cut exit hole.
    b. larger, clean-cut entrance hole and a smaller, saucer-shaped exit hole.
    c. larger, saucer-shaped entrance hole and a smaller clean-cut exit hole.
    d. smaller, clean-cut entrance hole and a larger, saucer-shaped exit hole.

22. When a shot is fired from a very short range or from a very long range, it is easier to determine whether or not a bullet has broken the glass by:

    a. examining the entrance hole of the glass.
    b. examining the exit hole on the glass.
    c. examining the radial and concentric fractures.
    d. locating the projectile.

23. Determining the direction of the bullet when penetrating glass can be done easily by a visual inspection of the smooth entrance hole and the crater-shaped exit hole or by:

    a. examining the glass particles.
    b. running the fingers across the surface of the glass.
    c. gunshot residue tests.
    d. locating rib marks on the glass.

24. In determining the angle of fire, when the bullet is shot from the right side, it will leave:

    a. considerable chipping on the right side of the glass and little chipping on the left.
    b. little chipping on the right side and considerable chipping on the left.
    c. a circular hole with chipping distributed uniformly.
    d. an elliptical hole with chipping distributed uniformly.

25. In determining which bullet hole was made first, the first bullet hole will have radial cracks that will be:

    a. complete and uninterrupted.
    b. terminated by the radial cracks of the second bullet.
    c. terminated by both the radial and concentric cracks of the second bullet.
    d. terminated by the concentric cracks of the first bullet.

26. In determining which bullet hole was made first, the second bullet hole will have radial cracks that will be:

    a. complete and uninterrupted.
    b. terminated by only the radial cracks of the first bullet.
    c. terminated by only the concentric cracks of the first bullet.
    d. terminated by both the radial and concentric cracks of the first bullet.

27. The best method of determining the type of weapon or ammunition used to make a bullet hole in a window when the spent bullets, the cartridges, and the weapon have not been located is to:

    a. measure the size and shape of the bullet hole to determine the caliber.
    b. examine the radial and concentric cracks on the window.
    c. test fire the different types of weapons into similar glass under similar conditions.
    d. make an educated guess based on the size of the hole.

28. When a laboratory glass examiner renders an opinion of positive identity, he is saying that this particular piece of glass _____ with a second piece of glass as part of the same window.

    a. is similar to the one that was joined together
    b. has properties consistent with the one that was joined together
    c. was joined together
    d. was either definitely joined or definitely not joined together

29. In a physical fit, not only are the two pieces of glass similar in surface pattern and shape but also they lock into place and resist movement because the _____ mesh.

    a. radial cracks   c. hackle marks
    b. concentric cracks   d. rib marks

30. In a hit-and-run motor vehicle accident, broken headlight glass is most important for:

    a. indicating the kind of car involved.
    b. establishing it was a car that injured the victim.
    c. indicating the cause of death.
    d. linking a suspect's automobile to the victim.

31. Before attempting a physical fit of the "known" and the "questioned" piece of glass, the laboratory examiner will first:

    a. wash and polish each piece carefully.
    b. screen the pieces to be certain they are similar in obvious physical characteristics.
    c. chip minute particles off each piece to check for density and refractive index.
    d. try to see if any of the other collected pieces fit.

32. Particles of glass from the same pane of glass _____ in chemical and physical properties.

    a. are usually identical   c. may vary greatly
    b. may vary slightly   d. are usually not similar

33. A substance will float or sink in a liquid depending on its _____ in comparison with the liquid.

    a. volume   c. density
    b. weight   d. refractive index

34. If two glass particles become suspended at the same level in a density gradient tube, it may be concluded that _____ come from the same source.

    a. they must have   c. it is highly unlikely that they
    b. they could have   d. they did not

35. If two glass particles become suspended at different levels in a density gradient tube, it may be concluded that _____ come from a different source.

    a. they must have
    b. they could have
    c. it is highly unlikely that they
    d. they did not

36. _____ is the bending of light when it passes at an angle through substances of varying density.

    a. Lucidity
    b. Translucence
    c. Reflection
    d. Refraction

37. When a clear glass particle is immersed in a clear liquid having the same refractive index, it will:

    a. fluoresce.
    b. reflect light.
    c. appear.
    d. disappear.

38. A hot stage is an attachment to a microscope used to determine the refractive index of a particle by heating the liquid it is immersed in until it reaches the same:

    a. temperature.
    b. density.
    c. refractive index.
    d. buoyancy.

39. By comparing the "known" particle with the "questioned" particle, the glass examiner may conclude any one of the following except:

    a. identity of source.
    b. non-identity of source.
    c. probability of source.
    d. possibility of source.

40. The degree of probability that a glass particle has come from a particular source is determined by:

    a. a mathematical equation based on the relative frequency of density and refractive index values.
    b. the FBI's statistical data on the relative frequency of density and refractive index values.
    c. the application of the laws of probability to the theoretical distribution of physical properties.
    d. an educated inference based on years of experience.

41. When collecting glass as evidence at the crime scene, the investigator should:

    a. collect all of the broken glass available.
    b. collect a generous sample from each broken glass object.
    c. be guided by the investigative purpose this evidence may serve.
    d. consult with the laboratory expert before collecting any glass.

42. When examining broken glass at the scene of a burglary, the investigator should first turn his attention to determining:

    a. if there is evidence on the glass such as blood or fingerprints.
    b. the direction of impact.
    c. if a physical fit is possible.
    d. the source of any particles found.

43. When collecting glass as evidence, several samples of approximately 1 square-inch should be removed from the area of the pane around the break, if the investigator is to:

    a. discover evidence on the glass.
    b. determine the direction of impact.
    c. establish a physical fit.
    d. compare particles for density and refractive index.

44. Collecting all of the glass from a broken window is necessary for each of the following investigative problems except:

    a. determining the direction of impact.
    b. determining a physical fit.
    c. determining if glass particles are from a particular window.
    d. determining which of several shots were fired first.

45. Glass can be marked for identification with all of the following except:

    a. a diamond point or carborundum point.
    b. a ball-point pen.
    c. adhesive tape with the investigator's initials on it.
    d. a grease pencil.

Answers:

1. c	p. 792, 2.	16. c	p. 798, 3f.	31. b	p. 804, 5c.
2. b	p. 793, 2b.	17. a	p. 798, 3g.	32. b	p. 804, 6.
3. c	p. 793, 2c.	18. c	p. 798, 3g.	33. c	p. 805, 6a.
4. d	p. 793, 2d.	19. a	p. 799, 3g.	34. b	p. 805, 6a.
5. c	p. 793, 2e.	20. d	p. 799, 3h.	35. a	p. 805, 6a.
6. d	p. 794, 3.	21. d	p. 800, 4a.	36. d	p. 806, 6b.
7. b	p. 794, 3a.	22. d	p. 800, 4a.	37. d	p. 806, 6b.
8. a	p. 795, 3b.	23. b	p. 801, 4b.	38. c	p. 806, 6b.
9. b	p. 795, 3c.	24. b	p. 801, 4c.	39. a	p. 807, 6c.
10. c	p. 796, 3c.	25. a	p. 801, 4d.	40. b	p. 807, 6c.
11. c	p. 796, 3d.	26. d	p. 801, 4d.	41. c	p. 807, 7.
12. b	p. 796, 3e.	27. c	p. 801, 4e.	42. a	p. 807, 7a.
13. a	p. 797, 3e.	28. c	p. 802, 5a.	43. d	p. 808, 7a.
14. d	p. 797, 3f.	29. d	p. 803, 5a.	44. c	p. 809, 7c.
15. c	p. 797, 3f.	30. d	p. 803, 5b.	45. b	p. 809, 7c.

Chapter 38

STAINS, TRACES, CHEMICAL ANALYSIS

Questions:

1. A(n) _____ is an arrangement of black lines on a photographic plate formed by burning a substance and having the resulting light dispersed through a prism. It is useful for analyzing inorganic substances, such as paint.

 a. x-ray diffraction   c. spectrograph
 b. electron microscope   d. spectrophotometer

2. A(n) _____ provides an absorption spectrum that detects tiny differences in organic materials, such as inks, dyes, and lipsticks.

 a. x-ray diffraction   c. spectrograph
 b. electron microscope   d. spectrophotometer

3. A(n) _____ analysis is useful for distinguishing substances with a crystalline structure such as grease stains, shoe smudges, and barbiturates.

 a. x-ray diffraction   c. spectrograph
 b. electron microscope   d. spectrophotometer

4. A(n) _____ is useful for examining clue materials such as dust, metals, fibers, inks, and other materials whose particle size and distribution cannot be differentiated by less sensitive instruments.

 a. x-ray diffraction   c. spectrograph
 b. electron microscope   d. neutron activation analysis

5. _____ measures the wavelength and intensity of the radiation given off by the evidence sample after it is subjected to stream of neutrons. It is an effective tool for determining the presence of gunpowder residue on the back of the firing hand.

 a. X-ray diffraction   c. Chromatography
 b. Electron microscope   d. Neutron activation analysis

Answers:

 1. c p. 818, 1b. 3. a p. 820, 3.   5. d p. 821, 5.
 2. d p. 819, 2.   4. b p. 821, 4.

Chapter 39
FIREARMS

Questions:

1. _____ , the only Federal agency to have authorized access to the records of gun manufacturers, importers, wholesalers, and retailers, established the National Firearms Tracing Center in 1972.

    a. ATF   c. IRS
    b. FBI   d. OSI

2. If a gun found at the crime scene had been lost or stolen, a firearms trace will lead to the identification of the:

    a. lawful owner.   c. the finder.
    b. the user.   d. the thief.

3. The minimum description of a firearm should contain the following information in the order given: _____, serial number, and finish.

    a. type, caliber, make, model   c. caliber, make, model, type
    b. make, model, caliber, type   d. caliber, type, make, model

4. Colt, Iver Johnson, and Smith and Wesson are examples of a firearm's:

    a. model.   c. type.
    b. make.   d. caliber.

5. _____ is a term describing in general the manner of operation such as revolver, automatic, and semi-automatic.

    a. Model   c. Type
    b. Make   d. Composition

6. _____ is a term that describes the color and surface of the firearm such as blue, nickel, and parkerized.

    a. Color   c. Material
    b. Finish   d. Composition

7. The main reason why a serial number alone does not always identify a particular firearm is that:

    a. the firearm may be stolen or lost.
    b. the firearm may have its number altered.
    c. the firearm records may have been lost.
    d. there may be several firearms with the same number.

8. Firearms identification is concerned primarily with two problems: first, from a bullet or cartridge case found at the scene of the crime to determine the kind of firearm used; and second, whether a(n) _____ "suspected" firearm was used.

a. particular make of
b. particular model of

c. individual
d. particular type of

9. The _____ are the properties of a bullet which remain intact after firing and serve to indicate the nature of the firearm for which it was intended.

a. individual manufacturing characteristics
b. general or class manufacturing characteristics
c. individual rifling impressions
d. general or class rifling impressions

10. The _____ are an additional set of characteristics which are stamped on a bullet after it is discharged which helps in identifying the type and make of the gun.

a. individual manufacturing characteristics
b. general or class manufacturing characteristics
c. individual rifling impressions
d. general or class rifling impressions

11. The _____ are a set of individual characteristics which are impressed on a bullet after discharge which serve to identify an individual gun.

a. individual manufacturing characteristics
b. general or class manufacturing characteristics
c. individual rifling impressions
d. general or class rifling impressions

12. Among the general manufacturing characteristics of a bullet are the knurled grooves on the curved surface called:

a. cannelures.
b. contour or shape.

c. land impressions.
d. groove impressions.

13. Shotgun pellets are identified by:

a. cannelures.
b. the diameter.

c. contour or shape.
d. size and weight.

14. The _____ is the result of cutting grooves in the barrel and serves to impart spin to the bullet.

a. rifling
b. diameter

c. caliber
d. pitch

15. The _____ are the raised ribs running in a spiral lengthwise through the barrel.

    a. lands   c. pitch
    b. grooves   d. cannelures

16. The lands are impressed on the barrel by the cutting of:

    a. ridges.   c. pitch.
    b. grooves.   d. cannelures.

17. There are a(n) _____ number of lands than (and) grooves on the interior of the barrel.

    a. greater   c. equal
    b. lesser   d. uneven

18. Lands and grooves are important to firearms identification because they impart _____ the bullet when the gun is fired.

    a. spin to   c. direction of spiral to
    b. a smooth surface to   d. impressions on

19. Individual characteristics on a fired bullet are caused by imperfections in the barrel from all of the following except:

    a. manufacturing.   c. wear and rust.
    b. storage.   d. repeated firings.

20. In order to determine whether the fatal bullet was fired from a particular gun, the evidence bullet is compared with a test bullet fired into:

    a. the air.   c. water or cotton.
    b. a mattress.   d. metal or some other hard surface.

21. In order to determine whether the evidence bullet and the test bullet were fired from the same gun, both bullets are studied under the comparison microscope to discover matching _____ caused by the lands and grooves of the gun barrel.

    a. spaces   c. smooth areas
    b. striations   d. spiral indentations

22. _____ , a class characteristic of the case, can be divided first into rim, rimless, and semi-or auto-rim, and second into straight, tapered, or necked.

    a. Caliber   c. Manufacture
    b. Composition   d. Shape

23. _____, which is a class characteristic of cases, may be brass, nickel-plated, copper, plated steel, paper, or plastic.

    a. Caliber   c. Manufacture
    b. Composition   d. Shape

24. Firing pin indentations, breech face markings, extractor marks, and ejector marks are important _____ characteristics of _____.

    a. class... bullets.   c. individual...bullets.
    b. class... cases.   d. individual...cases.

25. The common type of powder used in ammunition for small firearms is:

    a. smokeless.   c. semi-smokeless.
    b. black.   d. grey.

26. When a gun is fired, invisible primer residues are dispersed throughout the area within _____ feet of the discharge.

    a. 2   c. 10
    b. 4   d. 20

27. In the Gunshot Primer Residue (GSR) Test, invisible particles of gunshot primer, particularly the elements of antimony and _____, are collected from the hands of a shooting suspect.

    a. barium   c. nickel
    b. lead   d. copper

28. If the Gunshot Primer Residue (GSR) Test is positive, that is, elevated levels of gunshot primer elements are present on the hands of the suspect, it indicates that:

    a. the suspect fired a firearm.
    b. the suspect handled a discharged firearm.
    c. the suspect was in the presence of a discharged firearm.
    d. no conclusion can be drawn.

29. If there is a negative result from the GSR Test, that is, elevated levels of gunshot primer elements are not present on the hands of the suspect, this indicates that:

    a. the suspect did not shoot a firearm.
    b. the suspect had not handled a firearm.
    c. the suspect was not in the presence of a discharged firearm.
    d. no conclusion can be drawn.

30. Failure to detect gunshot primer on the hands of a suspect who actually fired a gun could be due to all of the following reasons except:

 a. The GSR Test is often inaccurate.
 b. Too many hours had elapsed and the primer residue rubbed off.
 c. The suspect washed his hands.
 d. 22 caliber ammunition often does not contain antimony and barium.

31. When a victim of a fatal shooting has gunshot primer particles on his hand, one can conclude that:

 a. there was a homicide.
 b. there was a suicide.
 c. there was a struggle for the gun.
 d. no conclusion can be drawn.

32. GSR evidence is collected by swabbing the hands of the suspect with a 5 percent solution of:

 a. hydrochloric acid.
 b. nitric acid.
 c. sulfuric acid.
 d. hydrogen peroxide.

33. GSR evidence can be tested by any of the following methods except:

 a. neutron activation analysis (NAA).
 b. atomic absorption spectrophotometry (AA).
 c. trace metal detection technique (TMDT).
 d. scanning electron microscopy/energy dispersive x-ray analysis (SEM/EDX).

34. The Walker test for powder detects the presence of _____ and is designed to reproduce the pattern of powder residue about the bullet hole.

 a. antimony
 b. barium
 c. nitrites
 d. lead fouling

35. All of the following types of photography and radiography can be used to provide a pattern of the powder residue around the bullet hole area except:

 a. process film photography.
 b. infrared photography.
 c. soft x-ray radiography.
 d. neutron radiography.

36. Trace Metal Detection Technique (TMDT) is a useful means of determining whether a person's hand or clothing has recently been in contact with:

 a. a metal object.
 b. a gun specifically.
 c. gunshot powder residue.
 d. explosives.

37. In TMDT the surface (usually the hand) to be examined is treated with a test solution and then placed under:

 a. incandescent light.
 b. ultraviolet light.
 c. infrared light.
 d. soft x-rays.

38. A photograph of the fluorescent pattern of a gun will show the metal trace pattern in colors that are characteristic of the metal. This photograph can be compared to photographs of distinctive patterns or _____ which are specific to types, makes, models, and calibers.

    a. archetypes   c. specimens
    b. examples   d. signatures

39. An identifiable fingerprint is _____ found on a gun used in a crime.

    a. always   c. rarely
    b. commonly   d. never

Answers:

1. a	p. 828, 2.	14. a	p. 835, 6a.	27. a	p. 840, 8.		
2. a	p. 829, 2.	15. a	p. 835, 6a.	28. c	p. 840, 8a.		
3. c	p. 830, 4.	16. b	p. 835, 6a.	29. d	p. 840, 8a.		
4. b	p. 830, 4b.	17. c	p. 835, 6a.	30. a	p. 840, 8a.		
5. c	p. 830, 4d.	18. d	p. 835, 6a.	31. d	p. 841, 8b.		
6. b	p. 831, 4f.	19. b	p. 835, 6a.	32. b	p. 841, 8b.		
7. d	p. 831, 4g.	20. c	p. 836, 6a.	33. c	p. 841, 8d.		
8. c	p. 834, 6.	21. b	p. 836, 6a.	34. c	p. 842, 9.		
9. b	p. 834, 6a.	22. d	p. 837, 6b.	35. d	p. 843, 10.		
10. d	p. 834, 6a.	23. b	p. 837, 6b.	36. a	p. 843, 11.		
11. c	p. 834, 6a.	24. d	p. 837, 6b.	37. b	p. 843, 11.		
12. a	p. 834, 6a.	25. a	p. 839, 7.	38. d	p. 845, 11d.		
13. d	p. 835, 6a.	26. c	p. 840, 8.	39. c	p. 845, 12.		

Chapter 40

TESTS FOR INTOXICATION

Questions:

1. In a homicide investigation, it is important to determine the relative sobriety of:

    a. the suspect only.   c. both the suspect and the victim.
    b. the victim only.   d. neither the suspect nor the victim.

2. All of the following are effects of alcohol consumption except:

    a. acting as a stimulant.   c. slowing down brain activity.
    b. acting as a depressant.   d. loss of coordination.

3. The taking of samples of blood and urine for intoxication tests is considered:

a. to be a violation of a suspect's rights.
b. not to be a violation of a suspect's rights.
c. to be legal only under a court order.
d. to be legal only if the suspect does it voluntarily.

4. The most direct and reliable way of measuring alcohol concentration in a person's blood is by means of an analysis of:

a. physical movements.
b. blood.
c. urine.
d. breath.

5. Breath tests are most commonly used in _____ investigations.

a. homicide
b. assault
c. suicide
d. motor vehicle accident

6. Blood specimens should be taken by:

a. by the investigator.
b. trained forensic laboratory personnel.
c. a physician or trained medical personnel.
d. by either a physician or an investigator.

Answers:

1. c   p. 850, 1.   3. b   p. 852, 6.   5. d   p. 853, 7.
2. a   p. 851, 2.   4. b   p. 853, 7.   6. c   p. 853, 8.

Chapter 41

TRACING MATERIALS AND DETECTIVE DYES

Questions:

1. Methylene blue, which in the presence of moisture turns into a deep-staining dye, and uranyl phosphate, which fluoresces under ultraviolet, are examples of substances called:

a. tracing powders.
b. taggants.
c. radioactive tracers.
d. chemical detectors.

2. A tracing material which on touching the skin will be converted to a dye by the moisture is called a:

a. staining powder.
b. fluorescent powder.
c. chemical detector.
d. taggant.

3. An ultraviolet lamp is used to detect _____ on the hands of suspects who have come into contact with this tracing material.

    a. staining powder
    b. fluorescent powder

    c. chemical detectors
    d. radioactive substances

4. Tracing materials may be useful in investigating all of the following crimes except:

    a. systematic petty larcenies.
    b. false alarms.

    c. random acts of violence.
    d. bombing cases.

5. Both chemical detectors and fluorescent substances can be used as tracing materials in:

    a. burglaries.
    b. gasoline thefts.

    c. false alarms.
    d. bombing cases.

6. As an aid to investigating explosions, it has been suggested that _____ could be added to explosives which upon detonation could be collected and traced to the source of the explosive.

    a. staining powder
    b. fluorescent powder

    c. chemical additives or taggants
    d. radioactive substances

7. A survey meter will detect _____ used as tracing materials.

    a. staining powders
    b. fluorescent powders

    c. chemical additives
    d. radioactive substances

Answers:

1. a	p. 857, 1.	4. c	p. 858, 3.	7. d	p. 861, 4.
2. a	p. 858, 2a.	5. b	p. 861, 3d.		
3. b	p. 858, 2b.	6. c	p. 861, 3e.		

Chapter 42

HAIRS AND FIBERS

Questions:

1. When comparing the evidence sample (a) and the standard sample (b) of hair under the microscope, possible findings may be any one of the following except:

    a. a and b are from the same source.
    b. a and b are possibly from the same source.
    c. a and b are probably from the same source.
    d. a and b are not from the same source.

2. The first step in the laboratory microscopic examination of hair found at the crime scene is to determine whether:

    a. the hair is the suspect's or the victim's.
    b. the hair is from a male or female.
    c. it is a human hair.
    d. the suspect or victim had a dog or cat.

3. The parts of a human hair include all of the following except:

    a. the shaft or innermost core.
    b. the medulla or core.
    c. the cortex or body surrounding the medulla.
    d. the cuticle or outer covering.

4. All of the following are deductions concerning the source of a hair specimen that a laboratory expert using a microscope might make except:

    a. the sex by the thickness and length.
    b. the age by the color of the hair.
    c. the race by the shape of the cross section.
    d. the physical size by the inner structure of the hair.

5. Some other deductions that a laboratory expert could make from a microscopic examination of hair include all of the following except:

    a. occupation, such as painter, from foreign matter in the hair.
    b. social standing by the health and the quality of the hair.
    c. poisoning, such as arsenic, from traces in the hair.
    d. murder weapon by the impression left on the hair.

6. Hair analysis is an excellent means of determining:

    a. short-term drug use.   c. short-term alcohol abuse.
    b. long-term drug use.   d. long-term alcohol abuse.

7. Hair samples are analyzed to determine drug use using the same techniques that are used for urine analysis, namely:

    a. scanning electron microscope.   c. immunoassay and gas chromatography.
    b. neutron activation analysis.   d. x-radiography.

8. Hair analysis may be a more effective means than urine analysis for determining drug use for all of the following reasons except:

    a. it uses a more reliable system of analysis.
    b. opiates and cocaine disappear from the system in two days.
    c. it is a less intrusive method of testing.
    d. samples can't be switched because the hair can be plucked out by the person doing the testing.

9. A victim of a violent assault in defending himself may rip out hair roots from an assailant. A DNA analysis of these cells compared with a DNA analysis of blood taken from a suspect could _____ the suspect as the assailment.

    a. positively identify
    b. probably identify

    c. possibly identify
    d. only exclude

10. Fibers from the clothing of persons involved in violent crimes often prove more valuable as clues than hair because fibers usually have _____ identifying characteristics when examined under a microscope.

    a. a few more
    b. the same number of

    c. fewer but more distinctive
    d. many more

11. An examination of rope, cloth, and string found at the crime scene is done primarily to determine:

    a. how it was used.
    b. its source.

    c. its construction.
    d. its type or kind.

12. Fibers may be divided into the following classes: animal, vegetable, mineral, and:

    a. artificial.
    b. natural.

    c. synthetic.
    d. chemical.

13. When there is a large sample of evidence available, the investigator may make a preliminary test to determine whether a fiber is animal or vegetable by:

    a. smelling it.
    b. feeling it.

    c. soaking it.
    d. burning it.

14. A laboratory expert will make a microscopic examination of fibers when comparing _____ specimens found at the crime scene with _____ specimens in the laboratory in order to establish similarities and differences.

    a. known...known
    b. known...unknown

    c. unknown...known
    d. unknown...unknown

Answers:

1. a	p. 862, 1.	6. b	p. 863, 2f.	11. b	p. 865, 3.
2. c	p. 863, 2a.	7. c	p. 864, 2f.	12. c	p. 866, 4.
3. a	p. 863, 2a.	8. a	p. 864, 3.	13. d	p. 866, 5a.
4. d	p. 863, 2d.	9. a	p. 865, 3.	14. c	p. 866, 5b.
5. b	p. 863, 2d.	10. d	p. 865, 3.		

Chapter 43
INVISIBLE RADIATION

Questions:

1. _____ is slightly longer in wavelength than visible light.

   a. Ultraviolet radiation   c. An x-ray
   b. Infrared radiation   d. Neutron radiation

2. _____ is slightly shorter in wavelength than visible light.

   a. Ultraviolet radiation   c. An x-ray
   b. Infrared radiation   d. Neutron radiation

3. When ultraviolet radiation strikes a surface, it is absorbed by some substances and its energy is transformed and radiated back in light of different colors. The object is the said to :

   a. absorb light.   c. fluoresce.
   b. reflect light.   d. radiate.

4. Ultraviolet light is used directly by means of a special:

   a. lamp or flashlight.   c. fluoroscope.
   b. ultraviolet film.   d. radiograph.

5. The widest use of ultraviolet light in criminal investigation is in:

   a. detective dyes.   c. fingerprint powders.
   b. stain location.   d. document examination.

6. Ultraviolet examination is helpful in all of the following areas except:

   a. paper examination.   c. suspicious package examination.
   c. ink comparison.   d. forgery examination.

7. By using ultraviolet light in rape cases, semen and urine can be readily found on a garment by means of their:

   a. light absorption.   c. distinctive colors.
   b. light reflection.   d. fluorescence.

8. In processing a _____ surface for latent fingerprints, a fluorescent powder can be used. The fluorescing fingerprint can then be photographed in ultraviolet light to achieve the desired contrast to the background.

   a. light   c. multicolored
   b. dark   d. single

9. The appearance of an object in the infrared must ordinarily be studied:

    a. by means of the fluorescent effects visible to the naked eye.
    b. through the use of an infrared lamp only.
    c. through the medium of a photograph.
    d. by means of a night-viewing device.

10. The utility of infrared rays is attributable to the fact that certain substances are opaque to this radiation while others are:

    a. reflective.   c. fluorescent.
    b. transparent.   d. refractive.

11. Infrared examination has its widest use in criminal investigation for:

    a. preliminary screening tests for materials such as cloths and paints.
    b. detecting powder marks around bullet holes.
    c. detecting and differentiating stains.
    d. document examination.

12. When ink has been used to obliterate writing, if the obliterating ink is transparent to the infrared and the lower writing is opaque, it is a relatively simple matter to render them legible by means of:

    a. a magnifying glass.   c. infrared photography.
    b. an infrared lamp only.   d. a night-viewing device.

13. X-rays are useful in detecting the presence of:

    a. metallic objects in metallic surroundings.
    b. metallic objects in non-metallic surroundings.
    c. non-metallic objects in metallic surroundings.
    d. non-metallic objects in non-metallic surroundings.

14. X-rays are electromagnetic radiations differing from light in that they have a _____ wavelength, a characteristic which gives them great penetrating power.

    a. much shorter   c. much longer
    b. little shorter   d. little longer

15. Film exposed by means of x-rays is called:

    a. x-ray film.   c. a radiograph.
    b. x-ray screen.   d. an electron radiograph.

16. The source of x-rays is a _____ containing a cathode and an anode.

    a. battery   c. an x-ray lamp
    b. transistor   d. a vacuum tube

17. X-rays penetrate non-metallic objects. When they are blocked by metallic objects, these latter produce what can best be described as _____ on the photographic plate.

    a. a photograph   c. an outline
    b. a shadow   d. a detailed image

18. If the voltage is increased, the wavelength of the x-rays become shorter and the radiation is more penetrating. The longer wavelength and less penetrating x-rays, in the range of 4-25 kilovolts, are called:

    a. soft x-rays.   c. gamma rays.
    b. hard x-rays.   d. electrons.

19. The shorter wavelength and more penetrating x-rays are called:

    a. soft x-rays.   c. gamma rays.
    b. hard x-rays.   d. electrons.

20. For a quick inspection of an object under x-rays, a small box with a viewing aperture for both eyes called a _____ is used.

    a. borescope   c. snooperscope
    b. fluoroscope   d. microscope

21. Of the following applications of x-rays to criminal investigations, soft x-rays would be most effective in detecting:

    a. lead fouling around a bullet hole.
    b. a bomb in a parcel post package.
    c. loads in dice.
    d. a firearm hidden in luggage.

22. Hard x-rays would be most effective in detecting:

    a. differences in similar specimens of paper.
    b. differences in similar specimens of fabric.
    c. metal objects hidden in furniture.
    d. differences in imitation and real diamonds.

23. _____ radiation, which can be obtained by means of radioactive substances such as cobalt-60 or radon, is extremely hard radiation, useful in dealing with metal objects that are impenetrable to ordinary hard x-rays.

    a. Gamma   c. Secondary
    b. Electron   d. Neutron

24. A(n) _____ radiograph is a picture of secondary radiation caused by x-rays hitting a substance and that substance emitting electrons. It is useful for examining the surface and lower layers of a painting or a document.

a. gamma
b. electron

c. hard x-ray
d. neutron

25. A(n) _____ radiograph is produced by atomic particles bearing no charge which can penetrate substantial objects. It is especially useful in examining concealed bombs, where it can reveal the inner arrangement and components and even detect the presence of fluids.

a. gamma
b. electron

c. hard x-ray
d. neutron

Answers:

1. b	p. 870, 1.	10. b	p. 874, 8.	19. b	p. 880, 13a.		
2. a	p. 870, 1.	11. d	p. 875, 9a.	20. b	p. 882, 16.		
3. c	p. 870, 2.	12. c	p. 875, 9a.	21. a	p. 882, 17a.		
4. a	p. 870, 3.	13. b	p. 877, 11.	22. c	p. 884, 17b.		
5. d	p. 871, 4a	14. a	p. 877, 12.	23. a	p. 885, 17c.		
6. c	p. 871, 4a.	15. c	p. 877, 12.	24. b	p. 885, 17d.		
7. d	p. 872, 4c.	16. d	p. 880, 13.	25. d	p. 885, 17e.		
8. c	p. 873, 4f.	17. b	p. 880, 13.				
9. c	p. 874, 7.	18. a	p. 880, 13a.				

Chapter 44

DOCUMENTARY EVIDENCE

Questions:

1. The investigator will find that documents in one form or another will account for approximately _____ percent of the physical evidence he will encounter.

a. 20
b. 40

c. 70
d. 90

2. The most common document problem is that of:

a. questioned authorship.
b. decipherment of erasures.

c. typewriter identification.
d. the age of a document.

3. The opinions formed by an investigator concerning a questioned document _____ in an investigative report.

  a. should always be included
  b. should always be included along with the document examiner's opinion
  c. should be included only if the document examiner declines to give one
  d. should not be included

4. All of the following are rules that should be followed when handling documentary evidence except:

  a. Initially handle the document with tongs.
  b. Retain the document in a transparent envelope.
  c. Routinely mark each document for identification by writing the case number, the investigator's name or initials, and the date on the back of the document.
  d. Routinely test for fingerprints by dipping the document in a solution of silver nitrate.

5. Conclusions concerning documentary evidence should be made by:

  a. the investigator alone.
  b. the laboratory expert alone.
  c. either the investigator or the laboratory expert.
  d. both the investigator and the laboratory expert.

6. The group of characteristics which form an individual's script are:

  a. always changing and identifiable.
  b. always changing and unidentifiable.
  c. permanent and identifiable.
  d. permanent and unidentifiable.

7. In addition to the quality of the lines that form the letters, all of the following handwriting characteristics will form the basis of the examination except:

  a. the formation of the letters.
  b. the spacing between letters, words, and lines.
  c. the spelling and punctuation.
  d. the choice of pen and paper.

8. In the majority of handwriting comparisons, particularly in forgery cases, the laboratory expert _____ reach a conclusion.

  a. will always   c. does not
  b. does   d. usually does

9. The purpose of this chapter is to train the investigator to:

  a. be a handwriting expert.
  b. recognize suspicious documents.
  c. conclude which documents are not authentic.
  d. turn over all documents to the laboratory expert.

10. A(n) _____ is a specimen of writing of known authorship which can be used by the expert in a comparison.

a. exemplar
b. request standard
c. non-request standard
d. questioned document

11. A(n) _____ is a specimen of writing of known authorship which has been written prior to the investigation.

a. exemplar
b. request standard
c. non-request standard
d. questioned document

12. A(n) _____ is a specimen of writing of known authorship prepared at the behest of the investigator.

a. exemplar
b. request standard
c. non-request standard
d. questioned document

13. In order that an exemplar be admitted in evidence, its _____ must first be established.

a. date of writing
b. legibility
c. suitability
d. genuineness

14. An exemplar should be prepared with materials _____ those apparently used for the questioned document.

a. exactly alike
b. similar to
c. dissimilar to
d. entirely different from

15. A ball-point pen should not be employed in preparing an exemplar unless:

a. a suspect requests one.
b. he never used one before.
c. the questioned document was written in ball-point.
d. the questioned document was written with a fountain pen.

16. The exemplar should correspond in word and form to the questioned document. Correspondence in _____ means the use of similar writing materials in preparing the exemplar.

a. word
b. form
c. word and form
d. characteristics

17. Ordinarily, the suspect should be required to write:

a. the actual text of the document.
b. a different text but one which will include key words and letter combinations.
c. a different text that will display every letter and punctuation mark.
d. any text selected by the investigator.

18. All of the following statements concerning the preparation of exemplars are true except:

 a. The suspect should write on only one side of the paper in the same script as that found on the questioned document.
 b. The investigator should dictate the text without suggesting punctuation, spelling, or paragraphing.
 c. The material should be dictated several times, each time increasing the speed of dictation.
 d. Each exemplar, as it is completed, should be left with the suspect to guide him in making subsequent copies.

19. If the questioned writing consists only of a signature _____ copies will suffice. If it consists of a few paragraphs _____ will suffice.

 a. fifty...twenty   c. twenty...five
 b. forty...fifteen   d. five...two

20. When the questioned document is obscene, the subject should be required to:

 a. write the actual text anyway.
 b. write the text leaving blanks to substitute for the obscene words and descriptions.
 c. write a substitute text using many of the words and letter combinations found in the original.
 d. trick the subject into creating his own text to see what kind of language he would use.

21. Specimens which do not repeat the questioned writing are called:

 a. non-request standards.   c. non-request exemplars.
 b. auxiliary request standards.   d. auxiliary exemplars.

22. Check exemplars should be prepared on:

 a. photocopies of checks.
 b. blank checks similar to the ones under investigation.
 c. on many different kinds of blank checks.
 d. regular lined paper because only the signature is important.

23. The Supreme Court, in _____, held that a suspect may not decline to provide a handwriting sample.

 a. *Gilbert v. California*   c. *Gideon v. Wainwright*
 b. *Schmerber v. California*   d. *Gilbert v. Sullivan*

24. If the subject refuses to provide specimens of his handwriting, the investigator should:

    a. force him to write using a court order for justification.
    b. confiscate any letters sent to his lawyers.
    c. obtain non-request standards from personal papers and official documents.
    d. obtain his signature by sending a package to him that he has to sign for.

25. Even when request standards are given freely, the investigator may also want to have non-request standards available primarily because:

    a. the more evidence available the stronger the case.
    b. the subject may deny making the request standard.
    c. a jury may not believe that the suspect wrote the request standards.
    d. the investigator may want an indication that the request samples reflect the subject's normal writing habits.

26. When sending documentary evidence to the laboratory expert, in the letter of transmittal the investigator should:

    a. tell the expert which documents are thought not to be genuine and why.
    b. request the expert to determine the authenticity of the documents completely on his own in order to avoid any charge of bias.
    c. include the full report of investigation so that he has as much information as the investigator.
    d. list only the names and numbers of the documents plus the bare facts of the case.

27. Forgers may disguise their writing in two ways: (1) they may _____; (2) they may invent an entirely new style of writing.

    a. spell names and words incorrectly.
    b. combine together two different writing styles.
    c. attempt to make perfect letters.
    d. imitate the handwriting of another person.

28. All of the following are common methods of disguising handwriting except:

    a. forming the letters perfectly.
    b. changing the direction of the slant.
    c. writing very rapidly or very slowly.
    d. using the left hand instead of the right.

29. When writing with the unaccustomed hand, the normal characteristic of the person's handwriting will _____ be detected.

    a. rarely   c. usually
    b. always   d. never

30. Non-guided writing can be detected by:

   a. abnormal letter formations.
   b. abrupt changes in direction.
   c. misalignment and poor spacing of the letters.
   d. a style that is smooth and controlled.

31. The writing of an illiterate is characterized by an absence of style and the appearance of:

   a. unorthodox designs.
   b. grammatical errors.
   c. misspellings.
   d. peculiar phrasing.

32. The forging of an illiterate's writing can be detected in the grammatical errors, misspellings, and peculiar phrasing because it is difficult for the forger:

   a. to make that many mistakes.
   b. to express himself properly with such limited literary skills.
   c. to know the form which an illiterate's expression will take.
   d. to deliberately to misspell words.

33. Handprinting, because it is so rarely done, is marked by distinct peculiarities such as the design and form of letters and:

   a. the alignment of letters.
   b. misspellings.
   c. the slant of the letters.
   d. the choice of large and small letters.

34. The existence of family similarities in writing, the use of non-European writing, and ideographic writing such as Chinese or Japanese, will each provide _____ in detecting individualities.

   a. great difficulty
   b. a different set of problems
   c. little difficulty
   d. a different set of rules

35. When obtaining standards for a typewriter examination, it is important to determine:

   a. who the usual typist is and how he types.
   b. has the typewriter been repaired since the questioned document was prepared.
   c. the year the typewriter was manufactured.
   d. has anyone else used the typewriter beside the usual typist.

36. To determine whether a questioned document was produced by a particular typewriter, it is necessary to compare the questioned document with:

   a. the typewriter itself.
   b. other documents produced by a similar typewriter.
   c. standards prepared with the typewriter.
   d. the ribbon only.

37. If the ribbon is new, it is important to submit it for examination to determine:

    a. if it is the same type of ribbon that produced the document.
    b. if the typewriter ribbon is changed often.
    c. if there are portions of the text on the ribbon.
    d. the kinds of documents prepared on this typewriter.

38. All of the following statements concerning the preparation of typewriting standards are true except:

    a. The text of the questioned document should be copied exactly.
    b. Each copy should be on a single sheet of paper similar in quality and color to the original.
    c. The entire keyboard should also be typed.
    d. Always use the same ribbon that produced the questioned document.

39. To detect dirty, defective, or scarred type, a _____ of a page of the text should be produced.

    a. carbon specimen   c. photograph
    b. photocopy   d. heavily inked copy

40. A class characteristic will enable the examiner to determine the make and model of the typewriter. An example of a class characteristic is:

    a. the alignment of the letters.   c. the slant of some of the letters.
    b. a broken typeface.   d. the design and size of the letters.

41. When a letter on a typewriter will print in the middle of an imaginary space in which all the letters and figures occupy the same area, the typewriter is said to:

    a. "on its feet."   c. have perfect letter design and size.
    b. be in perfect alignment.   d. have perfect letter slant.

42. The most prevalent typescript is _____ in which ten characters occupy an inch length of paper.

    a. pica   c. roman
    b. elite   d. gothic

43. On a page of typing, all characters are aligned:

    a. horizontally only.   c. both horizontally and vertically.
    b. vertically only.   d. neither horizontally nor vertically.

44. When the typeface no longer strikes the roller with equal pressure on all its parts causing variations in the density of the ink impression, the typeface is said to:

    a. be out of alignment.   c. have defective slant.
    b. be "off its feet."   d. be broken.

45. A single-element typewriter often has characteristic defects in the typeface which take the form of:

    a. broken typeface.   c. defective slant.
    b. raised beads.   d. misalignment.

46. The maximum age of a typewritten document can be set by determining the make and model of the typewriter and when it was:

    a. first manufactured.   c. used widely.
    b. last manufactured.   d. last sold.

47. All of the following are useful in determining the typist of a document produced with an electric typewriter except:

    a. characteristic grammatical construction.
    b. arrangement of material on the paper.
    c. the "touch" of the typist or the amount of pressure used in striking the keys.
    d. the use of unusual characters or symbols.

48. Suspected additions to a typewritten document can be detected by looking for all of the following except:

    a. erasures.   c. use of a different make of typewriter.
    b. misaligned additions.   d. spelling and punctuation errors.

49. To determine whether a sheet of paper came from a particular pad or a check from a particular checkbook, it is necessary to:

    a. find distinguishing marks on the sheet of paper or the check.
    b. match the perforated edges.
    c. find the watermark.
    d. compare the sizing or fiber composition of the paper.

50. To determine the manufacturer of a piece of paper, the investigator should first examine the _____ of the paper.

    a. physical characteristics   c. loading materials
    b. fiber composition   d. watermark

51. A reference file for the paper used in checks is maintained by the FBI and is called the:

    a. Paper Reference File.   c. Safety Paper Standards File.
    b. Checkwriters File.   d. National Fraudulent Check File.

52. All of the following files are maintained by the FBI except:

    a. Anonymous Letter File.   c. National Fraudulent Check File.
    b. Bank Robbery Notes File.   d. ink dye pattern file.

53. "Taggants" made from rare-earth elements are used to identify the manufacturer and the age of:

    a. papers.   c. typewriting ribbons.
    b. inks.   d. watermarks.

54. A skilled forger may make a document appear older than it is. This is important in cases involving:

    a. anonymous letters.   c. fraudulent checks.
    b. kidnap letters.   d. wills and contracts.

55. Determining the exact date of a document can only be done by:

    a. textual references to events.   c. knowing the age of the materials used.
    b. an eyewitness to the signing. d. chemical tests of the materials.

56. In determining the approximate age of an old typed contract, all of the following techniques can be used except determining the:

    a. age of the ink used for the signature.
    b. year of the introduction of the typewriter make and model.
    c. first production date of the typewriting paper.
    d. first appearance of a physical defect in the typeface on a dated document.

57. The more specific date indicators of a document would be found in:

    a. the production dates of the typewriter and the paper.
    b. the chemical and physical properties of the materials used.
    c. the information from the textual content of the letter and the envelope cancellation mark.
    d. the style of arranging the various elements of the document.

58. Discoloration around the edge of a paper clip or the absence of discoloration under it is an indication that the paper clip:

    a. is made of an unusual substance.
    b. has been attached to the paper for a long time.
    c. has been attached to the paper recently.
    d. has been used many times previously.

59. The document examiner is by necessity also a:

    a. criminal investigator.   c. photographer.
    b. psychologist.   d. office machine technician.

60. On first receiving a questioned document, the examiner will photograph the front and back and use the photograph as a substitute for the original. He will do this:

    a. because the evidentiary characteristics are clearer in the photograph.
    b. in order to examine the front and back of the document at the same time.
    c. so he can print a number of copies for the examiners.
    d. to avoid the unnecessary touching of evidentiary materials.

61. _____ is the process whereby an enlarged image is achieved on the negative.

    a. Photomicrography   c. Filter photography
    b. Photomacrography   d. Infrared photography

62. In _____, the photograph is made with a microscope objective and eyepiece in order to achieve a magnification of at least ten times.

    a. Photomicrography   c. Filter photography
    b. Photomacrography   d. Infrared photography

63. To superimpose a traced signature over a genuine signature _____ is used.

    a. filter photography   c. photomacrography
    b. infrared photography   d. a set of transparencies

64. In obliterated writing cases, it is often necessary to discern writing that lies beneath other writing. If the two writings were made with different colored inks, a photograph is made using a _____ of the same color as the upper ink.

    a. transparency   c. filter
    b. negative   d. lamp

65. Inks and papers, which appear similar in visible light, often look strikingly different under _____ , which cause some substances to fluoresce.

    a. ultraviolet light   c. soft x-rays
    b. infrared light   d. colored filters

66. Because some inks are transparent and others are opaque to _____, photography using it will sometimes restore legibility to obliterations and erasures.

    a. ultraviolet light   c. soft x-rays
    b. infrared light   d. visible light.

67. The texture of two apparently similar papers can be differentiated in a radiograph made with:

    a. ultraviolet light.
    b. soft x-rays.
    c. hard x-rays.
    d. gamma radiation.

68. If spuriously added writing crosses the original writing, the document examiner by using _____ can sometimes determine which writing was made first.

    a. chemical testing
    b. a microscope
    c. soft x-rays
    d. hard x-rays

69. Punch holes can be examined for the presence of ink stains. If the punch was made after the writing, the edge will:

    a. reveal an ink stain.
    b. not reveal an ink stain.
    c. be bruised by the pen.
    d. be avoided by the pen.

70. If ink writing is added after a paper has been folded, the ink will:

    a. dry faster at the fold.
    b. dry slower at the fold.
    c. ordinarily be unaffected by the fold.
    d. bleed into the fold.

71. Adding an extra zero to the amount of a check is called " _____ " the check.

    a. altering
    b. raising
    c. adding on to
    d. lifting

72. If an original writing is made on a pad of paper and the top sheet is removed, it may still be possible to decipher the writing from an examination of the sheet immediately under it. This is called an _____ writing problem.

    a. illegible
    b. altered
    c. obliterated
    d. indented

73. When a document is covered with a polymer film which is charged electrically and sprayed with a toner, an image of indented writing will become visible. This is called:

    a. electrostatic imaging.
    b. iodine fuming
    c. testing by indented writing solution.
    d. indented writing photography.

74. If the investigator receives an anonymous letter identifying a criminal from a person witnessing a crime, he should:

    a. reject all anonymous "tips."
    b. accept the "tip" and test its reliability.
    c. accept the "tip" only if the source can be identified.
    d. find out from the criminal who he thinks informed on him.

75. In committing the crime of _____, the criminal obtains property from another with his consent induced by the wrongful use of force or fear.

a. extortion
b. blackmail
c. kidnapping
d. robbery

76. Blackmail is a form of extortion in which the criminal uses a(n) _____to convey the threat.

a. announcement
b. telephone call
c. telegram
d. letter

77. Of the four categories of anonymous letter senders, the member of a large organization who "drops a letter" describing the improper actions of a rival, would be included under:

a. persons with information.
b. persons with criminal intent.
c. malcontents.
d. cranks.

78. Characteristics of the obscene letter is the description of:

a. how to contact the writer.
b. normal sexual activity.
c. abnormal sexual activity.
d. his occupation and his physique.

79. In anonymous letter cases involving a series of letters and a complainant, the investigator should instruct the complainant on receiving a letter to:

a. open it to make sure it is from the same person.
b. throw it away unopened because if the writer is ignored he will stop.
c. confront each of his associates with the letter in order to detect a guilty reaction.
d. submit the unopened letter to the investigator to be processed for fingerprints.

80. In an anonymous letter case, if one or more suspects have been identified, the most practical method for the investigator to obtain conclusive evidence is by means of:

a. an undercover operative to watch each suspect.
b. confronting each subject with a letter and demanding that they admit sending it.
c. a "plant," such as stationery marked with an invisible number in fluorescent ink.
d. forwarding the letter to the FBI to see if they have a similar one in their Anonymous Letter File.

81. _____ ink has long been used for entries in record books and for business. It is considered the best permanent ink for document purposes.

a. India
b. Logwood
c. Iron gallotannate
d. Nigrosine

82. _____ ink is a natural coloring material extracted from a tree.

   a. India   c. Iron gallotannate
   b. Logwood   d. Nigrosine

83. _____ ink is a water solution of a synthetic black compound prepared from aniline and nitrobenzene.

   a. India   c. Iron gallotannate
   b. Logwood   d. Nigrosine

84. _____ ink and other carbon inks, such as Chinese, are among the oldest writing substances known.

   a. India   c. Iron gallotannate
   b. Logwood   d. Nigrosine

85. To determine whether two documents were written with the same type of ink, they should first be:

   a. examined under a microscope.
   b. compared visually for color.
   c. tested with a 5 percent solution of hydrochloric acid.
   d. examined under ultraviolet light.

86. To distinguish between iron gallotannate (turns light blue), logwood (turns red), and nigrosine or india inks (both unaffected), a 5 percent solution of _____ is used.

   a. sodium hypochlorite   c. nitric acid
   b. sulfuric acid   d. hydrochloric acid.

87. To distinguish between nigrosine (turns brown) and carbon ink (unaffected) a 10 percent solution of _____ is used.

   a. sodium hypochlorite   c. nitric acid
   b. sulfuric acid   d. hydrochloric acid

88. Without the use of a "taggant" added to the ink, it is _____ to determine the age of inks.

   a. still easy   c. very difficult
   b. moderately difficult   d. practically impossible

Answers:

  1. c   p. 893, 1.   31. a p. 907, 19.   61. b p. 928, 45.
  2. a   p. 893, 2.   32. c p. 907, 19.   62. a p. 928, 45.

3. d	p. 894, 3.	33. d	p. 909, 20.	63. d	p. 928, 46.
4. d	p. 894, 3d.	34. c	p. 909, 21.	64. c	p. 928, 47.
5. b	p. 895, 4a.	35. b	p. 910, 24.	65. a	p. 929, 48.
6. c	p. 896, 6.	36. c	p. 910, 24c.	66. b	p. 929, 49.
7. d	p. 896, 7.	37. c	p. 911, 24c.	67. b	p. 930, 50.
8. c	p. 896, 8.	38. d	p. 911, 24c.	68. b	p. 931, 53a.
9. b	p. 897, 9.	39. a	p. 911, 24c.	69. b	p. 931, 53b.
10. a	p. 898, 10.	40. d	p. 912, 26.	70. d	p. 932, 53c.
11. c	p. 899, 10.	41. b	p. 913, 26b.	71. b	p. 932, 54.
12. b	p. 899, 10.	42. a	p. 913, 26b.	72. d	p. 932, 55.
13. d	p. 899, 11.	43. c	p. 913, 26b.	73. a	p. 933, 55.
14. b	p. 899, 12.	44. b	p. 914, 26d.	74. b	p. 937, 64a.
15. c	p. 900, 12b.	45. b	p. 915, 26f.	75. a	p. 939, 64b.
16. b	p. 902, 13a.	46. a	p. 915, 27.	76. d	p. 939, 64b.
17. a	p. 902, 13a.	47. c	p. 916, 28c.	77. c	p. 939, 64c.
18. d	p. 903, 13c.	48. d	p. 917, 29.	78. c	p. 941, 64d.
19. c	p. 903, 13d.	49. b	p. 918, 30b.	79. d	p. 941, 65a.
20. c	p. 904, 13f.	50. d	p. 920, 32c.	80. c	p. 942, 65e.
21. b	p. 904, 13f.	51. c	p. 921, 34c.	81. c	p. 943, 67a.
22. b	p. 904, 13h.	52. d	p. 921, 34d.	82. b	p. 944, 67b.
23. a	p. 904, 14.	53. b	p. 921, 34d.	83. d	p. 944, 67c.
24. c	p. 905, 15.	54. d	p. 923, 36.	84. a	p. 944, 67d.
25. d	p. 905, 15.	55. b	p. 924, 38.	85. b	p. 945, 68.
26. a	p. 906, 16.	56. a	p. 924, 39.	86. d	p. 945, 68.
27. d	p. 906, 17a.	57. c	p. 925, 39.	87. a	p. 945, 68.
28. a	p. 906, 17a.	58. b	p. 926, 40e.	88. d	p. 945, 69.
29. c	p. 907, 17c.	59. c	p. 926, 41.		
30. d	p. 907, 18.	60. d	p. 927, 44.